THE LIBRARY OF CONSTRUCTIVE THEOLOGY

THE END IS NOT YET

THE END IS NOT YET:

A Study in Christian Eschatology

By

ULRICH E. SIMON

DOCTOR OF DIVINITY
FELLOW OF KING'S COLLEGE, LONDON

JAMES NISBET & CO. LTD
DIGSWELL PLACE

Published by
James Nisbet and Company, Limited
Digswell Place, Welwyn, Herts.

© *1964 Ulrich E. Simon*

First Edition 1964

236
si SS

7804259

PRINTED IN GREAT BRITAIN AT
THE UNIVERSITY PRESS
ABERDEEN

For Tony and Deirdre Bland

GENERAL INTRODUCTION

BY THE EDITORS

Times change, and our words change with them. The passage of thirty years, crowded with events which have shaken the foundations of our society, make necessary some addition to the original Preface to this series. From a new vantage point further down the stream of time, earlier landmarks take on a new perspective. There are phrases in the original Preface which their authors, writing afresh today, would not now employ, not because they would repudiate their meaning, or feel constrained to some major retraction, but because the continually changing vocabulary of theological conversation has rendered blunt and inapt words which were formerly clear-cut and apposite.

About the main stresses of their original intentions the Editors remain convinced and very sure that the 'Library of Constructive Theology' has still an important work to fulfil. That silent crisis of our time, which they saw to involve not only a questioning of authority but a revolt against it, has not only persisted but intensified in such manner as to sharpen the questions facing Christian men as they seek to bring home their message to a largely estranged contemporary mind. It is true that the last decades have seen an important return to authority, a return in many churches to positive elements in the holy tradition of the past, in the revival of dogmatic theology in Continental Protestantism, in the increasingly fruitful Ecumenical conversation, and in the emphasis on the dogmatic content of Biblical theology.

In part this has been a result of the context of the time: the new perils and heresies, and notably the challenge of totalitarian ideologies, have driven Christian men to consider the great unchanging affirmation of their faith. They have also been the logical consequences of the explorations of historical, dogmatic, and Biblical studies themselves, pursued by a generation of scholars. But if theological studies have advanced, new knowledge has accumulated in the field of science, new problems of philosophical discussion, such that in itself a return to authority can only sharpen the acuteness of the crisis provoked by the relation of Christian belief to the modern mind. 'The effort to think out anew, in the light of modern knowledge, 'the foundation affirmations of our common Christianity' is not less but rather more urgent than in the years before the rise of National Socialism and the Second World War, and the recent discussions about 'De-Mythologizing' and the problems raised by 'Logical Positivism' have shown that the Christian enquiry may turn out to be even more drastic and thoroughgoing than a previous generation had envisaged.

The Editors stressed the value and validity of religious experience, widely defined to include the moral and spiritual experience of the whole human race. Now 'existential' seems to be replacing 'experience' in the jargon of the schools. Modern philosophic discussion has pursued the lines of a century-old debate, but it too has been drastically affected by the shattering experiences of contemporary life, in a disrupted, shattered world where the old familiar stable patterns of existence have been dissolved, and where the age-long problems of the human soul have to be reconsidered against a life setting of pain and anxiety and frustration thrust in upon the human consciousness by events which the individual cannot alter and control, driving him to ask old questions with a new depth and poignancy. But here again the change of emphasis and vocabulary, and the new problems provoked for Christian exposition, have not altered but rather brought into deeper analysis the fundamental concern of religion, amid all the preoccupations with human solidarities, with the lonely and the contrite heart, and with a God who addresses men and women at the deepest level of their personal existence. It remains true that 'theology cannot exist without the religious consciousness and reflection upon it.'

Finally, the need for studies of these things which shall be intelligible to the general reader is as urgent as ever. Twenty years ago it was right to speak of a gulf between the pulpit and the pew: now perhaps we might add the perils of a gulf between the study and the pulpit, beside the great divide which separates the pew from the street. The problem of Christian communication meets us within and without the Church, hampering the endemic responsibility of the whole Christian community from carrying out at every level an ever-renewed and renewing theological conversation, and, above all, imperilling the evangelical commission to the Churches to bring their gospel home to the heart and mind of a bewildered, distraught, and hungry age.

*   *   *

The Editors of this series are convinced that the Christian Church as a whole is confronted with a great though largely silent crisis, and also with an unparalleled opportunity. They have a common mind concerning the way in which this crisis and opportunity should be met. The time has gone by when 'apologetics' could be of any great value. Something more is needed than a defence of propositions already accepted on authority, for the present spiritual crisis is essentially a questioning of authority if not a revolt against it. It may be predicted that the number of people who are content simply to rest their religion on the authority of the Bible or the Church is steadily diminishing, and with the growing effectiveness of popular education will continue to diminish. We shall not therefore meet the need, if we have rightly diagnosed it, by dissertations, however learned, on the interpretation of the Bible or the history of Christian doctrine. Nothing less is required than a candid, courageous, and well-informed effort to think out anew, in the light of modern knowledge, the foundation affirmations of our common Christianity. This is the aim of every writer in this series.

A further agreement is, we hope, characteristic of the books which will be published in the series. The authors have a common mind not only with regard to the problem but also with regard to the starting-point of reconstruction. They desire to lay stress upon the value and validity of religious experience and to develop their theology on the basis of the religious consciousness. In so doing they claim to be in harmony with modern thought. The massive achievements of the nineteenth and twentieth centuries have been built up on the method of observation and experiment, on experience, not on abstract *a priori* reasoning. Our contention is that the moral and spiritual experience of mankind has the right to be considered, and demands to be understood.

Many distinguished thinkers might be quoted in support of the assertion that philosophers are now prepared in a greater measure than formerly to consider religious experience as among the most significant of their data. One of the greatest has said,

'There is nothing more real than what comes in religion. To compare facts such as these with what is given to us in outward existence would be to trifle with the subject. The man who demands a reality more solid than that of the religious consciousness seeks he does not know what.'[1]

Nor does this estimate of religious experience come only from idealist thinkers. A philosopher who writes from the standpoint of mathematics and natural science has expressed the same thought in even more forcible language. 'The fact of religious vision, and its history of persistent expansion, is our one ground for optimism. Apart from it, human life is a flash of occasional enjoyments lighting up a mass of pain and misery, a bagatelle of transient experience.'[2]

The conviction that religious experience is to be taken as the starting-point of theological reconstruction does not, of course, imply that we are absolved from the labour of thought. On the contrary, it should serve as the stimulus to thought. No experience can be taken at its face value; it must be criticized and interpreted. Just as natural science could not exist without experience and the thought concerning experience, so theology cannot exist without the religious consciousness and reflection upon it. Nor do we mean by 'experience' anything less than the whole experience of the human race, so far as it has shared in the Christian consciousness. As Mazzini finely said, 'Tradition and conscience are the two wings given to the human soul to reach the truth.'

It has been the aim of the writers and the Editors of the series to produce studies of the main aspects of Christianity which will be intelligible and interesting to the general reader and at the same time may be worthy of the attention of the specialist. After all, in religion we are dealing with a subject-matter which is open to all, and the plan of the work does not require that they shall delve very deeply into questions of minute scholarship. We have had the ambition to produce volumes which might find a useful place on the shelves of the clergyman and minister, and no less on those of the intelligent layman. Perhaps we may have done something to bridge the gulf which too often separates the pulpit from the pew.

Naturally, the plan of our series has led us to give the utmost freedom to the authors of the books to work out their own lines

[1] F. H. Bradley, *Appearance and Reality*, p. 449.
[2] A. N. Whitehead, *Science and the Modern World*, p. 275.

of thought, and our part has been strictly confined to the invitation to contribute, and to suggestions concerning the mode of presentation. We hope that the series will contribute something useful to the great debate on religion which is proceeding in secret in the mind of our age, and we humbly pray that their endeavours and ours may be blessed by the Spirit of Truth for the building up of Christ's Universal Church.

PREFACE

'If this world is not to our taste, well, at all events there is Heaven, Hell, Annihilation—one or other of those large things, that huge scenic background of stars, fires, blue or black air.' So wrote E. M. Forster in *A Passage to India*; I know no better way to introduce another book on the End, the Last Things, Eschatology. Another book? Indeed, libraries exist on the subject, and yet the bigness of the subject justifies another attempt to grapple with the unknowable. As long as men are aware of Beginning and End they will transcend the present.

In this book, after setting out the quest for life in general terms, I present the reader with what I would call the material relevant to Christian thought. Both the Bible and the Tradition, covering the thought of thirty centuries or so, provide the sources for our somewhat telescoped survey. It had to be kept in bounds. I have had to omit much. Only the most important references are given, for a host of footnotes, as we all know, clutters up the page and causes the reader to faint. The books mentioned in the text contain themselves hosts of references and books for further study. They may be found in the bibliography at the end of this book.

In Part II I have adopted the form of a dialogue. The characters are not chosen arbitrarily, but their artificiality cannot be denied. They are spokesmen, representing points of view, and nothing else. Their failing in the debate is that they are much too polite. In real life they would articulate their dislikes in no uncertain terms. Yet, I hope, they bring to life a debate which no straightforward account could do by itself. All arguments in theology suffer from endless qualifications. We look over our shoulders, we sense the antagonist, we say 'although' and 'In view of the fact that', we wish to show that we know the whole round of possible views and are aware of monographs on the subject. The resultant tedium is difficult to bear. The dialogue, which invites the reader to look at Eschatology through many spectacles, is meant to save him from this labour. Our debt to Socrates and Plato is acknowledged herewith.

In this dialogue, the protagonists first try to establish the scope and nature of the problem. After disagreeing on that, they proceed to investigate some common experiences relevant to eschatology and go on to explore the motives of, and the criteria for, the study of the End. Lastly they argue in turn on the End and Truth, the End and Goodness, and the End and the Beautiful.

Following out of the aesthetic argument Part III goes more fully into the whole symbolism associated with the End. The form of dialogue had to give way to ordinary descriptive writing. There is less controversy in this field of symbolism once (a big 'If') this type of language is admitted to speak for itself.

Part IV nearly remained unwritten, for it is much easier to sit on the fence and to go on presenting contrasting views without even hinting at a decision. But the ease of impartiality is no defence against the indictment of cowardice. Certain things have to be stated unequivocally. In this section the traditional doctrine is taken for granted and an attempt is made to test it, interpret it, and offer it to the judgement of the contemporary reader. Whereas the dialogue allowed the speakers to spread themselves and to quote from other sources to support their theses, this section is quite unadorned. I have numbered these final doctrinal theses, if only because this format cuts out anything superfluous. I have also pared down the sentences to the bare minimum in the hope that they may invite discussion. Eschatology solicits not only passionate convictions but also the exchange of many views in the pursuit of this Hope.

If I were asked what I want to convey to the reader above all, it is the enriching complexity of my subject. Eschatology deals with facts: men have lived and acted in the belief that they will not taste of death and that the end is round the corner. Eschatology deals with fancy, for the belief has been discredited by events. Eschatology deals with scepticism, for scorn has been poured on a world of fancy now exposed to the light of evidence. Eschatology deals with ideals and hopes which by their very warmth and beauty refuse to be tied down to the laws of evidence. Eschatology deals with doctrine which would avoid the extremes of sceptical denials on the one hand, and fanatical affirmations on the other.

Clearly the reader will be helped if he can keep an open mind and allow all these streams of different and sometimes opposing data to bear upon the main point which is this: the world in which we live is meaningful because God not only created it but also sustains it to a further purpose. All things move towards a tremendous climax, but the 'end' is not yet, though we have already a glimmering of the eternal vista through the risen and glorified Christ and the gift of the Spirit. Our whole temporal existence then is at stake against the canvas of the universal and eternal consummation in, and of, God.

My thanks are due not only to the various authorities which are mentioned in the text, but also to Dr W. R. Matthews, Dean of St Paul's, without whose constant encouragement and help this book could not have been written.

August 1963   U. E. S.

CONTENTS

PART I

THE GROWTH OF A TRADITION

CHAPTER I

THE QUEST FOR LIFE ETERNAL

The End is a term which defies definition. Strictly speaking we do not know an End in the absolute sense, and from a scientific point of view there can hardly be a discussion of the End. The End is not subject to experiment and tests of verification. It remains obdurate to the making of a scientific model, for the very conception of the End presupposes that time has ended, and with it existence such as we know it. In the absence of a scientific reality there is no point in discussing the probability of the existence of the End. All probabilities include the possibilities of existence; if therefore we deny the possibility of the End we also must infer that there is no probability of the termination of existence in time.

But this somewhat discouraging analysis and its negative conclusions only apply to the End in an absolute sense and not to an End which is qualified and thereby made relative to other realities. For example, we can quite well and validly speak of the end of John Smith, because he has died; or of the End of the state of Lithuania, because it has been annexed; or of Mithraism, because it no longer appeals to anyone's belief. There is therefore an end in time, after which time goes on, for a particular subject once existed in time and now no longer does so.

We do not know when the human race, or some members of it, were first concerned with this phenomenon of limited ends. Our own civilization never seems to have been quite free from it, and it is possible that even pre-historic cultures favoured the mental conception of the End in human affairs. For example, the seasonal impact upon life always brought in its train an awareness of the beginning of the fertile season as well as of the end; as soon as man began to sow crops he was wholly under the sway of a given calendar which the sun governed. Nor was he oblivious of the phases of the moon. The shepherds particularly celebrated the new and the full moon. Thus the natural life under the open sky required an awareness to periods of time which always began again after they had come to an end: years, months, weeks, and days were not abstractions but communal experiences. Hence it is not surprising that in the four millennia before Christ there is already

3

in the Ancient Near East an observance of the cycles of life; every inauguration of the New Year implies also the cessation of the Old.

In Mesopotamia, always threatened by the unruly waters of the Tigris and the Euphrates, the New Year Festival recalled in its words and action the emergence of order out of chaos. The destructive floods were not only a memory but a contingent possibility: what had brought to an end previous attempts at settled life might so easily overthrow all present hopes of peace and security. Thus there grew up a myth-ritual pattern for the New Year in which the end of chaos and its succession by the created order was not only celebrated as a fact of the past but as a present reality to be achieved. The King, or his representative, acted out in priestly liturgy the Epic of the Creation, and in this liturgy the theme of the End was never far from actors and spectators. The King enacted here death and resurrection; he conquered his enemies and was enthroned as victor; he was crowned and married; the royal procession proclaimed his life-giving victory. But behind the liturgical façade and the yearly repetition of the rite there lay the conviction that chaos and death, which had been overcome at the beginning, still had the power to end prosperity and life itself. The dark forces were hostile to man and had to be placated and overcome. If this were not done the new life would be stifled and all things would return to the primeval chaos.

The famous remains of Ugarit suggest that the same concern for the insecurity of life and the menace of the End was felt further south in Syria. Here also words of an epic nature seem to yield a pattern of a religious cultus which may have prevailed in varying forms and degrees throughout that region. Ageing gods, destructive powers, realms of death, evil conspiracies, etc., must be prevented from blowing out the lamp of civilized order. At Ugarit the god Baal goes through many vicissitudes before he also conquers and proceeds to his triumph.

All these evidences are defective in the sense that we cannot be certain what sort of action went with the words. The actual performance remains a conjecture. But there can be no doubt that the End loomed as large in these performances as it does in the texts and that, more importantly, the End was associated with chaos, death, enmity, and everything undesirable. The pagan cultus did not wish to speed the End but to ward it off, just because it acknowledged the threat of a universal return to the beginning of the cycle, and thus to chaos.

The focal point of the rituals of the End is Death: the death of vegetation, the death of the king, the death of the community, and possibly also death among animals. But when death began to strike society in itself as strange, unwelcome, hostile, and as an element, natural and supernatural, which evokes wonder and repulsion, it is far more difficult to say. Pre-historic man does not paint death on his caves, although the death of animals is his concern. Pre-historic man has left no words to tell us about his fears and hopes, but he has left burial mounds and upright stones, dolmens, menhirs, and the like, all of which suggest that he buried his dead with care, not only to have them safely out of the way but also to ensure for them a future. The death of man must have become a puzzling problem at some time, for it is obvious that it was not simply accepted as a natural phenomenon even in those early days when the ice receded from the islands and continents of Europe. Whether the dead were thought of as residing still on earth, or even in the air and thence in the sky, we may again not deny nor affirm with any certainty. Whether, in fact, we are entitled to think of man before the dawn of history as thinking and feeling uniformly alike is more than doubtful. What is not open to doubt is that at some time among some people Death, as the end of the life of the individual, was not accepted but experienced as a challenge to the survivors whose own coming death linked them to their predecessors.

When the veil of the unknown is partly removed by historical texts we cannot be surprised to find that Death is seen to occupy the central point in the quest after life. Man dies: must man therefore vanish?—this question is put and answered differently by different civilizations. In the Near East itself we meet optimism (if to live after death may be assumed to be a good thing) and pessimism. In Egypt the King at least lives for ever, for he is god even during his life-time and the funeral rites ensure his well-being after burial in the pyramids. His subjects may not always have felt the same degree of confidence in the hereafter, seeing they were ordinary mortals and their slaves and animals certainly died to live no more. In Mesopotamia the royal cultus, however, does not seem to have infused enough hope to sustain a belief in a real life after death. Hence the experience of death evokes here a much sharper reaction and the international story of Gilgamesh typifies both the general search for life and its tragic failure.

This epic of the legendary king of Uruk is altogether remarkable. It has come down to us in several versions and represents traditions of the third millennium before Christ and memories of even earlier times. It provides the words to the muted evidence of archaeological remains, such as the Royal Cemetery at Ur. Here,

unlike in Egypt, the immolations for the dead and the offerings of
the kings to the gods of the underworld do not presage a blessed
future but rather the inevitable departure of all to the land of no
return, to the underworld of lost shades, the pit of destruction and
death. There may have been more hopeful vistas seen and entertained by others: Gilgamesh also hears through Utnapishtim of a
better world and even in his own travels seems not far away from
the earthly Paradise of the gods. Indeed the natural man, represented by Enkidu, his great friend, appears to have lived once in
the innocent world of an immortal harmony which the animals
shared. But all this is now outside Gilgamesh's reach, try as he
may to regain it with all his daemonic energy, itself an endowment
of his semi-divine parentage on his mother's side. He must fail,
for according to the story, as reconstructed, death is no accident
but the result of forces greater than man. Enkidu dies because
he and Gilgamesh have overreached themselves. In their search
for knightly adventure they have killed the giant Herdsman, the
evil Humbaba, ignoring his prayers for mercy and his divine status.
Worse still, Gilgamesh and his friend spurn the attentions of the
goddess Ishtar, and Gilgamesh, a victim of his own ignorance, slays
the Bull of Heaven—who personifies the seven years of drought
sent by the angry goddess to avenge her humiliation. Thereafter
not even the gods of Sun and Wisdom can protect our hero and the
forces from below exact punishment. First Enkidu must die, then
Gilgamesh must start on his pilgrimage to win back his friend and,
if possible, to avert his own death. But eternal life is elusive and
as the serpent snatches the secret plant from his hands all hope
is lost.

The fascination of this epic lies not only in the articulation of
vain hopes but also, and perhaps even more, in the general setting.
Good and evil, friendly and hostile powers, the world above and
the world below, add dramatic complications to the plot. Gilgamesh and his people are not alone in the universe but their
destiny is determined by constellations greater than themselves.
Hence the End is certainly not to be viewed as an isolated experience, merely as the end of biological functions or of communities,
although the epic reflects without a doubt a situation of political
unrest and economic consequence (demand for timber and metals).
The End involves issues of retribution after moral choice and
cosmic dimensions provide the canvas upon which Mesopotamian
culture paints its images of the life of gods and man. Babylonian
astrology knits not only human affairs to the course of the stars
but identifies the gods with the stars. The conflict among the gods,

from which human battles proceed, is also bent on a dénouement, a catastrophic climax which must affect the whole world. The 'overtones of anxiety' (H. Frankfort) in Mesopotamia spring from the apprehension of a possible End to all life. Men may be crushed by the gods, but the gods also may be crushed by a cosmic fate. This insecurity of the higher powers in the Near East is immortalized in Greek mythology, where the offspring of the gods endeavour to dethrone their progenitors and replace the old by the new. Thus Zeus, himself the usurper of Cronos who, before him, got rid of Ouranos, remains like all Olympic gods subject to calamity. Nemesis can overtake the celestial potentates as well.

Both Persian and Greek sources proliferate richly entertaining ideas about the End. Iranian Apocalyptic starts from a dualistic conception of the Universe. The highest God Ahura-Mazda stands in irreconcilable antagonism to Angra-Mainyu, the great principle of evil. Throughout the seven thousand years of the creation they fight for the possession of the world. The world-epochs culminate in the judgement and the destruction of the known world by fire, but this world-conflagration is not the end of all life, for there is a double Resurrection: individuals receive their reward after death before the general resurrection consummates the destiny of the world. In this resurrection Shaoshyant, benefactor of the human race, takes a leading part in the somewhat materialistically conceived restoration, which is itself part of a cosmic event in which angels and spirits share.

But Persian thought was itself developed out of Babylonian and Eastern patterns of belief which, in their turn, flourished in the Hellenistic Age. The Greek writers reflected a common cultural inheritance in which, for example, journeys to the Realm of the Dead were celebrated. From Homer to Virgil[1] we have accounts of consultations with the dead in Hades where they disclose future events and secrets of the beyond. Like Gilgamesh the heroes travel and descend to the underworld, which is composed of several tiers, as in Orphic mythology.

Plato uses the common theme in his *Phaedo* when he describes a cosmos of ascending beauty: below everything is distorted, but in the higher realms colourful beauty increases. The deep is full of filth, stink, and fire—partly for punishment, partly perhaps for purgation; above man ascends to the Elysian fields of merited pleasure. The freed immortal soul can enjoy the better world through change and growth. The notion of such an ascent necessarily opens the cosmos to souls which pass from the isles of the

[1] *Aeneid*, Book 6.

blest to the upper regions and take time in reaching their perfection.

Thus intermediate states suggest themselves, and these agree in some measure with the structure of the Universe, the circles of the planets and the grades of the spiritual beings which inhabit the spheres. Daemons and gods are met with on high, whereas evil daemons and titans guard the way to Tartarus, for every division of these realms has its own non-human inhabitants. The Universe is alive and moves through the Great Year to its point of origin, the new age of gold. The cycle of one age is succeeded by the new cycle; thus the End of time becomes also the beginning of time.

The evidence, therefore, suggests that awareness of the End grew with the advance of civilization. Man in his brutish state has nothing to fear. Man as a conscious animal has much to fear and perhaps a little to hope for. A complex society favours the conglomeration of different motifs of the End, partly to ensure stability and success, partly to vent deeply felt wants. Thus materialistic considerations jostle with mental speculations and spiritual quests. The End and its cultic rites, for example, provides for an easy passage from one year of fertility to another, inspires scientific calculations about the calendar and the spheres of the stars and, incidentally, the making of suitable instruments, and at the same time stimulates the individual soul in its craving after endless existence. Even if the antique world did not possess one single myth-ritual pattern, its awareness of the End was everywhere a potent force on all levels of public and private life. Yet it was not destined to reach the Western world unchanged, for the irony of history saw to it that the pattern was re-patterned first through Israel's prophetic inspiration and then through the Christian proclamation.

CHAPTER II

ISRAEL AND THE END

The Old Testament reports the doings and aspirations and fears of generations of a people who regarded themselves as a continuous nation in history. These children of Israel always looked back to their forefather Abraham who had set out from Ur near the Persian Gulf some time in the second millennium B.C. He and his immediate friends and descendants carried with them a cultural heritage into Syria and Palestine, in which the End was known and feared. Yet in the Scriptures which purport to reflect their feelings and actions the Patriarchs entertain none of the complex notions then apparently current in Mesopotamia. Of myth-rituals there is nothing in these traditions of ass-riding semi-nomads, though there is plenty of danger and struggle. Abraham meets with terrors, especially in dreams and visions; Jacob fights mysteriously with angels and gods. But their main concern is to fulfil their vocation in the design of the strange God who severed them from the consolations of a settled life with the promise of a better future in an unknown land. These men, practical and peaceful as they are, seem obsessed with the idea of the future; the procreation of children, and the welfare of their families, constitute their great hopes. Calendar feasts and melancholic reflections on mortality are quite alien to them, although they are constantly harried and speak openly of their troubles and sorrows. But when death comes the fact is accepted with dry matter-of-factness and decent burials mark the end of physical life.[1] Abraham buries his wife in the cave of the field of Machpelah which he had bought for the purpose[2] and where he himself would lie later.[3] Yet somehow this is not the end, for without bothering us with details the narrator tells us that these people 'were gathered to their people'.[4] A cairn marked the spot where the bodies lay, but where the tribe gathered after death we are not told. The details may have been suppressed at a later stage, but no subsequent censorship can delete the fact that these wandering Aramaeans had a future, not only on earth among their seed, but also among their fathers beyond death. The last of the Patriarchs, Joseph, does not need to be touched with the

[1] For Death and Funeral Rites, cf. R. de Vaux, *Ancient Israel*, pp. 56ff.
[2] Gen. ch. 23.   [3] Gen. 25:9.   [4] Gen. 25:8; 35:29; 49:33.

9

optimism of Egypt to embrace this belief as a new thing: it was already there. Only the custom of embalming the dead and their interment in a coffin gives an Egyptian nuance to the end of this epoch.[5] But this simplicity of an unspecified belief in Life after Death was lost in Egypt among the oppressed Hebrews . . . and it was never to be regained.

The history of Israel explains this increase in complexity. Several stages may be detected, but these did not follow one another but existed side by side. After the flight from Egypt and the conquest of Palestine the tribal confederacy consolidated its hold on the land by assimilating its traditions to the common culture of Canaan. Although the Lord Yahweh was enthroned at Shechem, Shilo, and later at Jerusalem, and although the Ark recalled the mighty past of Moses and the desert, the forces of Canaan were even mightier in their hold on the people. One of these forces was the by now familiar agricultural calendar of the year and the prominence given there to the renewal of life. At the sanctuaries of Canaan a myth-ritual pattern obtained, shorn, it would appear, of all its finer and more reflective moods and pessimism. Here sexual orgies were part of the cultus which was responsible for the safe passage from one year into the next and for the averting of dangers, sicknesses, spells, magic and also death. The simple belief in the life after death became part of a much greater belief in the End—of seasons, of crops, and imaginary issues connected with life after death.

It is, however, never quite easy to imagine what really went on at these pagan gatherings, already foreshadowed by the dance around the Golden Calf at the time of Moses. These ecstatic and possibly savage rites seem to have nothing to do with ultimate things. And yet the cult of the dead evidently loomed large at these popular centres. Witches and wizards presided over the consultations of the dead. The account of Saul's visit to Endor[6] may stand as an example of what was attempted in necromancy and how it succeeded: the ghost of Samuel is forced up by incantation, but the ghost's state is not further defined. The dead exist below and can be summoned; at the numerous High Places, near the cemeteries, these rites were connected with child-sacrifice in fire and ceremonial lamentations, such as the weeping for Tammuz.[7] Even the bodies of the great prophets were venerated and treated as sacred and powerful relics.[8] This popular religion moved on a level of functional purposefulness and did not wish to raise

[5] Gen. 50:26.   [6] 1 Sam. ch. 28.
[7] 2 Kings 17:17; Ezek. 8:13.   [8] 2 Kings 13:21.

questions about the End; the dead were enlisted to help the living.

In Jerusalem, however, the official cultus moved on a much higher level, even though it may have confirmed previous customs and borrowed quite a few features from extraneous sources. Whether a New Year Festival in the proper sense was always, or at any time, celebrated there we do not know, but the Psalms which have come down to us suggest that at least the common themes of the End were known among the priests. The very choice of Zion as the sacred mountain of Israel, though a sanctuary for centuries before David, indicates that the cultus of Yahweh found here an appropriate home. Its language is almost always concerned with the praise of God in connection with a super-human struggle; victory is still to be won, assistance in the ordeal requested; if unworthiness precludes Israel from gaining success penitence is uttered and penance promised; if failure has resulted, lamentations go up to God. The Psalms adumbrate the tensions of a battle which enrols Israel in a strife which leads to the End and which looks into the past for encouragement; but it is also the conflict of the whole world—*multum in parvo*. Hence the themes of the End are interwoven with cosmic phenomena and supernatural tribunals, assizes, and judgements. Death and the departed figure here,[9] not in isolation but in the grand setting of all the first and ultimate issues. The King speaks and acts for his people, sometimes in his own person, sometimes through his court-poet or through his priest: the *I* and the *We* of the Psalms are always personal but they represent also the whole people and even the whole world. Thus the *I* of David speaks for every man of God. Similarly the Enemy in the contest is personal, concrete and recognizable: sometimes in the poor sick man, who suffers from a disease at which the wicked mock, or in the bewitched, who writhes under the lash of the spell, or in the entrapped victim whom the demons have seduced. Every righteous man meets with the attacks of the wicked and undergoes humiliation. Thus the royal ritual of suffering in an ordeal, dying in a conflict, conquering death, rising to life, receiving the crown, of enthronement, marriage, and triumphal procession, brings the End within reach not only of the King but of all who identify themselves with him in the Temple. At the same time the cultus is not 'eschatological' in a technical sense, for the ritual brings the future into the present by the realism of the victory.[10]

---

[9] For example, Pss. 14, 16, 73, 88, 118.

[10] Hence Mowinckel is right in qualifying very carefully the eschatological content of the Psalms; cf. note viii in *The Psalms*, with references to the text of the book.

These stages in the ritual are scattered over many Psalms and need not be investigated here.[11] What is not always quite so easy to discern is the theme of the End in the Psalms. Psalm 29, for example, does not mention the word 'End' at all, nor does death concern the poet; yet the power and the glory which he invokes here is clearly the majesty which once mastered the chaos and will once again end the enemy's grip; he who sat upon the flood will be the King of the future Kingdom and will give the security (shalom) which such a victory ensures. The present tension, then, looks back for encouragement and forward in hope. All the great royal Psalms (92–100) deal with ultimate issues. The exultant affirmation of God's sovereignty stands in contrast to present needs: it mortgages the future. Thus the conquest of death (68 : 20) belongs to a triumphal procession which acclaims this future act of God: he will be our guide even unto and beyond death (48 : 14). The King is the leader and the shepherd in this movement and will therefore behave wisely and perfectly (101 : 2). The Messiah's perfection alone fits into the universal scheme of a cosmic victory which extends to all the corners of the earth. Hence homage to the King —the kissing of his feet (Ps. 2), the acclamation of the reborn from the dawn (Ps. 110)—assures the worshippers of their place in the Lord's original triumph over chaos in creation and his coming victory over the Enemy. The drama challenges the worshippers to obey the summons.

This emphasis on obedience is another End-theme in the Psalter. It has a flavour not found outside the Bible, for it links the cosmic drama to the history of Israel in Egypt and in the desert. The tradition pointedly repeats that disobedience led to chaos and disaster and that, in reverse, only obedience can meet with the divine favours. Therefore to hear is to reply, to listen is to obey. But this insistence means that no End-salvation comes from the ritual itself, but only from the response to the ritual. Even the King is subject to this restriction, for he is not God, not even in a representative sense, but always acts within the sacred tradition of freedom which acknowledges the sovereignty of God. The King acts as shepherd because the Lord is his Shepherd, the King reigns because his Lord is God. All authority is derived. Hence the glorious End is not a human victory nor a national achievement, but a divine act which comes with power to a covenanted people and king.

Israel's adaptation of the myth-ritual pattern was a process which began under Moses and culminated in the work of the great

11 For example. Pss. 16, 18, 22, 24, 45, 47, 73, 81, 95, 96, 104, 130.

prophets. Not only necromancy but all aspects of orgiastic fertility rites came under their condemnation. Hence even the person of the King and the ritual of the Temple came to reflect the constant opposition which the prophetic tradition exerted upon Israel's institutions. Both King and people were committed to a covenant with Yahweh, who steers the world as King, both in creation and in history. Hence the annual renewal of nature was not to be acclaimed in the pagan way, as a link in the circular movement back to the End, but all the gifts of God were to evoke a response of gratitude towards God. Thus during the formative period of the Exodus, Moses had directed the people away from pagan mythology towards Law and Promise. The sequence of all the trials in the desert—at Sinai and at the many springs, especially at Kadesh—was the purified community, a model to the whole world in righteousness and peace. Israel's political achievement after military success fulfilled the divine law and did not depend upon ritual but upon God's providential Presence. In the Mosaic tradition Law is always concrete and quite unmythical: certain cases are judged according to custom, and having set a precedent they establish statutes for the generations to come; but these laws are themselves derived from the Ten Commandments, the categorical words of God, the substance of the Covenant. Some prophets who followed Moses in Canaan sometimes lost sight of this tradition and opted for the pagan ecstaticism. But under the attacking fervour of Elijah and his followers this Baalistic practice crumbled and the prophets of Yahweh reverted to the tradition of Law and Promise. This ideal was hammered out particularly in the eighth century. Although Temple, King and the annual ritual continued alongside the prophetic preaching they were to be transformed in a radical manner.

In this transformation, then, the End was re-interpreted; ultimate issues were revolutionized. Amos, above all, expresses the moral calculus whereby Israel must be defeated, humbled, and punished, and this sad and awful fate belongs to 'the days which will come' (Amos 4 : 2). The future is morally conditioned; because men have offended against the norm, against the created order, the Lord, who formed the mountains and created the wind and unfolded his purpose to man, will abolish the abnormal excesses (4:13). The Lord, who orders the stellar constellations and turns deep darkness into morning and the day into darkness and controls the waters and the rains, will make his Day an occasion of deep darkness (5:8, 18). The New Year's Day, the Victory celebrations, will turn into ashes in the face of reality: this is the End which the

rotten summer fruit, seeping juicily through the basket, enunciates:
Harvest becomes End! (Amos ch. 8). All the prophets which follow
proclaim the sombre note of a great reversal, of a national judgement which must ensue because the right way of life has been
profaned by Israel; the cultus, instead of purifying the sons of Levi,
underpins the proud parody of truth. Even after so-called purges
and reformations and after the fall of Israel, Jeremiah can still
complain in Judah, a few years before the fall of Jerusalem, that
the land mourns, the herbs of every field wither, for the wickedness
of the inhabitants: the end stands at the threshold and the national
catastrophe finds its echo in the melancholy death of nature, the
silence of birds, the quaking of the earth, the desolation of vine-
yards and cultivated fields and gardens, the complete breakdown
of civilization. Suffering and anguish, thirst and famine, captivity
and death terminate the age of delicate clothes and cosmetics and
ornaments. Kingdom and priesthood, rich and poor, share in the
terrible fate which they have brought upon themselves. It is the
fate of chaos and formless void, which the ancients feared, but now
about to be realized in no mythical manner but in the hard realities
of wars lost and alliances shown up for their hollowness. And this
End on earth is appropriately accompanied by a pall of smoke, a
blackness which seems to wrap up the heavens, as if the whole
universe also stood in flames and mourned its dissolution.[12] No
one seems able to escape from the disaster; no life after death
compensates for loss on earth. Indeed, the prophets do not even
opt out of the End themselves and do not arrogate for themselves
an eternal life in consolation for present despair. They are content
to proclaim the oracles of the End and to transmit this new truth to
the circle of devoted disciples who bequeath it to posterity. For
them and for their masters the rest is silence.

And yet hope rises in the seedbed of despair. All the prophetic
oracles are complex and the voice of new confidence is heard when
it is least expected. Scholars often stress the later date of some
of these hopeful passages which seem so out of key with the rest.
Few, for example, would expect Amos to reach the bathos of
predicting the restoration of David's throne more than a century
before its collapse. But such isolated instances of subsequent
glossing cannot discredit the surge of prophetic hopefulness which
looks beyond the End of chaos to restoration in terms of world-
wide salvation under the leadership of a new Israel. The End-
beyond-the-End is conceived of as a perfect Kindom in which God
reigns himself in the hearts of men and especially through the son

[12] Jer. chs. 4, 12, and elsewhere.

of David. This new age abounds in unknown wealth: the ploughman overtakes the reaper and the treader of grapes the sower of seed: the whole world becomes fruitful and civilization flourishes as never before.[13]

Hosea also anticipates this new age when the Lord revives his people and raises the wounded and the dead.[14] Micah looks to Bethlehem, David's birthplace, as the home of the perfect ruler who will initiate the glorious harmony of righteousness so that all nations will be drawn spontaneously to acknowledge God in Israel and its sanctuary of Zion.[15] This hope of a universal acclamation of God, which coincides with a complete moral reformation of mankind, was evidently held in common by many prophetic schools. Isaiah, the greatest of their leaders, also holds up high the mountain of God, Zion, although he above all, and out of a deep knowledge, condemns the Temple institutions and the abuses of priestly and royal privilege of his day. He sees beyond his day to the imminence of catastrophe, and from catastrophe to the reversal in which God builds his kingdom. His spiritual realism pairs with his political awareness: the coming perfection is not an esoteric mystery for a few, but a world-wide movement of the Spirit. In this setting he envisages the birth of a child, a child which will embody the Presence of God; this Immanuel will take up with himself the old battle-cry of Israel 'God with us' and bring it to perfection in his own person; all the divine epithets of dignity and power are ascribed to this coming wonder-child who is chosen to sit upon the Throne of David. At last kingship will become divine because the elect child has nothing to do with self-seeking despotism but represents the Everlasting Father as Prince of Peace. God endows him with his Spirit, wisdom, and knowledge. Then destruction on earth ends and yields to perfect universal peace.[16]

The rise of the great world-empires contributed a political flavour to the religious expectation. When the Assyrian Empire cracked up in the seventh century Nahum greeted this event as 'the Lord's Revenge'. In his vision the burning of defeated chariots comes in the same category as the melting of the hills and the drying up of the sea. Zephaniah compares the same events to a grisly banquet at which God bids his guests take their share in the prepared sacrifice: 'The Day of the Lord is near', he proclaims, and thus blends the political and military situation of the moment with the pathos of the divine punishment, the howling and crashing of the great Day of Wrath. When the trumpet sounds it is for the

[13] Amos 9:13ff. [14] Hos. 6:2.
[15] Mic. 5:2; 4:11ff. [16] Isa. chs. 7, 9, 11, and 32.

alarm of unprecedented distress and a speedy extirpation of all inhabitants. This extreme gloating over the crumbling Assyrian Empire may have had the effect of inducing unjustified hopes of peace and relief among Israelite listeners, for it is remarkable that their self-confidence reached absurd degrees as a result of a total misreading of the political situation. Some of the extreme oracles of the Coming Day may well have been responsible for this. Jeremiah, at any rate, despised ill-founded optimism and, realist that he was, he proclaimed instead the inevitability of Babylonian rule. In his view God orders world-empires to succeed each other, and anyone who refuses to bow down to them must suffer the consequences: plague, famine, death. Jeremiah robs the notion of the End of its political romance.

Nevertheless, when the sword had struck and the first batch of Jews found themselves exiled in Babylonia, Jeremiah changed his tone. For them, and for them alone, there is hope. Those who have been carried away will continue to exist, for their future is bound up with God's purpose. Therefore even Jeremiah the realist, who despises wishful thinking and ill-conceived nationalism, can say: 'There is hope in the end',[17] and he demonstrates his conviction by the surprising decision, taken in prison, of buying a piece of land, not far from Jerusalem and occupied by Babylonian troops, which belongs to his family. He is the first great prophet to demonstrate the fluid nature of Hope, touched by the perspective of the divine purpose and the power of human history. He removes the hope from the narrow concern of life after death and from cultic drama.

After the Exile in 586 B.C. things were never to be quite the same as before. Even after the return to Jerusalem from Babylon there was to be no king. Yet this return was also deemed to be fulfilment of prophecy: after the crime and its punishment God had consoled his people and annulled the final death sentence. Israel would live again as the People of God to be a redeeming blessing to all the peoples of the earth. For the Second Isaiah[18] the advent of the Kingdom requires God's own participation in human affairs, for man's condition is mortal and only the word and the spirit can endow man with life. But God prepares salvation within the drama of history and in his saving action he unfolds himself as the End of all purposes. The missionary vocation of Israel is to unfold to the world the hollow wickedness of Babylon and of all secular power. Upon paganism God has already pronounced the verdict of death and it bears the seeds of extinction: all pagan villainy will

[17] Jer. 31:17.   [18] Isa. chs. 40–55.

culminate in exposure and in shame. But Israel, purged and separated from pollution, will experience a new Exodus and receive a new Law and extend the new Covenant, which Jeremiah had predicted,[19] to all who turn from darkness to the light. In this triumph of righteousness a great deal of suffering, even unto death, is inevitable, for the world hates Israel, and all that is bad in Israel hates the righteous remnant, and even the nucleus of disciples forsakes the perfect Servant of God. But in his humiliation and death the Servant not only atones for the sin of the world but is lifted out of the depth of degradation and death to the life beyond where he receives the recompense for his self-oblation. This treasure is no longer of this world, but is a spiritual felicity which endures beyond all earthly existence, because it is united to God himself who is the author of the loving sacrifice. When the Second Isaiah, therefore, calls men to decision and holds before them a glorious future of eternal communion he includes the tragic death of the Servant as the permanent mark of the blessed life which lies in the future. The End is now conceived as the turning point not only of history —of Israel, and even the whole world—but of human existence. It is the beginning of real life, the fulfilment of the creation. The End is not a return but the goal and achievement of a humanity which transcends its nature to attain to god-likeness in reflecting the Creator. No such thing existed before, not even in the mythology of the golden age. It is a new thing. Therefore the last things are now also rightly called the new things and man's latter end (*acharith* in Hebrew) points to the New and unprecedented (*chadash* in Hebrew).

Future writers and schools never reached again the high note of cohesion and inspiration found in the Second Isaiah, although his work remained a source of comfort and a challenge to action in the centuries to come. Yet the lure of political entanglement remained strong in Israel and for a time at least there was the temptation to press for a human king again at Jerusalem. The book of Zechariah, for example, still shows signs of Messianic hopes which reduced the transcendental End to a manoeuvre of earthly expediency. Fortunately these hopes were short-lived and the Jews settled down in a state of unaccustomed normalcy which lasted from 540 B.C. until well into the second century B.C. During this period Israelite thinkers received a great impetus from Persian sources and they developed their conception of the End on a broad front. The visionary element becomes a convention of speech and much that is written about the End is couched in apocalyptic language which

[19] Jer. ch. 31.

is not to be taken literally. When Zechariah, for example, intro-
duces horses, horns, carpenters, measuring angels, the Branch of
the Tree, the golden candlestick, the olive trees, the flying roll, the
woman in the ephah, the four chariots and the crowns of kingship,
he is mingling symbols, ancient and modern, to set the people in
a state of elation.[20]   This enthusiastic movement found its active
expression in the rebuilding of the Temple, and in the fifth century,
in the restoration of the walls of Jerusalem.   The victory of
Nehemiah and Ezra established a working hierarchy and orderly
government.   In these centuries of rebuilding the symbolism of the
End, its intimations of angelic assistance and celestial help, served
to rouse the low morale of the people.   Without it Judaism might
never have been born.   In later generations, however, the extremism of the language became somewhat stereotyped and the educated
members of the nation grew heartily tired of it since they knew
the dangers of religious hysteria.   Until the great crisis of the
second century, therefore, the trend of Jewish works of literature
is on the whole against bizarre prophecies and favours a saner
course in its Wisdom writings.

The tradition of Wisdom acts as a welcome antidote to the
fantastic images of apocalyptic contrivers. Yet it is by no means
just sober reflection or down-to-earth piety. Who, for example,
could speak in more poetical richness of style than Job and his
adversaries? But we are not concerned with style, but rather with
speculations regarding the End in all the sonorous chords as enunciated in the various schools. In that respect the Wisdom literature
retreats from previously gained insights. The large book of
Proverbs is quite bereft of the summons towards the universal
End-goal; the Preacher (*Ecclesiastes*) denies not only the providential End to the world, but even the final goal to Israel and an
immortal destiny for the individual. The soul leaves the body
upon death: the latter returns to the dust, the former to God who
made it. All is vanity because everything has been before and
every effort ends in death and oblivion. The aristocratic hauteur
which carries along these soliloquies enunciates not despair but a
deistic, if not agnostic, resignation to the inevitable.

We move here in a different atmosphere which almost deliberately ignores the traditions of Israel, even if some of the material
is very ancient. Take the love songs collected in the Canticles,
conventionally ascribed to Solomon so as to gain their admittance
to the Canon of the Old Testament. This praise of erotic love
stands in direct contrast to the pessimistic note of the Preacher: life

[20] Zech. chs. 1–6.

in the spring is good and we skip happily on this earth while we may. But although love is said to be stronger than death by way of poetical exaggeration[21] the reader is not meant to believe that the loving pair will enjoy each other because they will live for ever. Rather the moment of ecstatic enjoyment seems to cancel out the fear of death. But what of the moment of ecstatic misery? What of age, poverty, need, failure, and the very snapping of the marrow of life?

The author of the book of *Job,* who uses the old folk-tale of God and the Enemy, their wager, and the final reward of the tested victim, comes to a very pessimistic conclusion; for although Job's roarings are rewarded with vindication and his friends shown up to be in the wrong, the consolation is not of another world. 'I know that my redeemer is alive, will vindicate me, and I shall see': the corrupt text[22] cannot conceal the absence of a positive belief in the life after death. On the contrary, the author assumes with his contemporaries that if there is a place after death it solves nothing for the living, for this Sheol is simply the common grave from which there is no return.[23] Man is like the flower and like the beast: all perish, and with them thoughts, desires, and virtues. It is true that this gloomy pit may at least grant the peace of indifferent oblivion to the persecuted and suffering, for 'there the wicked cease from troubling' and rest and quiet envelops all.[24] Consolation and vindication, the author maintains with conviction, are to be found here, and only here, in our vision of reality as it is. Kingdoms, Messiah, world-wide salvation, life after death, recompense, change and glory, etc., do not belong to the human lot.

This new school of thought, which protested against a fanatical and fantastic conception of life, flourished even against the background of the Israelite institutions, for so liberal was the Hellenistic Age that a member of the priesthood could easily reconcile the delightful scepticism of Wisdom with his duties as an agent of positive tradition. There was born the type of religion which has succeeded in taming the wild spirit of romantic behaviour and which falls back upon a metaphorical interpretation of difficult supernatural beliefs. Under such circumstances the End no longer played a decisive part. Among the sophisticated leaders even the belief in a life after death probably only lingered on in a pale fashion under the guise of the immortality of the soul. This Greek conception satisfied the new demands of reasonableness and particularly removed the dying of individuals from the whole sweep of

---

[21] Song of Sol. 8:6.   [22] Job 19:25ff.
[23] Job 7:9; 10:21.   [24] Job 3:11ff.

cosmic events. There must have been a time when the union of
Socrates and Moses appeared to have been achieved, if not in
Jerusalem then certainly among the Dispersed who read their Old
Testament in Greek.

At the same time the old traditionalist outlook and the embers
of the prophetic fire remained alive, especially among the poor outside the capital. When the second century dawned and nomina-
tions to the priesthood in Jerusalem induced serious bickering and
Syrian intervention, no one on the spot could have guessed that
within less than half a century the whole country would be up in
arms, not only against the invaders from the North but against the
whole tolerant, secularized, Hellenized way of life within Judaism.
As the Maccabbees hit back they gained more than a military
victory at great cost. They completely changed the mental climate
among the Jews; from now on, for better or worse, the issues concerning the End really took control of everything else. Once again
the trumpet sounded the alarm and the noise of the chariots heralded
the shaking of the foundations.[25] The old hope had only slum-
bered: it was not dead. The great and terrible Day—of which the
prophets had spoken[26]—was here.

The book of *Daniel* acts in the Israelite tradition as a kind of
watershed. The old waters of prophecy flow down to the past, the
new waters of apocalyptic flood the future. In order to encourage
the loyal Jews in a desperate struggle these revivalist and mysterious
chapters draw on the great names of the heroic age and their appeal
is to past deliverances which will inspire the warriors to effect
victory in the present crisis. To this end, however, the old must
blend with the new, and types, symbols, secrets, and new doctrines
bring about a new pattern. The End is now many things at the
same time. The description of the great statue of gold, silver, brass,
and clay (ch. 2) symbolizes the collapse of all world empires and
their last menace, the Syrian king. Again Ram, he-goat, great
horn, and little horns (ch. 8) traverse the same political ground.
Most impressive is the imagery in ch. 7 which pictures the succession of beastly kingdoms: the lion with eagle wings, the bear, the
leopard with four wings, and the last horrible beast, all yield before
the unfolding thrones of judgement and the triumph of the Son of
Man who receives on behalf of the godly the Kingdom of God.
This Kingdom is the 'stone cut without hands' (ch. 2) which in
dreams and visions is already seen as victorious, for within God's
providential rule all tyrannies are weighed, judged, and numbered.
But this is a mystery, for the *Mene, mene, tekel, upharsin* is written

---

[25] Joel ch. 2.   [26] Isa. 26:20; Joel ch. 3; Zeph. 1:2–3; 3:8.

on the walls of those who do not themselves understand but perish in the very solution of the mystery (ch. 5). Yet, however mysterious, the relief for the outnumbered fighting forces must come soon, if they are to hold out, and so the element of waiting renders their hope poignant to the point of near-despair. To their expectancy comes the answer that it is but a little time, a period which can be measured in years and even days which will bring the great reversal and the longed-for salvation. This numerological bias[27] looks to the present reader more fantastic than it was originally intended to be. On the contrary, for the entrenched guerilla fighter, this was an element of absolute realism in an otherwise frenzied world, in which even angelic forces appeared to be engaged on the side of friend and foe. The meaning of the battle remains hidden until the unprecedented time of trouble when Michael, the prince of Israel, stands up for his people. All the stars and elements are involved in this cosmic fight which is, therefore, not a parochial hole-in-a-corner affair but a universal sweep affecting all mankind. The forthcoming victory embraces every creature, it is final and irreversible. Even those who have suffered and died to restore human rule to humanity in the place of brutal oppression will share in the unprecedented glories. The dust of the earth will not prevent them from waking out of the sleep of death and rising to the realm of light: like stars they shall shine, and their new life is eternal. At the same time the treacherous villains will not find in death a final refuge, but they also will give an account for themselves and receive their due punishment.[28] The valley of dead bones, which Ezekiel pictured as revivified by the Spirit at the time of the Exile (ch. 37), is now converted into a heavenly sphere of risen individuals, who through their own decision incurred suffering even unto death and accordingly are rewarded with life. This surprising *dénouement* alters the whole course of existence in Israelite thought, for now life is not restricted only to what is known but extended also to the unknown. It begins anew when everything else is broken down: the Lord eats up death and destruction and consoles the sorrowing as the earth is made to cast out her dead bodies.[29]

The book of *Daniel* not only reflects and illustrates this great conflict but it contributed decisively to the victory, although its time calculations proved quite wrong. The final capitulation of the Syrian garrison in Jerusalem did not occur until 142 when Judas Maccabaeus had been dead some twenty years. But by this time

[27] Dan. 7:25; 9:24–27; 12:6–12.   [28] Dan. 12:2–3.
[29] Isa. 25:6ff; 26:9.

the fight had gone beyond its original religious stake, and soon, against all the principles of the Hasidim and of apocalyptic hopes, a Jewish kingdom had come into being which owed everything to the force of arms and diplomacy.   This empire of the later Hasmonaean line was great in size but little in godliness.   The book of Judith expresses the enjoyment of worldly victory and power, an enjoyment which was not shared by the conservative and pious folk. They still cherished the apocalyptic hopes in which the wicked world must make room for the divine city, the godly commonwealth, the Israel of God, the Kingdom of eternity.   Once again this extremism displeased many educated leaders and literary men in Jerusalem.   Compositions of a distinctly anti-apocalyptic flavour began to circulate and propounded a Hellenistic conception of Wisdom, as in the *Wisdom of Solomon* which, while subscribing to the doctrine of universal immortality, deleted the radical hopes of a new world to be gained by miraculous intervention.

But history was on the side of extremism, for the land of Palestine was discontented with poverty and oppression and a mental climate which could not acquiesce in things as they were. Before Roman power arrived decisively in 63 B.C., when Pompey captured Jerusalem, the Jewish leaders had already brought Temple and Priesthood into disrepute.   The ascendancy of Rome and the puppet régime of hated Idumaeans were not likely to pacify the land.   If the second century had seen in Daniel a book of singular relevance the first century became a seed-bed to a host of books, nay libraries, of an apocalyptic character.   The historical element, however, recedes increasingly, as does the dependence upon tradition.   The new writers are no longer content to gloss the books of Jeremiah and Daniel as before, but they invent new heroes and create a style far more extravangant than their predecessors.   These books are, however, not products of the private study but belong to a period when Judaism itself became split into factions and a certain sectarianism took the place of the former schools.   These sects were often perfectly orthodox; indeed, they deemed themselves to be more orthodox than the traitors in high places.   The *Testament of the XII Patriarchs,* for example, encourages the adherents of the Pharisees to counter sin, to oppose Beliar, a personification of evil. He will eventually be bound[30] and cast into the fire for ever.[31]   The Messiah will come and reign after the general resurrection and the last judgement.   Then the saved will reside in Eden.[32]   Moral goodness and sincere piety give a foretaste of the good things to come.   The author of *Jubilees* seems to be a spokesman of the Essenes

[30] Levi 18:12.   [31] Judah 25:3.   [32] Daniel 5:10–13.

who, according to Josephus, Philo, and Eusebius, practised austeri-
ties rare among the Jewish people. He refers constantly to heavenly
tablets and is much concerned to show that all feasts are essentially
heavenly. The people of God are holy and must obey a calendar
which is not polluted with heathen influences, as the established
calendar seemed to the author to be. He commends the strict way
of segregation. But pride of place among the many Apocalypses,
as regards influence and wealth of ideas, must be accorded to the
so-called Ethiopic *Enoch,* which was probably begun in the second
century and received additions until about 75 B.C. No wonder
Enoch is a work of contradictions.

In Enoch the celestial and supernatural almost oust the earthly
and natural. Angels and giants, though fallen, still seduce men
into wickedness, but their final doom is imminent. Enoch travels
from sphere to sphere and sees their place of future punishment and
thence he proceeds to visit the perfect world whose centre is Zion.
The long second Book of the so-called Similitudes of Enoch (chs.
37–71) mingles the world assizes with the phenomena of the weather
and the stars. Here the Son of Man is the future Messiah who
pronounces judgement upon the whole world and leads the righteous to their eternal triumph and the earthly rulers to their doom.
Enoch watches the consummation of this universal act in Heaven.
The next Book makes the celestial sights its main object. The same
religious *leitmotif* pervades these chapters: man has tainted the
world, but divine providence restores perfection. Book Four out-
lines the saving history from the Flood until the dawn of the
Messianic Age, and the last Book shows how human history divides
up into ten eras, of which the last three—defeat of the wicked,
exposure at the Judgement, and the Messianic Age—are still to
come. On this note of the finality of the Last Judgement the work
ends with exhortations. Throughout it abounds in vivid and fantastic imagery. Shepherds and symbolical animals together with
celestial fires adumbrate the scene. The heavenly vocabulary, however, cannot disguise the main message of the Book which is terrestrial. Apostate Jews are the enemies in one place, the Gentiles
who oppose the righteous Jews in another. The righteous must
enjoy their triumph at last, not in Heaven, but on earth. In the
early sections this is achieved without the aid of a Messiah and
without expectations after death, whereas in the Similitudes the
Messiah and the Resurrection provide the climax of the victory.
As to the wicked, the final chapters (103) contemplate no resurrection but the eternal torment of their spirits in the underworld; but
even there darkness, chains, and fire seem to work for annihilation

in the end rather than existence for punishment. Later Apocalypses
—especially those written after the débacle of the fall of Jerusalem
in A.D. 70—develop this theme of punishment and revenge on the
one hand, and of a consolation of the victims on the other, be it on
earth or in Heaven, before death or in an after-life.

The impression made by the Apocalyptic literature is easily
misleading; for a perusal of these books makes little sense except
as a genre of poetry. Yet recently acquired evidence has quite
revolutionized our estimate of this body of apparently contradictory
beliefs. The New Testament had already familiarized us with a
very lively religious world, in which Saducees, Pharisees, and
Scribes enjoyed privileges at the expense of Galilaean peasants
and brave zealots. The coming of the Baptist John evoked according to the Gospels a stream of mass repentance which brought
thousands to the river Jordan in expectation of the Kingdom. But
this astonishing movement of about A.D. 27 seemed to stand in
inexplicable isolation historically and in the Gospel narrative only
served to introduce the story of the Baptism of Jesus and the initiation of his Ministry. Only those who could read between the lines
sensed that Jesus belonged to a generation of Jews many of whom
were on the brink of a new life, or at least were living in the hope
that the promised fantasies would come true. Some were expect-
ant in the military field and reduced the struggle to an anti-Roman
appeal. They were living again in the second century, in the age
of Daniel, when fighting on earth would mean gaining merit in
Heaven. But there were also others, who were neither militarists
nor law-abiding Pharisees and who longed to *anticipate the End* by
beginning a new life.

The ruins and the literature from Qumran constitute the evidence for the tradition of apocalyptic living carried out on earth.
Here the 'as if' fantasy was implemented in concrete terms of a
community. Its identification is not our business, though it seems
to us certain that the people of Qumran were Essenes. This movement started in the ranks of Pharisaic separatism as a further protest
against the abuses alleged to have been perpetuated by the priesthood in Jerusalem. The place which they occupied near the wady
Qumran had seen Israelite occupants before: they had returned to
withdraw from the corrupting luxuries of the settled life to live the
ideal life of disciplined freedom.

Qumran, with its buildings, assembly-rooms, scriptoria, cisterns,
aqueducts, pottery workshops and kilns, with its finds of coins,
animal bones in special jars, its cemetery, its evidence of the cultivation of corn outside the camp, and above all with its libraries in

the cliffs overlooking the Dead Sea, is not and never has been a romance. It is the answer of the archaeologist to the question: how did people live who pretended that the End was virtually in sight and that they could and must live *as if* the End had already dawned for them? Here was a community which practised what the book of Jubilees preached and which believed what Enoch predicted. Hence they embraced practices which were not even traditionally Jewish: they seem to have lived a life dedicated to celibacy (the evidence in the cemetery with the bones of children and women *outside* the main cemetery does not necessarily contradict the main undertaking of celibacy); goods were held in common for the benefit of all; novices were accepted according to a rule of initiation in which purifications, by water and confession and deeds, preceded their advancement through grades of perfection. In the scorching heat of the region of the Dead Sea these men co-operated not only to keep alive in a wicked world but in order to prepare the way for the work of God in their own lives. As they toiled in the parched fields, repaired their water supplies, made and sold pottery, wrote out manuscripts for themselves and for corporate gain, they were looking forward to the coming of the Kingdom and the King. They interpreted the scriptures of the Old Testament messianically (e.g. Isa 52:14 reading *meschachti* for *mischchat,* i.e. *I have anointed him* for *so marred*) and re-lived the oracles of the End as meant for them. Their righteous teacher was a martyred judge, who would chastise the wicked who oppressed the righteous. The Habbakuk commentary enunciates clearly that the enemy is a wicked priest, the man of the lie, a caricature of priesthood. Against this the community maintains the true hierarchical order of precedence which is strictly observed when the members come together for their common meal. Hierarchy and eschatology are united in sacrificial living.

But the community of Qumran also leaves many questions unanswered. The End inspires a way of life but not a system of thought. The Messiah at times becomes divided into two Messiahs —of Aaron and of Israel—and these seem to be colleagues of the Prophet who is to come.[33] The status of the Messiah varies a great deal and depends upon the conception of the enmity between Light and Darkness, the two eternally opposed realms. The Messiah must come from the former realm to fight against Satan, the head of the league of evil powers. But this conception contradicts the equally powerful strain of the omnipotence of God and his providential care for men and the ease with which he inaugurates the

[33] I. Q.S. ix, 10–11.

new Age.   Again this somewhat complacent confidence—enunciated
in the Thanksgivings (Hodoth)—cannot square with the serious and
sacrificial heroism which pervades the Manual of Discipline and
the War Scrolls.   In the Manual, however, human actions and
normal considerations for good neighbourly relations contradict
the absoluteness of the End.   The gradual building up of character
and the care for institutional health simply belong to a compartment
of life in which angels and celestial watchers and Belial seem singularly out of place.   Yet the Zadokite Fragment, which existed
also outside Qumran and shows that the spirit of Qumran was not
unknown in Palestine and even outside Palestine, makes the Covenant an ethical, this-worldly document with tangible stipulations
about daily life in which demonic assaults, for example, are as real
a danger as heathen practices.   This is 'the rule for such camp-
communities as may come into existence throughout the Era of
Wickedness—that is, until the priestly and lay "messiah" again
assume office.'[34]   But the obscurity reaches its climax for us with
the puzzle of the Scroll of the War of the Sons of Light and the
Sons of Darkness.   All the indications are that these communities
were peaceful and even dedicated to non-violence.   Were they even
pacifists, in the sense in which the religious are pacifists in the
Christian tradition?   Were they, in fact, 'monks in a monastery'?
The War Scroll describes Battle Dispositions whose every detail—
the names of the squadrons and the standards and military orders
—stresses the apocalyptic nature of the battle.   Yet it seems to be
a real battle spread out over many years.   God and his angels join
the ranks to achieve the final victory.   The language of the document seems to exclude a purely metaphorical warfare with figurative weapons.   The writer of these odes, and those addressed by
them, could not know that their prophecies would be overtaken by
events and that Qumran would fall to the troops of Vespasian in
A.D. 68.   The sacred buildings became the garrison of the legion-
aries, the members of the community were killed unless they got
away to Transjordanian safety whither the Jewish Christians also
fled.   All that remained, as always, is the Word.

But even the sombre events of Roman triumph did not wholly
terminate speculations and hopes of an End which God would
effect.   The Christian Apocalypse is but one example of this renewed outbust of an expectation so great that it surmounts the
horrors of the moment.   The so-called Apocalypse of Ezra reaches
a high-watermark of literary achievement and religious thought, for
here the sufferings of Israel and all the appearances contrary to

[34] CD xii, 22.

God's rule are taken seriously. The End is not the fulfilment of things but their utter repudiation, and the coming of the new Age will be sudden. The Messiah ('My Son') will rule for four hundred years and die with his generation: then the primeval silence prevails for seven days and the general resurrection and the final judgement will inaugurate the age to come. Only a few Jews will be saved, and the heathen must perish. Zion, barren for a long time, appears as the New Jerusalem. A Man from the Sea gathers his peaceful followers and the new commonwealth prospers in safety. Thus the seer, who verged on despair and remains sensitive to the tragedy around him, can proclaim bliss in the future. The Apocalypse of Baruch teaches the same lesson with a highly contrived symbolism: the cedar tree, the last enemy, is executed by 'My Messiah' who is represented by the vine. A vision of dark and bright waters illumines the dark and the bright pages of Israel's history, now to be ended by the Messiah who subjugates the enemies of Israel. But despite these notes of triumph this Apocalypse also conveys to posterity a sense of frustration and gloomy pessimism. The reconstruction of Jerusalem, the gathering of the twelve tribes of Israel and the destruction of the heathen, are hardly events to be expected within history; a sense of unreality attends the Resurrection and celestial glories.

Yet another stroke of defeat was needed in Israel to discredit finally the apocalyptic hopes: at the time of Hadrian, Bar-Kochbah, the self-styled son of the Star, attempted a rebellion, which gained even the support of wise men like Rabbi Akibah; it ended in another and even deadlier defeat. Jerusalem became Aelia Capitolina in A.D. 135 and the Jewish State ended for over eighteen hundred years. The resurgent forces in Judaism had more than enough of Utopian dreams; they set themselves the task of salvaging tradition from the ruins. But in Christianity the old hope merged with the new Faith.

CHAPTER III

THE NEW TESTAMENT

All aspects of the hopes and fears associated with the End appear in a new and more intense light in the New Testament, for Jesus the Christ is in the Church's proclamation the One who was to come. The central message in every document is always the same: He has fulfilled the predictions made about God's gracious acts. But this assertion of the completed work of Christ does not exclude an intensified hope that he who has come will also come again and that what was begun in the Birth, Life, Death, and Resurrection will be consummated in a cosmic event at the end of time. The New Testament reflects different situations of Church life in which the present is governed both by the past fulfilment and the hope of the future. Owing to the Church's life in the Spirit and her confession of 'Jesus is Lord' the New Testament no longer permits us to distinguish between the teaching of Jesus before his death and the proclamation of the Gospel after his Resurrection. What the Lord taught and enacted before his death is the substance of the Church's belief about him after his Resurrection. Hence the Lord's assertion that the Kingdom has come, that Satan is exposed, that from now on divine Power dwells with men, that his own sacrifice will and must usher in the new Age of the Son of Man, and that he will lead the redeemed Israel after his death as the victor over death cannot be divorced from the Apostolic preaching: Jesus is Lord.

The New Testament as a whole accentuates, therefore, the problem of the End in a specific manner, for its writers and preachers do not suppress the question: 'When will you restore the Kingdom to Israel?'[1] They feel the paradox of the triumphant Christ and a world which is on the brink of destruction. They speak as men who have had the Spirit and experience the miracles of healing and world-converting preaching while they await the Lord's Coming.[2] The world's framework is already waning[3] and the anguish of the times is such that the end of the world may be acclaimed with relief.[4] 'The time is at hand',[5] and salvation round the corner.[6] Yet at the same time until the final winding-up there

---

[1] Acts 1:6. [2] Jas. 5:8; Heb. 10:37. [3] 1 Cor. 7:31.
[4] 1 Cor. 10:11. [5] Rev. 1:3. [6] Rom. 13:11.

remains the work; this is no time for indolence or disappointment, but rather for a determined effort to engage in the present conflict.[7] It is in this atmosphere of being on tip-toe with expectation and of responsible decisions that the Apostolic community transmits this Gospel by written and spoken word; not a single passage in the New Testament can be understood unless this tension of a life before the End be borne in mind.

The Parables never fail to reflect the quest of the Kingdom of God as a present reality, announced by Jesus, and as a final destiny, involving the Coming of Jesus. If the latter be left out of account misinterpretation is sure to follow: the tares, the hidden treasure, the goodly pearl, the drag-net, the unmerciful servant, the labourers in the vineyard, the two sons, the marriage of the king's son, the ten virgins, the talents, the sheep and the goats, the seed-bed growing secretly, the householder, the two debtors, the good Samaritan, the importunate friend, the rich fool, the servants watching, the wise steward, the barren fig-tree, the great supper, the king going to war, the piece of money, the prodigal son, the unjust steward, the rich man and Lazarus, the unprofitable servants, the unjust judge, the Pharisee and the publican, the pounds (to take first parables occurring in one Gospel only), the leaven, the lost sheep (in two Gospels), the sower, the mustard-seed, the wicked husbandmen, the fig-tree (in three Gospels)—all these Parables lose their incisive edge if they are treated only as allegories of life, as it is lived or ought to be lived. Rather the parabolic figures describe a life whose beginning is meaningless apart from the End, an End which summons the members of the new Israel to make a new beginning. Against a background of inextricable good and evil the Kingdom moves forward into a future which, because it is God's future, opens eternity at the point of Judgement. Hence even stories which appear to move on an earthly level involve the hearer in other-worldly concerns: for example, the penitent decides to turn not for moral reform but in order to gain the eternal Kingdom; or again, the creditor forgives in order to obtain a higher recompense. Every virtue—such as generosity and diligent justice—is portrayed as going beyond itself and feeding on the Perfection which does not belong to this world, just as every vice—such as laziness and hardness of heart—receives its real condemnation only at the End when Evil is fully exposed in the glare of the divine assizes. The general air is, therefore, one of expectation: 'watch ye' remains the only possible refrain accompanying all human existence, and it is the Gospel which answers to the watchfulness of the elect because it

[7] 1 Thess. ch. 5; 2 Thess. ch. 3; 1 Cor. 15:58.

opens up the vista of the eternal Christ who was and is and is to come. Hence even the secret growth of the seed, though it not only permits but even encourages a patient building-up of character in the individual and of the well-knit society of the people of God, is not felt to contradict the equally pertinent law of the end of growth; for when all things have matured to the point which God has ordained the time of the harvest begins, and this harvest is not the death of all effort but its justification.

The delay of the so-called Parousia or Christ's Return coupled with the unpalatable fact that the elect were still subject to death and, in fact, did die, led some to doubt. We lack the necessary evidence to know whether the impatience of disappointed faith was widespread, but it seems to have been sufficiently militant and persuasive to invite serious rebuttals. After years of waiting men would say: 'Where is the promise of his coming?' and complain that all things continued in the same way as they always had been.[8] The flagging of this hope was never accepted as a natural development but repudiated as part of a general tendency towards sin and apostasy. The Apostles are seen to fan the flame of hopeful expectation, and their exhortations to faith and good deeds coincide with the consolation that the future will bring back the Lord and culminate in a glorious End. The premature death of Christians, perhaps the greatest obstacle to hope, is not to be misinterpreted. The dead and the living attend together upon the Christ when he descends from Heaven with the acclamation of universal triumph, and the dead rise with the living to meet the Lord in the air—'so shall we ever be with the Lord.'[9] But the consolation which derives from this assurance must not lead to speculation concerning dates. The Lord's return comes unexpectedly, 'like the thief in the night';[10] to prepare for it is to live now in this expectation with thanksgiving and an abundance of good works. Thus the expectation itself, by creating a great moral and spiritual readiness, remains the mainspring of Christian existence. It acts as consolation and challenge by the anticipation of the Kingdom.

But this insistence on the Reign of God as a present fact could not fail to lead to further reproaches within the Churches. The future at least could be settled by assurances; the present was a very different proposition. On all sides, St Paul admits himself, the enemy is ranged. First Jewish, then pagan opposition, mob violence, perverted justice, and soon open hostility on the part of the State assail Christian existence from outside, while within rivalries prepare the way for serious splits and even treacherous apostasies.

[8] 2 Pet. 3:4.   [9] 1 Thess. 4:13ff.   [10] 1 Thess. 5:1ff.

Against this canvas of dangers and suffering the problem of the death of individuals recedes. The whole question of God's sovereignty in the world is raised by the predicament of historical existence in the world, and the New Testament offers two answers side by side. On the one hand the world is already on the way out and the forces of evil have been exposed in their futility;[11] on the other the present is worked into a dramatic whole and made part of a sequence leading to the End.

In this dramatization of the conflict the figure of Anti-Christ becomes part of the expectation. Within the Church Antichrist is recognized as the seducer who denies, and causes others to deny, that Jesus is the Christ and that Jesus, if Christ, was human.[12] Thus the Christians experience in their special sphere of 'Faith' the attacks of Antichrist before the Antichrist, and the Last Hour before the Last Hour.

It remains, however, the centre of the Gospel that Satan and his host were defeated by Christ's obedience on the Cross and God's vindication of Christ in the Resurrection. The persistent increase in Evil is still ascribed to the onslaughts of wicked forces which will until the Last Day operate with unequalled ferocity, just because their ultimate defeat is already certain. The 'mystery of lawlessness' is already at work and will induce a general falling away in apostasy until the 'man of sin'—'the son of perdition, that opposes and exalts himself against all that is called or worshipped as God'—makes his final attempt to dethrone God and put himself in the place of God. This attempt at usurpation on the part of fallen angels reflects the rebellion of a whole hierarchy of ungodly powers and is, in its turn, reflected also by the evil tyrannies which make historical existence a fearful burden.[13] At the same time these passages in the New Testament make it clear that resistance to evil is not only possible but a matter of duty and that in some parts of the world at least it can be mastered without actual martyrdom.[14] Indeed, according to the best interpretation of Thess. ch. 2, the authority of the State, i.e. of the Roman administration, is by no means to be identified with the Enemy but rather with the restraining influence which at least provides a semblance of order and thereby an opportunity for the Church to exist and to expand. Hence the New Testament with all its dramatic expectation of the slaying of the Serpent, the Dragon, the Anti-Christ[15] contains several passages which express a positive estimate of the state, for 'rulers are not a terror to the good work, but to the evil'.[16] 'Honour

[11] 1 John chs. 14–17.
[12] 1 John 2:18, 22; 2 John; 1 Tim. 4:1.
[13] 2 Thess. ch. 2; Eph. 6:10ff.
[14] Heb. 12:4.
[15] Rev. 12:7.
[16] Rom. 13:3.

all men, love the brotherhood, fear God. Honour the King!' is an important principle,[17] whose advocate at the same time articulates 'Be watchful: your adversary the devil, as a lion, walks about seeking whom he may devour'.[18] The dramatic sequence of events, as experienced by the people of God living in history, thus accommodates the 'present age' in the cosmic unfolding of the 'age to come'. As long as it is possible Christians must resist Antichrist and be fortified by the hope that at the End they will be victorious with Christ. If the State, however, openly sides with Antichrist then, it would appear, the restraining hand has been withdrawn and the final act of the drama of redemption is about to dawn. Thus the hopelessness of the times creates a pattern of hope: at the end Christ will triumph and defeat the enemy.

In the emergent pattern contemporary trials appear in a setting of predictions and revelations, such as are given in the apocalyptic chapters of the Gospels (especially Mark ch. 13) and the monumental unfolding of the Apocalypse itself. It belongs to the nature of the pattern that it uses a narrative form in which one event is depicted as succeeding another. Thus the impression is gained that earthly history figures in a cosmic narrative of super-human dimensions. According to Mark ch. 13 the teaching is given privately in answer to the disciples' request for a date. The purpose of the Lord's answer is to warn them against false Christs and to inspire them with a sense of endurance, 'for the end is not yet'. After conceding that during the delay the whole world must be brought within the compass of disintegration, partly by wars and partly by natural catastrophes, the Lord dwells again on the disciples' particular duty in the time of crisis. Their share in the drama is to bear witness for Christ, not by way of prepared apology, but by the unpremeditated inspiration of the Holy Spirit. Almost casually the Lord puts off the hour of the End—'the gospel must first be preached unto all the nations'. Endurance to the end, therefore, means the acceptance of the delay and of all the hateful consequences of confessing Christ: expulsion from Israel, from the family, from the world. The exhortation suggests that *only* the heroic witness, i.e. 'he who endures to the end', can and will be preserved. But Mark makes mention of a specific historical crisis (the siege of Jerusalem or an earlier crisis?) when flight and not endurance is the right measure. This tribulation, which seems to overtake all irrespective of religious loyalty, is so serious that it looks like the End. Surprisingly it turns out to be only the precursor to further existence, for God shortens the days of intolerable

[17] 1 Pet. 2:13ff.   [18] 1 Pet. 5:8.

sufferings. A long interval follows and then the cosmic upheavals
announce the Son of Man's coming with great power and glory.
The End has come and culminates in the gathering of the elect from
all the corners of the universe. The date of this event is known only
to the Father, but it is near, so near that the hearers are admonished
again to watch and pray for the coming of their Lord: 'This generation shall not pass away, until all these things be accomplished.'

The pattern consists of the warp and woof of contradictions.
Its paradoxical inconsistency becomes even more marked in the
Apocalypse where repetitions complicate the design. But if the
convention of the narrative—as a report of successive events—be
ignored the pattern may be freed from its chronological fetters and
be understood as a prophecy:

(1) EARTHLY EXPECTATIONS OF THE CHURCH:
     world-wide testimony and gradual success
     conversion of nations and Jews
     dissensions within
     persecutions without

(2) THE PRESENT WORLD:
     condemned but temporarily reprieved
     increase of lawlessness
     tribulations, wars, famines
     advent of abominations and Antichrist
     approaching End within a calendar of time

(3) THE ACT OF JUDGEMENT:
     Individuals' Death and Accountability
     Exposure of the Enemy and forces of Satan
     The Assizes: Trial, verdict, sentence, mourning
     Resurrection of all Flesh
     Retribution and Vindication
     The Millennium: Kingdom of Saints
     Intervals of waiting, Possibilities of Purgation
     and Ascent

(4) THE COSMIC END:
     The Last Day
     Portents in Heaven: Sun, Moon, Stars
     Universal Catastrophe
     Christ's Return in Glory
     Punishment of evil angels
     Final Reversal
     Light conquers Darkness
     Consummation of Christ in God

This four-fold ordering corresponds to no timetable but to the early Christian Community's acclamation of Christ, as the Saviour of the world, as the risen Victor and Conqueror of the world, as the Son of Man and Judge of all men and of all things, as the Son of God who restores the Kingdom to the Father. It demonstrates the Church's involvement in history, in the day-to-day struggle in, and against, and on behalf of, the contemporary world, together with the Church's conviction of present victory and future glory in a realm freed from the contingencies of power and temporal vicissitudes. Thus the apocalyptic pattern responds to the task in the present world and to the eternal anchorage of faith, and accommodates the richly variegated past. Moreover, the pattern attempts to combine the dramatic suddenness, the unexpected givenness of the divine action, the uncompromising 'Either-Or' faith (salvation-or-damnation), together with the undoubted gradualness of growing churches and the slow maturing of human personality in the realm of faith. Hence the pattern permits on the warp of eternity the existence of such woofs of intervals and change as mitigate the severity of the crudely stated themes of the End.

The life of the Church shows even in New Testament times that the continuation of earthly existence did not run counter to the End-hope. There is throughout the New Testament writings an awareness of the community as an orderly people of God whose institutions reflect in their simplicity the Reign of God which has already begun. The Body of Christ, as St Paul insists, is the Israel of God, not bound by human laws but by faith in God who is the author of loving, orderly concord. Enthusiasm must never swallow up the rational and responsible existence of the united Body, which is to be built up and not to be pulled down. Wrecking ecstacy has no place in a community which serves God in Christ. Thus the Church as bearer of the End-hope prepares for the End by strengthening all the conservative forces of goodness, such as the family, in a deliberate and rational manner. Moreover the wealth of spiritual gifts does not minister to apocalyptic confusion, but rather to a form of hierarchical government which, free from human jealousies, reflects in its institutions the building-up purpose: apostles prophets, teachers, miracle-workers, healers, ecstatics, interpreters are encouraged in their work.[19] Similarly members are instructed and baptized and break bread in a liturgical manner which develops 'until the Lord come'.[20] Indeed in the rites of the Church the End-pattern is set forth and experienced by an act of 'remembrance', which grants a participation of the glorious future.

[19] 1 Cor. ch. 12.　　　　　　　　[20] 1 Cor. 11:26.

The sacramental life of the Church is particularly designed to wed the ecstatic End-hope to the order of the Church. Both in Baptism and in Eucharist the saving history of Israel is remembered to show how the release from the bondage is fulfilled in the final release from sin and Satan: thus the act of memorial is no pious exercise but a recall of the mighty acts which pass into the present reality. Those about to be baptized escape from the imminent condemnation and enter the ark of life; those who feed on the Lord share in the Bread of Life, which in its turn points to the future consummation when the celestial banquet awaits those who have become eligible and worthy of the Kingdom. In as much as the Lord's Death and Resurrection are central to every Christian act of worship it is impossible for the sacramental institution to become a self-contained act. Similarly the Christian life turns upon an imitation of him who brought to an end the old, and ushered in the new, age.

This identification with Christ—who was, is and is to come;[21] yesterday, today, tomorrow—reaches its highest measure in suffering and martyrdom, for when men are persecuted for the Name and even have to give their lives for the Name they recall the Passion and Death in their own bodies and stake their belief in the Living and Crucified Lord, not only as the cause of their sufferings but also as their hope. They share in his cross and will share in his glory.[22] Their personal decision thus draws together Christ past, present, and future in the continuum of time and history. The First Epistle of Peter gives the classical exposition of suffering as the condition of genuine hope.

The Fourth Gospel goes furthest in freeing the Christian hope from apocalyptic excesses and interprets the End in terms of the organic union between Christ and his own. The faithful share in the Life of Christ, and the Kingdom of God is the eternal Life which his Presence as the shepherd and door renders possible and which the living Bread, Wine, and Water sustain beyond physical limitations. Men who prefer darkness and death, and not demons, make up the apocalyptic anguish. Human life in the flesh terminates in the perdition which God's Son has come to avert by living in the flesh. Life itself is wholly relative; unless it is lived in the Son, in the loving and knowing faith-union, it is not life in the real sense of the word. The work of Christ is eschatological because he has eternal Life and God has sent him to raise up the elect at the last day—the constant refrain in ch. 6. But this process of life-saving is already beginning: 'the hour comes and now is' when the

---

21 Rev. 1:8; Heb. 13:8.   22 Rom. ch. 8; 2 Cor. ch. 4.

tombs open and the dead come out.[23]   Present fulfilment does not
rule out future hope; on the contrary, the work of Christ inspires
every hope for the future.   Thus John has not abandoned the common New Testament eschatology[24] but has universalized that personal experience of which St Paul could say: 'I live, yet not I, but
Christ in me.'[25]   This 'in-Christ' existence could have become the
mystical cancellation of the End-hope if Christianity had been conceived merely as a personal experience.   Instead, according to the
fourth Gospel in true Pauline feeling, this mystical sharing in Christ
feeds the hope for the future with an unfolding of further stages of
apprehension: truth, not yet to be tolerated, will be given and the
Christ-like will advance from glory to glory in inconceivable
radiance.   Thus world-judgement can now be understood as world-
salvation,[26] for the Holy Spirit dwells in the Church and authenti-
cates her mission by those whom Jesus sends.   The Spirit 'places
the world in the position which it will occupy at the last judgement'
and 'the Spirit is thus the eschatological continuum in which the
work of Christ . . . is wrought out.'[27]   Thus the possession of the
Spirit, as bestowed by the living Christ from the Father, prepares
for the future.

First-century Christianity did not discreetly drop the End-hope.
The possession of the Spirit controlled its excesses and transformed
some of its features, which naturally varied from place to place.
No doubt individual taste and convictions played their own part,
as can be seen from the inscriptions on, and the iconography of, early
Christian tombs.   Optimism and pessimism alternated as in any
other society.   The events of the century served to discredit dated
expectations.   Jerusalem had fallen in A.D. 70, the Jewish Christians
became dispersed and soon disappeared from the scene, Christianity
became and remained illegal, oppressive measures increased, the
generation of the Apostles was passing away, the Lord had not
come.   Yet the earliest slogan, which St Paul quotes in Aramaic
in 1 Cor. 16:22—Maranatha!—lost none of its force.   Whether it
conveyed originally a sense of past, future or imperative—the Lord
has come, the Lord will come, Lord come!—it is now impossible
to judge.   But in the last book of the New Testament the writer
uses its theme to look again to the future.   'Behold, he comes with
clouds', he begins[28] to unveil the cosmic drama in which the Lamb
sets out with his angelic host to annihilate 'Babylon' and the wicked

---

[23] John 4:23; 5:25 ff.
[24] Cf. C. K. Barrett: *The Gospel According to St John*, p. 57; C. F. D. Moule:
The Birth of the New Testament, 1962, p. 98.
[25] Gal. 2:20.   [26] John 3:17; 12:47.
[27] Barrett, *op. cit.*, p. 76.   [28] Rev. 1:7.

beast. To the sound of the trumpets the elect witness the Advent of the Coming One in his heavenly Jerusalem. The victories and triumphs of martyrs and virgins are consummated in the celestial company of the Lamb while the wicked perish with Gog and Magog in Satan's confusion.

The Apocalypse did not easily gain universal approval, and for a long time the East resisted its admission as divinely inspired Scripture. The closing years of the first century, however, as well as the terrors of the second, provided only too suitable a background for its ultimate place in the New Testament. This document more than any other committed the Church to an End-hope which could not be explained away rationally or obscured by her own institutions. Thus the Church set forth on her spiritual conquest by offering salvation to the world in such terms as excluded a purely this-worldly success. Evangelism and worship still converged upon 'that day', namely the Judgement and the Consummation of all things.

CHAPTER IV

THE CHRISTIAN TRADITION OF THE END

'He shall come with glory to judge the quick and the dead: of his kingdom there shall be no End', 'I expect the Resurrection of the Dead and the life of the age to come'. Thus articulated the Church the primitive faith of first-century Christians and, despite an inevitable waning of the imminent hopes of consummation, this portrayal of the End became part of the Creeds of the new universal religion. No one could be taught the Faith, undergo Baptism, and share in the Eucharistic food, without being reminded by common confession that he himself was a pilgrim on the road to an eternal destiny and that his pilgrimage was part of a vast cosmic process of redemption, which reaches its End with the annihilation of evil and the Triumph of the returning Christ. Clearly the so-called disappointment arising out of Christ's failure to return did not deprive the Christian Church of her End-hope. On the contrary the End always remained in sight and the message of hope prominent.

The bare propositions of the Creed cannot, however, tell the whole story. The message of the End certainly became an *articulus stantis aut cadentis ecclesiae*—the Church had to stand by maintaining it or fall by giving it up. It was an article firmly embedded in the belief in God and Christ. It became part of the history which it caused and inspired, for by expecting the End in the terms of judgement and glory the Church entered the history of the world in a very peculiar way. It met the world as something outside itself, something to be won over, something to be resisted, something to be condemned if need be. Until it became safe to be a Christian in the Roman world the End-hope fortified the Church in her mission. The New Testament pattern still prevailed and strengthened morale and conviction: the Church could regard herself as the bearer of the hope and her ecclesiastical institutions could be seen to serve a cosmic End.

The simple relationship, however, was not destined to last, for if the End-hope caused history to be made, history also caused the End-hope to be modified. As the Church left behind the Jewish background and enrolled Gentile members new attitudes and feelings obtained. The new geographical and ethnic orientation could not but affect the Church's framework of eschatological beliefs.

38

Alongside the Greek discussion of ideas the Latin ascendency favoured their use in the support of law and order. In the West the centralization of power in the Bishop of Rome, and the final recognition of this power by the State, gave a new look to the End-hope. In the East the influence of the monks and the prevalence of ascetic practice stressed new conceptions of perfection which had had no place in the primitive pattern of the Kingdom of God.

A perusal of Patristic literature shows that certain inconsistencies of belief could not be avoided. The Fathers had to work with a dialectic which did justice to both the present triumph of Christ and the future reign of God. They held to the literal interpretation of the Biblical texts and combined these with the idealism of philosophy. Thus they arrived at a 'vertical' time-concept which, unlike the 'linear' notion of duration, could accommodate eschatological claims; for example, they could affirm that Christ is really present in the Sacrament and yet will come again: he is down here, in time; up there, in eternity. Similarly they combined a materialistic expectation of the End with a spiritual awareness of life and light in the world to come. Yet their grip on the principle of eternity did not prevent some of them from working out time-schedules (Lactantius reminds one of British Israel in this respect), for they did not think of the world in evolutionary terms, such as favour the Christian religion with a steady progress, but rather as a battle heading for a climax. Although the nuances of the different writers vary, everything is for them on earth but a foretaste of total salvation at the End.

Throughout the succeeding centuries, then, the credal statements continued unchanged but the impact of history modified and developed the meaning of the doctrine of the Last Things. The tension between East and West, the several devastations of Italy and Rome, the onslaught of Islam, the waves of invaders from Asia, left their marks on interpretation. The history of Europe after the Dark Ages rekindled the hope. However rent asunder by wars and insecure in its institutions, Christendom revived its belief in the future. Despite schisms and lasting divisions the Kingdom of God could not be dismissed as an illusory hope.

The events of the sixteenth century freed eschatology from its Catholic anchorage. Against the wishes of the Reformers the End-hope becomes again the possession of independent dreamers, ranters, and sectarians, whose allegiance to ecclesiastical institutions is so frail or non-existent that it becomes in their hands a political and religious force in its own right. The flood-gates are again open and uncurbed eschatology reaches the ordinary people.

The Reformers detested and feared unbridled eschatology as much as Papal claims. For them the Reformation itself was an eschatological event and the reformed Faith was the key to the Kingdom of God and the present tribulation the point of its actualization. Neither Luther nor Calvin freed themselves entirely from the medieval world-view and their Biblical outlook did not help them to reconcile apocalyptic expectations with the present task. They had to oppose the anticipatory eschatology of Rome and the fanaticism of the sectarians, but they did not work out a system of their own, and it is probably no accident that they shied away from the interpretation of the Apocalypse.

Yet despite the influence of the new humanism the Reformers still retain the pattern of the Judgement and the Second Coming. Calvin, indeed, perpetuates the dialectic of salvation and damnation with great emphasis on its final and eternal character. All the same, the final hope loses something of its cosmic breadth, and instead the individual, at the hour of death, looms large. For Calvin, in particular, the doctrine of the immortality of the soul, as set forth in the Psychopannychia of 1542, in which he combats, among other things, the view of the soul-sleep after death (against Luther), is a firm buttress of belief. In as much as it may be said that this is derived from Plato rather than from Christ one may perhaps detect signs of the spirit of the age. Once again, Biblical realism and Gentile reflection are brought to bear upon eternal problems which are historically conditioned. Thus Calvin, without abandoning belief in the final deliverance of Christ's Kingdom to the Father, depicts the future in such transcendent terms as to spiritualize the End of the world. Unwittingly the Reformers paved the way to the modern Protestant dislike of literal eschatology.

Enough has been probably said to make the point that the so-called Christian tradition of the End exists only in a broad sense, for it is always subject to regional, ethnic, and historical fluidity. In this great complexity we can, however, detect a few constants which may change their outward shape without loss of stability. Above all, the varying conceptions of the End depended always, and from the first, on the recognition of the enemy: this hostile force was identified with the ANTICHRIST of the New Testament. The Biblical passages, taken out of their context, built up a formidable picture of the mysterious dark power, the devil incarnate, the unique source of all lies, the false Messiah, whom— as was quite wrongly alleged—the Jews expect. Sorceries and heresies evidence his potential power in the world. This Antichrist became the exact counterfeit of the true Christ whom he imitates:

born a Hebrew of unclean or of fantastic parentage his advent coincides with the end of the Roman Empire; he favours the Jews, deceives the elect, and rebuilds the Temple where he has himself enthroned, though he is an apostate and a murderer. He has at his command unlimited miraculous powers; only at the end, after making war on the saints and sending portents of destruction, are his days numbered, and the destroyer with his false church is himself destroyed.

As can be seen, the anti-Jewish element in the Patristic identification of Antichrist is very pronounced and historically conditioned. But every new situation could accommodate other interpretations, since Nero had already in the primitive Church served as a famous figure of Antichrist. Every age can boast its Beast or Scarlet Woman and every century has its candidate for the mysterious number six-six-six. Traitors within and oppressors without induce the reaction: 'Antichrist is here!' In this vein Justin exposes Trypho the Jew (c. A.D. 160), Irenaeus denounces anonymous Gnostic leaders (c. 180), Tertullian indicts Marcion (c. 210). Hippolytus denounces the imitator-Christ, the would-be lion of Judah (200); similarly Jerome accuses Bishop John of Jerusalem (415). Endless are the curses heaped upon Origen in Justinian's decrees (542), for Origen, who taught the pre-existence of the soul, the passing character of punishment, and the ultimate reconciliation of demons, became the very type of heretic whose godliness made him more influential, and therefore more dangerous, than the open enemy. Such men, it was felt, deserved the solemn 'Anathema'.

Yet these labels and slogans also helped to curb the expectation of the End, for it became obvious, as John of Damascus stated, 'there are many Antichrists before the Antichrist' (742). Such a philosophy of history enabled the Church to move forward to the great age of her dominion in Europe. Islam swept across two continents and was hailed as a divine punishment (by Methodius of Para c. 670). Wars, losses, and splits occurred on a large scale; yet from the days of Charlemagne onwards the Church could proclaim *Christus Victor* as a visible fact. The confidence in Christian power established on earth led to aggressive policies, for the Church, no longer shaking under the threat of the End, tried to reconquer lost territories in the name of the End-hope. In 1146 St Bernard of Clairvaux preached the second Crusade against the Prince of Lies and many nobles responded with zeal. Although the cruel persecutions of the Jews and military failure in the East marred Bernard's gratification the crusading spirit against Antichrist was to remain alive for several centuries. Even if many Crusaders were attracted by unworthy motives of gain and violence the Utopian spirit was never absent from these ill-starred undertakings.

The detection of Antichrists knew no bounds. Not only infidels, Jews, Muhammadans had the convenient label attached to them, but Popes and Emperors also were not exempt from this term of denunciation. St Bernard called the Antipope Anaket II Antichrist. Wordly success seemed to favour the charge; for example the more splendid the reign of the Hohenstaufen Emperors became the less did they remain acceptable to the Sovereign Pontiff. Barbarossa was excommunicated in 1152 as Antichrist. Gregory IX called Frederick II the 'evil monster from the sea' (1239), the precursor of Antichrist. Less than a century later Dante indicts the Popes and looks to Henry VII as the redeemer of evil times. Pope Boniface VIII (1294–1303) is the High Priest of wickedness, fit to rot in Hell[1]; from his corruption and excesses the world will suffer until the ideal monarchy brings Reason and Charity to rule in the world and in the Church. Dante himself, however, lived long enough to be disillusioned and at the end of his life no longer believed in a simple political victory over Antichrist. Not so his successors, who still expected salvation from the defeat of Antichrist on earth. For Savonarola the wrath of God hangs over Rome in 1492, and he looks for Charles VII as the Messiah to restore the City of God and to convert the Muslims. According to such like him, to be for Christ is to be against the Church; for Pope Alexander VI is Antichrist, the scourge of God.

Wyclif and Luther were of a goodly company to call the Pope Antichrist and to identify their own day with the impending End. But after the Reformation the proliferation of Antichrists increased, until it became a convention, as in the Westminster Confession of 1647, to settle matters of faith by abusing the other side. But even within the reformed camp Antichrists began to abound in proportion to the hatred which Lutherans had for the Reformed, and the loathing which both felt for Anabaptists and revolutionary sectarians. The latter were not always slow to react and, following Thomas Müntzer (1489–1525), to believe that the ungodly, i.e. all but themselves, had no right to live. Yet there was a limit, too, to the persecution of Antichrist in the name of enthusiastic Utopianism, if only because the kingdom of the Saints or 'Zion' often discredited itself by its reign of terror. At Münster, where the so-called Johannes von Leyden reigned as king in 1536, immorality reached grotesque proportions. Gradually the theme wanes as order returns.

[1] Inferno xxvii:70.

Judas-Antichrist becomes almost a figure of fun, as in the burlesque and fantasies of Abraham a Sancta Clara (1644–1709).

The concept of the *Millennium* suffered a development sharply different from that of Antichrist, though intimately connected with it. The Thousand Years of the Messiah's reign were believed to follow upon the temporal defeat of the Anti-Messiah. In this form the doctrine had already been cherished in Jewish circles (Enoch chs. 13; 91; Ap. Baruch 40). It had also sustained the Christians; the 'binding of Satan' is a hope openly articulated in Rev. ch. 20. It was later given an arithmetic basis in the systematized arrangement of six word-epochs. This calculation used the poetic passage of Ps. 90, which declares that with God 'one day is like a thousand years'. The Sabbath of the Lord would accordingly coincide with the promised Thousand Years. On this fragile basis the early Christian writers took over the Jewish hope despite their hostility to Jewish beliefs. The Epistle of Barnabas, Justin, Irenaeus, Hippolytus, Lactantius and others do not scruple to use this doctrine in their controversies despite its often crudely materialistic portrayal of the first Resurrection of the righteous. In the fantastic world of the Millennium the Moon shines with the radiance of the Sun while the Sun increases its brilliance seven times; the wicked serve as slaves and the saints reign and enjoy carnal pleasures.

When extremists, such as the monks in Egypt, and sectarians, such as the Montanists, indulged in these sensual imaginations they unwittingly began to discredit all 'chiliastic' prophecies. The theologians of Alexandria, who were the spokesmen of a very different tradition, could not easily swallow the naive absurdities of thoroughly uneducated folk. Origen, above all, scorned the materialism implicit in chiliastic expectations. Nevertheless, the issue dragged on and would have continued to feed the fanaticism of further centuries if St Augustine had not tackled the thorny problem. He was particularly well equipped for the task since he had himself been attracted to what he now turned into a heresy (*City of God*, Book 20).

The weakness of the chiliastic hope lay, of course, in the dating of the world-epochs. When would the Thousand Years begin? According to one calculation the world should have ended in A.D. 195; this was based upon a passage in the Sibylline Oracles (VIII:148) and a figure given for the duration of the Roman Empire: 948 (from the Greek letters for ROME). Strangely enough, however, the absence of fulfilment never really worried the convinced chiliast. On the contrary, new dates would appear, calculations would be amended. St Augustine attacked the whole scheme of chiliasm. He had lost patience with dates as such. Boldly he identified the Thousand Years with the existence of the Church on earth, the Reign of the Saints with the Kingdom of God itself. He did not throw out eschatology nor the transcendent nature of the Kingdom. Indeed, he dwells at length on the Last Hour—'how long is this last hour', is his comment on 1 John 2:18. Through him interest in the dating of the seventh-world-epoch waned and the whole debate lost its sting of immediacy, for the Hope could be deferred to around A.D. 1000—which was a long way off.

The effect of Augustine's teaching was far-reaching. The millennium became quite simply the 'Jewish heresy' and was no longer officially expected at all. Its failure to appear caused no misgivings, especially as the slow return to civilized existence in Europe caused men to discount fantasy. Until the time of the Reformation the doctrine was both dead and forbidden. The Reformers had no more love for it. Calvin, for example, thought it 'childish'. But outside the recognized bodies of reform the chiliastic zeal suddenly reappeared with great force. The Anabaptists espoused the discarded hope. In England, too, the Independents came to dominate the political scene with a genuine expectation of the End. The Savoy Declaration looked forward to the millennium and until the disillusionment in 1654 there was under Cromwell an increasing enthusiasm among the 'Saints'. John Archer and Thomas Goodwin hailed the 'fifth Monarchy' as about to usher in the millennium after the fall of the four kingdoms. Ironically the Jews owed to this expectation the end of the ban on their residence in England, even if it be admitted that their return must also be accounted for on economic grounds. But in the seventeenth century belief and policy cannot be separated; for example, Bunyan's *Pilgrim's Progress* reflects a yearning after the New Jerusalem and the reign of the Saints, which is as deeply embedded in the social situation as in spiritual experience.

Although Milton, Newton, and Whiston bequeathed different forms of millenarianism to posterity the movement lost its fervour in England. Instead North America, Germany, and Bohemia provided a fertile seed-bed. In 1740 Bengel published his commentary on the Apocalypse and made chiliastic hopes respectable despite the fact that, unwisely, he committed himself to the year 1836 as the turning-point when the Beast's three-and-a-half years would terminate and the imprisonment of Satan begin. People of high standing, such as Lavater, spread the popular hope in Switzerland. Swedenborg gave the year 1757 as the start of the millennium. In the nineteenth century no less a person than Franz Delitzsch opposed the repudiation of the doctrine as implied by Reformation and Counter-Reformation alike. However, these verbal battles belonged largely to the study and perhaps the pulpit. The epoch-making, because world-transforming, millenarian movements seized the people on the American Continent, where all sorts of adventist sects created settlements from which states and institutions finally developed. 'Jerusalem on the American Continent' became a popular slogan, more or less connected with the traditions of Christian belief. From America Adventism spread through its missionaries, back again to Europe and, above all, to the African Continent. Here, however, it can be noted that the Christian affiliation tends to become weak and sometimes non-existent. Nationalist movements are apt to take over the hope of the rule of a Thousand Years in its entirety. In the ideology and propaganda of Hitler, for example, the *Tausendjährige Reich* is the very opposite of the Utopia built upon Christ and his Coming.

Despite the inherent absurdities of millenarianism the Christian tradition has remained attached to the hope that the LAST DAY, or the last hour, is about to approach. There is not a century without persons of some standing who either predict the imminence of the End or even believe that the last hour has already struck. Calculations and dates abound, despite the much-quoted 'But of that day or that hour knows no one except the Father' (Mark 13:32). Against this damper to speculative enquiry the de-coding of numbers, as given in Daniel and the Christian Apocalypse, has always retained its popularity. In Sub-Apostolic times an Ignatius can say: 'The last times have come', as he proceeds to his martydom. Tertullian in the second century awaits the Kingdom and the New Age as a moral necessity. Ephraem the Syrian (306–373) plays on the 'Holy Spirit Guitar' long lyrics on 'the End of the World'. Martin of Tours (316–397) anticipates Antichrist very soon. Commodian (third century) knows his age to be that of Antichrist. It would be tedious to cite all the authorities who, owing to the pressure of the evil in he world, are led to conclude that the End cannot be far off. Despite St Augustine's brake on such thoughts and the emerging self-assurance of the Church as a lasting institution, even when Islam had to be held at the gates of Europe, the cry of the End was always on men's lips. Later St Bernard, for example, though interested in the calculation of dates makes a point of refusing to accept the necessity, commonly granted, that the Last Day must dawn in his generation. Certain compromises could be made up, as by Rupert of Deutz (*c.* 1120) who deemed the seventh age to run side by side with the sixth. Some visionaries, such as Hildegard of Bingen (1098–1179) oppose speculations about the date, no doubt in order to preserve their own sanity and reputation. Others change their opinion, like Otto von Freising (*c.* 1143), who was convinced of the imminent End of the world and then corrected his gloomy predictions in the light of his nephew's (Barbarossa's) splendid successes.

The wave of excitement, always latent, reached its zenith in the preaching and in the writings of Joachim of Fiore (1130–1202), who looked for the Great Sabbath in 1260 and for the coming of the spiritual church. He is said to have encouraged Richard Lionheart against Saladin, who was considered to be the last of the six enemies before Antichrist. According to Joachim this Antichrist was in fact already alive, about fifteen years old and almost ready to pounce. Much of the popular piety of the age owes its existence to the abbot, not least the great *Dies Irae, Dies Illa,* which is ascribed to Thomas of Celano (*c.* 1250).

With the dawn of reason and the amazing advances in all the arts this Adventism was not likely to find favour among the hierarchy, but among the extremists Joachim's prophecies remained very much alive. The astonishing and depressing career of Rienzi (1313–1354) was certainly aided by them and the year 1367 was looked upon as a likely date of the End. Later the papal schism (1378–1417) lent itself to fresh interpretations of the End. The Taborites gave 1420 as the year for the Day of Vengeance and the Advent of Christ. Even as good and brilliant a Catholic prince as Nicholas of Cusa (1401–1464) calculated the date of the End; according to his figures the era 1452–1700 was the age of Jesus-Salvation before the end and this was to be followed by the Messianic birthpangs of horror until 1734. In this scheme of things Muhammed was now seen to have been the first beast whom others were yet to follow.

At the end of the fifteenth century Columbus set out to the Indies and reported to their Spanish Majesties on his discoveries; they were, he firmly believed, part of the greater eschatological design. The literature of about 1500 abounds in prophecies after the style of Joachim, and when the Reformation burst upon Europe, many, like Luther in his earlier period, hoped that the Last Day was before the doors. In 1521 Luther commented gloomily on the signs of the times, such as the planets in conjunction, the invention of the printing press and the making of books, not to mention new weapons of war. He hastened feverishly the publication of his translation of the book of Daniel lest it appear too late, for he doubted that the sixth millennium would be completed. Even Melanchton, certainly no lover of millenarianism, did not deem the

Day far off. Zwingly, this-worldly and yet also somewhat Platonic in outlook, can say 'The Lord is at hand', although he virtually regrets the presence of the Apocalypse in the New Testament.

After the Reformation new dates of hope abound everywhere. Suffice it to say that the achievements and the miseries of the seventeenth century in particular did not lack their eschatological flavour. For good and evil the Last Trumpet is lifted up and sounded as if to anticipate the great event. Even in the eighteenth century the deflation of the hope is not yet complete and the sectarians are as eager as ever for the coming of the Day. 'Wake up, wake up', calls the voice from heaven, but a note of caution creeps in now. Thus influential leaders, such as Bengel in Germany (1687–1752), make room to defer the fulfilment of the hope. They fix upon a day when they themselves will no longer be on this earth and can therefore not be held accountable for errors in the time schedule.

The many variations of the Advent hope have one thing in common: they are never divorced from real life. There may have been a few eccentrics who merely sat down to calculate dates, but they are not representative of that enthusiastic zeal which associated the call of the Last Trumpet with ambitious plans of transformation on earth. Just as primitive Christianity did not turn its 'waiting for the Lord' into mere passivity and followed, on the contrary, St Paul's advice to labour in all spheres, so the heirs to the End-hope lived out the same paradox: because the Day is about to dawn we must work while we can. In particular there were often attempts to display the Advent hope in such new social organizations as would return to, what was imagined to be, the perfection of the primitive Church. Just as orthodox communities practised poverty, celibacy, and obedience, the Adventist leaders attempted to give a definite social expression to a united brotherhood. Forms of Communism can be detected in every century. If such institutions could not be tolerated, or if divisions occurred within these revolutionary institutions, then these millenarian movements would seek their fortune elsewhere. Thus the Advent hope goes hand in hand with *Utopian schemes of world-improvement* and with pioneering movements and large-scale migrations.

The abbot Joachim of Fiore, whom Dante honours with a special place in Heaven (*Paradiso* XII:139–142), paired his expectation of the Coming of the Age of the Holy Spirit with plans for an ascetic life in which communism and evangelic poverty are woven together in an apocalyptic framework which never ceased to inspire some later sects and brotherhoods. These movements were often regarded as subversive of the established order, and men like Arnold of Brescia and Savonarola paid the penalty for their social reforms. But after the Reformation this enthusiasm found an outlet in appropriate channels. The eagerness with which schools, colleges and hospitals were founded and endowed by men, Catholic and Protestant alike, who genuinely believed in the speedy arrival of the End, characterizes the social usefulness of their hopes. The pursuit of the millennium led, among other things, to the creation of settlements in Europe and America, to the draining of swamps and the good husbandry of natural resources by technically advanced communities pledged to work for the common weal.

Many of these so-called brotherhoods derive from the monastic establishments and continue to work for the ideals of the *Fratres Communis Vitae*. In the face of the threatening chaos, with its ravages of war and the spread of venereal disease, they evolved a new type of perfectionism. The groups which take their name after Menno Simons (1492–1559) sought to express their millenarian ideals in a simple life of community. They detested war and they loved the common life. They practised community of goods but they did not proclaim the aggressive kind of Christian communism which stems from Müntzer. They would have abhorred Marxist Socialist doctrine. They were basically suspicious of science, but in order to build Zion in many different places they jettisoned their prejudices against learning. These brotherhoods were particularly popular in Bohemia before their migrations reached the ends of the world. They display a similar rhythm everywhere: millenarian utopianism provides the impetus and institutional prosperity ensues. When the Adventist spirit flags it is replaced by pietism of a softer note. But men like Count Zinzendorf (1700–1760), with his Herrn-huter foundation, and the Moravian settlements, prove that Utopian pietism still possessed the power to summon men to voluntary discipline and to great achievements in every sphere.

In the New World Adventism of many shades nourished the sectarian spirit. On this enormous continent, with a vast surplus of land, founders of religion with unorthodox and strong millenarian views found a strong following in the nineteenth century. The migration of the Mormons, for example, from New York State to Missouri and then through Illinois to the west, and their creation of the state of Utah, cannot be understood apart from the inner drive towards Utopia which comes to rest in conquest and achievement. Thus the Seventh Day Adventists lived out their dogma of the pre-millennial return of Christ by founding schools and colleges, publishing-houses and hospitals. The imminent destruction of the wicked and the translation of the living righteous to heaven did not prevent them from expressing their belief in progressive institutions. They see no contradiction in eschatological creed and humanistic practice.

These sectarian Adventist institutions may in course of time lose their original impetus of the Advent-hope in the same way in which orthodox Christianity may jettison its belief in the Coming One and the New Age. But the main Christian Tradition resists this tendency by its unremitting pursuit of *Mission*. As long as the Church herself is on the move and invades fresh territories by preaching and evangelistic activity it justifies its institutional nature by expansion. Behind these works, often involving sacrifice and martyrdom, lies the further belief that when the Faith has been preached to all nations the End will come, and not before. Hence the Advent-hope may sound a somewhat aggressive and even militaristic note of conquest. The famous 'Compel them to come in!' gave rise to forced conversions, and the great medieval advocates of coercion really believed that the extirpation of the ungodly was also to be undertaken in the interest of hastening the End. But on the whole the Advent-hope made not for intolerance but rather for peaceful means of persuasion through example. There is even a note of pacifism in some of the contemporaries of such warriors as Cromwell. Zion and the Reign of Christ provoked not only regicide but also the mission-preaching of James Fox, who combined his aggressive preaching with the principle of non-violence. As from the seventeenth century a new interest was taken in the heathen, just because, with the rise of tolerance, there grew up a feeling that the Gospel may bring real blessings to the whole world in preparation for the Reign of Christ. Men like Spener (1635–1705) and Francke (1663–1727), to mention only a few of this epoch, wished to gain Israel and the Gentiles for the redemption of Zion. The conversion of the Jews now re-enters the arena of the Messianic Hope; the study of the Epistle to the Romans and, arising out of it, a friendlier feeling for the Ancient People, quite reverse that earlier intolerance which, by identifying the Jews with Judas, cheerfully awaited their perdition in the last Day. The tremendous success of the Missions, more pronounced among the Gentiles than among the Jews (though not as insignificant among the Jews as sometimes imagined), revitalized the Advent hope. In the present century the old flame was rekindled by exaggerated claims of the conquest of all the continents for Christ.

The paradox of the God-given End and the work for the lasting Kingdom is deeply engrained in our Tradition. On the one hand we confront apocalyptic finality, on the other sensible husbandry. Yet the two aspects are not irreconcilable, for both are directed towards an *ideal of Perfection*. In the English language Blake has immortal-ized this longing in his 'Jerusalem'; this 'Emanation of the Giant Albion' combines with great originality the fervour and moral aspirations of Utopian perfection. 'Building Jerusalem' symbolizes the time-honoured ideal which only God's City can fulfil, and the challenge to which men must respond. Occasionally the ideal seems almost within the grasp of men, just as Rome appeared, however rarely, to embody the life of the promised perfect City (cf. Hymns of Prudentius). Ever since the days of St Augustine the tradition endeavours to have the best of both worlds, celestial and terrestrial. The latter ought to reflect the perfect harmony of the former and, as Gregory the Great saw clearly at a time of barbaric darkness, 'we in knowledge of the celestial country ought to rush towards it, as quickly as we can and in the shortest possible way' (*Commentary on Luke* 21:20). The monastic movement—as at Cluny—is itself a reflection of the celestial perfection, when it is moving at its highest level, just as the later brotherhoods, beginning perhaps with the Waldenses in Savoy, anticipate evangelic perfection by surrendering private property and civil rights, and, if necessary—like Abraham—betake themselves to the road into the unknown in the pursuit of the Millennium.

Thus both Catholic and Evangelical traditions encourage the work for the heavenly Jerusalem by commending a way of life at once humble and dedicated to the good of the whole of mankind. Heaven is the true and final *Patria*, Earth a place of banishment, but the way of perfection seeks to convert the latter into the former. This notion of social perfection is buttressed by a strong *individual-ism*, for it is the individual who responds to the call of perfection and will reap the final reward in the glorious future. Even when institutions lie in the dust on earth those who made them will be alive and continue their good work in eternity. Christian writers are understandably more detailed and eloquent in their descriptions of the fulfilment of personal merit than in their outline of the Kingdom of God as an impersonal state.

Man is immortal and heads for an eternal future. This basic tenet survived the flux of events and the threat of cosmic conflagra-tions. It came to dominate Christian eschatology. In the early days the promise of *eternal life* accounted for the Church's success; she summoned her members to perfection because perfection implies immortality. Eternal life is in that sense 'natural' to man, like night and day, or sleep and waking, or the germination of the seed (Clement of Rome, *c.* A.D. 90). But it is also more than natural, for the high calling to perfection involves sacrifice and even martyrdom. Thus Ignatius of Antioch (c. 110) typically considers his whole life a journey to God in the beauty of self-giving. He will become a true man if he allows God's wheat to sprout in him. To this end the temptations of the world need to be resisted and the passions mortified. The trials of men on earth betoken the bliss which is to come. Hence also the dead who lived before, and by hope and suffering anticipated Christ, have a share in eternity.

Death is sudden and the Resurrection, too, is abruptly dramatic, but the attainment of eternal life is portrayed by a gradual ascent. The immortal move forward 'to be built in among the angels', as the Shepherd of Hermas puts it, and to reach their deification in the City of God. This Christian apotheosis is thought of as 'progress among the stars' and is made to agree with the complex cosmology of the nine spheres and the respective orders of spiritual powers. The perfected rise from the lower spheres of the angels to the highest among Cherubim and Seraphim. A favourite traditional device pairs the number of the elect with that of the lost angels who, under Lucifer, rebelled before the world was made. Writers such as Origen and Anselm use this theme of the pre-mundane Fall to rationalize and harmonize the celestial status of man.

In this proliferation of different conceptions regarding the life after death we can detect a tug of war between spiritual and materialist tendencies and prejudices. Heavenly rewards vie with an other-worldly idealism which almost does away with the whole principle of continuity between conduct on earth and the glorious future. The apocalyptic prophecies, which work on a strict *quid pro quo* proportion of good works and fine rewards, are by no means palatable to all the Church Fathers. St Jerome, for example, stresses the fact that the new Jerusalem is more than the earthly Jerusalem renewed. St Augustine too looks to an eternal reality rather than to an earthly life perpetuated endlessly. Where deification is taken really seriously as in the East the very notion of perfection implies the cessation of earthly desires. The so-called Dionysus Areopagite (fifth century) conceives of immortality as a share in God's life; it is, therefore, immutable and apart from God there is no real sphere of life at all. The Oriental conception of light also helped to infuse discontinuity into the conception of the final bliss. It is true that the blessed are said to ascend in an ecstasy of apprehension of the eternal light and to that extent they retain their identity, but when they finally reflect the cosmic order in their hierarchical order little or nothing remains of the earthly and temporal. Educated men, who suffered and sought consolation in philosophy, such as Boethius, naturally embraced a doctrine which looked forward not only to the bright gaiety of Heaven and a rest after their trials but also to a complete detachment from activity. For the final rest is to know, and exist in, the truth after the removal of all the clouds of error and deception.

It is all the more remarkable that the Christian tradition did not surrender entirely to idealistic immortality. Right through the centuries the belief in the continuity of man—risen, changed, glorified—persists and obtains its credal sanction in the famous formulation of the *Carnis Resurrectio* which repudiates all notions of disembodied souls and of the transmigration of souls. Tertullian devotes a whole book to the Resurrection of the Flesh to establish with logical cogency the continuity to which all men are liable. It is not that flesh and blood cannot inherit the Kingdom of God; only corrupt flesh and blood are excluded from life, though not from punishment.

As we have seen before, what is needed is a synthesis which can comprehend the thesis of continuity and the anti-thesis of discontinuity: eternal life, which mounts on the wings of change to the transcendent changelessness. Thus the tradition looks to union with Christ as the meaning of eternal being, and Christ himself brings to the Resurrection the richness of continuity—'It is I'—and of discontinuity— 'touch me not—you will see me'. The great religious leaders never fail to stress the double nature of this meaning of eternal life which operates already in their midst. They commend virginity on earth in favour of a deferred marriage with Christ (St Jerome). They train for the contemplative life to prepare for the vision of Christ in glory (St Benedict). They place contemplation higher than thought, because it is in the state of contemplation that men ultimately replace the fallen angels (Isidore of Seville). But this state of contemplation is never reached apart from the perfecting of Love, for the ladder of ascent to the light is also a ladder towards perfect love (Johannes Climacus 579–649). Ascetic practice and mystical aim can never be divided, for, as St Bernard never tired of preaching, the alienation from self is the condition for the complete reflection of the heavenly light in man. The true freedom has to be won by mortification before God grants to us the final restoration of our bodies in freedom from all physical restraints. With good reason Dante appoints this Saint as his guide in Heaven to lead him from the earthly Paradise to the higher spheres of adoring love, where the unity of God is reflected in the ever-sustained desire of the perfected for the source of all perfection. Here the human is not lost in, but drawn into, the divine order, for humanity is enfolded in the hierarchy of Being. God gives all to man in Christ; his life is ours.

The climax of traditional eschatology was reached in the thirteenth century. Its doctrinal exposition is in the work of St Thomas Aquinas to which reference will be made more fully. Its architectural and sculptural perfection can still be admired in the great churches of this era, especially in France at Chartres, Amiens, and Bourges. Its musical and poetical creativeness has endured to this present day. In all aspects of human art, too numerous to be indicated here, the unique blend of the tradition asserts itself, binding together a scientific interest in cosmology and an awareness of moral perfection on the one hand, with a robust Christ-centred mysticism on the other. Eschatology never stands alone nor is it excluded from the day-to-day experience and feeling of the community. The present points to the future, and the future makes sense of the present; the here-and-now is an arrow towards the there-and-then. The classical notion of a general correspondence of reality sustains the magnificent edifice. The earthly microcosm is real because it corresponds to the macrocosm of the whole creation, God ruling over all, beginning and end.

But this medieval universe is never to be divorced from social and political realities. The End-hope is the key to the acknowledgement and power of justice. The highly ordered society derives its strength from an authority which is transcendental. The order is not an accident but sanctioned by the final order, the ideal Monarchy, the Kingdom of God. For earthly purposes this is perceived in the administration of justice, and justice is done, and seen to have been done, because rewards and punishments are meted out in the name of *the final retribution*. The threat of eternal punishment is to be understood in the forensic setting of maintaining order and warding off a return to barbarism. The tradition can only enunciate the bliss of Paradise if it gives an equal voice to the torments of hell. The symmetrical arrangement reproduces the typical Either-Or, by which the prophets stressed the severity of the Judgement. The verdict of the Court can be given only once and the sentence is irrevocable. Thus the retributive nature of punishment extends to all the nooks and crannies of the tradition which helps to protect the hard-won gains of a visible Christian civilization.

The lurid conceptions of the End do not necessarily belong to this conception of retributive justice. They can be traced back to the book of Enoch and the so-called Apocalypse of Peter, an anonymous work of the second century A.D., which enjoyed a certain popularity and sometimes even looked like being accepted in the Canon of the New Testament.   It is this Apocryphal document which articulates a strange delight in the sufferings of the tortured. When they cry for mercy they are told that the time for repentence is over.   This is common to the whole tradition, but the joy with which the righteous watch the torments of the damned is not.   In protest against this vulgar view Origen (185–254) went so far as to court defeat, for in pleading for the remedial nature of punishment he implied its temporal character.   He was the first of a long line of interpreters who postulated mitigating circumstances for the condemned.   He argued forcefully that guilt must be thought of as pre-natal.   If a man's sin is due to the Fall, which occurred before the world was made, his case is not hopeless, for justice demands that he be punished only for his own misdeeds.   Accountability must be paired with responsibility.   Furthermore, the End must ultimately also bring to an end sin and restore the perfection of the beginning.   Hence even the fallen powers and Satan must in acknowledging God escape from eternal torment.

The Christian tradition has never compromised with this or any other brand of *Universalism*,[2] for even in the view of mild thinkers, such as St Basil the Great (329–379) and his friends, the End is separation, dramatic and final.   The eternal fire radiates glory for the blessed and blazes avenging flames for those in Hell.   At the same time this refusal to bargain with Universalism, and the strength of the legal conception of Judgement, forced upon the tradition the need to deal with the majority of human beings who, according to Pope Gregory the Great (540–604) and many teachers in Rome, are neither damned nor can be considered in bliss immediately after death.   But if spiritual therapy in the hereafter is inadmissible and the gates are shut the case of the 'middle class' must become seriously problematic.   The tradition cannot really solve it by speaking, as does St Cyril of Alexandria (fl. 430–444), of the Church moving from corruption to her immortal existence, if the same possibility of progress and improvement does not lie within the grasp of individuals after their death.

It remains doubtful whether, in this connection, the concept of *Purgatory*—a paradox of reward and punishment—has ever really

---

[2] This is not to say that Universalism lacked its advocates at any time; there are many distinguished men *outside* the tradition, like Jakob Boehme (1575–1624), who plead for the reconciliation of evil powers.   Related in outlook is Annihilationism, put forward by Arnobius (fourth century) and condemned formally in 1513 by the Fifth Lateran Council, which quite simply puts non-existence in the place of torment. The modern version of Conditional Immortality was popularized by Edward White in *Life in Christ*, and found a lasting echo in the works of Martineau, Ibsen, Henry James, and (perhaps at least for a time) the Anglican Bishop and theologian Charles Gore.   In America a denomination carries the title 'universalist'.

found a happy place in the tradition. It is true that a whole culture
sprang up which rested upon the hope that, whereas Judas, Herod,
and the 'Rich Man' suffer endless privations in Hell—a typical
picture, used by John Scotus (810–877)—the 'normal' folk may just
get out of the devil's clutches as long as they are already saved.
This proviso is an important qualification on which all dogmatists,
beginning with St Gregory, insist. Eternal torments are never
reformatory and there is no mitigation of punishment for the
damned; only the penitent sinners can pay for the consequences of
their sins. It is a system of deferred payment in which others can
help by the weight of their prayers for the dead. Thus a gain is
available from which all can benefit within the strict terms of
Either-Or. The Church holds the trump cards against the impending
Day of Wrath by the offer of Baptism at the beginning and Unction
and Burial at the end, whilst Masses, Prayers, and Almsgiving continue to avail even beyond the grave of the deceased. This system
gives confidence to the dying, a sense of purpose to the living, and
translates pious hopes into practical action. Just because Purgatory
is not a middle state in the tradition but a realm of movement and
becoming, it can be used in such a way that present action makes
compensation for the future. On this basis, at any rate, capital,
which would not otherwise have been available, was subscribed to
pay for the building of schools, colleges, and hospitals.

The vehemence, with which the Reformers attacked the doctrine
of Purgatory and its relevant practices, shows, however, that the
system came to prove inadequate. Partly it had suffered from corruption, partly its abolition offered great prizes to the aggressors,
who curtly forbade the prayers for the dead. The Reformers believed in finality, discouraged speculation, and would have none
but the old bare bones of eschatology: all men rise in the Judgement
and receive their reward, nothing more, nothing less. The doctrine
of Justification by Faith could look after everything else and must
replace superstitions. By pruning the tradition of alleged accretions
it was made to return to its original centre: the fact of Death. The
ensuing scourges, which beset Europe in the violent centuries which
were to follow, confirmed only too cogently the inescapable core of
eschatology.

Personal piety comes to terms with Death in all sorts of ways.
Concern for the dead may oust every other consideration; then the
great themes of the Kingdom and cosmic consummation are virtually ignored. The Communion of the Saints can also become so
shadowy an affair as to lose its impact on the living. The Anglican
Prayer Book enunciates the hope 'to be delivered out of this present

world' but asserts that of future bliss with reserve. On the other hand there is a kind of piety, Catholic and Protestant, which exalts other-worldliness. Some famous hymns, among them the great chorales in the setting of J. S. Bach, perpetuate this feeling. Thus Paul Gerhardt sings: 'Ah, thou poor world', 'I am but a guest on earth', 'Come much desired hour', etc. This piety links a love for death with an intimate affection for Jesus and love for the neighbour: 'the duteous day closes' and with it sickness and pain depart. But there is in this nostalgia for death something fundamentally untraditional and unconvincing, if only because again the cosmic note of the Kingdom of God is abandoned in favour of a highly individualistic longing for an escape from living.

Another circumvention of Death, not wholly unlike in its piety, would deny the gravity of dying by offering the claim that death is already defeated in this life. Even as early as A.D. 1300 Meister Eckhart anticipated the many writers who believe in a 'Sea of Divinity', where the mystic experiences the immeasurable light, the incomprehensible love, and the divine union. Historical existence on earth does not worry them any more than Death: they are illusory. With men like Tauler (1300–1361) the Kingdom of God becomes the apex of the human soul; 'I' am the microcosmos of an entirely spiritual universe. After much controversy Pope Benedict XII succeeded in repudiating, if only by a narrow margin, such preposterous nonsense, and the Bull 'Benedictus Deus' (1336) restored, at least partly, the tradition that God will be seen at the time of universal fulfilment, and not before. But the mystics' tendency to spiritualize the state after death and to foreshorten the future suggests that the tradition of the End has an insecure base in the common experience of Death, which curiously enough, is its strongest, because universal, support.

In sum, the Western piety with regard to Death is exceedingly complex. Since the Tradition excludes Pre-existence and Reincarnation the Christian cannot postulate a simple logic of continuity. On the other hand he rejects the common experience of Death as final, for he holds all human souls to be immortal and personally accountable for their earthly existence. Partly he accepts Death as the happy gate-way to life, as if man were in training during this life for the hour of his death; partly he looks upon Death as a quasi-personal enemy, an obstacle to be dreaded and conquered. Death is 'natural', but in Balfour's words 'if there is no future life this world is a bad joke; and whose joke?' Love and Death are locked in a strife which no conceptions of the Hereafter can afford to ignore. Every death is as different as every life with its endless ramifications;

hence the intensity surrounding Death may vary from indifference to the deepest perturbation.

In the Tradition St Paul in his Epistle to the Romans, chs. 5–8, and St Augustine in his *Confessions*, Book IV, draw upon the vast range of death as an integral part of their theology of Hope, which is related and opposed to the philosophers' conception of Immortality. Death is real, as evidenced by the corpse's decomposition and the soul's agony, but the abyss of our dying is powerless against the life of Christ. Death is not, as to the Stoics, the natural order of things which cease to be but do not perish; rather it is the seal of perdition upon sin. Death represents the climax of our moral and religious disease from which Christ has come to save us. Death is last enemy, last after everything, including the devil: 'In the beginning death also came last—the counsel of the devil first, our disobedience next, and then Death.'[3] Death, though virtually defeated, is still to be put down, it is true, but—as Winklhofer finely observes—'whenever death occurs, there is a parousia of the Lord'. If the Christian experiences Death 'by dying daily' he already anticipates the miracle of the Resurrection. He matches despair with hope. 'The gospel does not show a way around the fear of death but a way through the fear of death to life in God' (Pelikan).

Thus the fine point of human mortality binds the Tradition of the End to every generation of men in their historical and personal existence.

[3] St John Chrysostom hom. 39, 4 in 1 Cor.

CHAPTER V

THE DOCTRINE OF THE LAST THINGS

No modern doctrinal statement of the things concerning the End can start out of nothing. Even if a modern theologian wishes to depart radically from formerly held beliefs he cannot change his data. These are given in a long tradition which begins in, or even before, the Bible and continues to our day. But within that tradition he must still turn to the Angelic Doctor of the thirteenth century; St Thomas Aquinas has treated of eschatology in such a systematic matter as can be comprehended even by those who know that six centuries of discoveries stand between them and his presuppositions.[1]

St Thomas does not treat the Last Things as the Cinderella of theology. If this part of the *Summa Theologica* supplements in a way what has gone before, and therefore really concludes the monumental work, it must not be imagined that he bestowed less care upon this section of theology. Eschatology is of one piece with the rest, and if it is here briefly summarized this can be done only on the strict understanding that the doctrines of God and Man, the Church and the Sacraments, enshrine the truth of which the future is a part.

At the same time a closer study of the relevant Quaestiones (LXIX–XCIX) will often reward the reader not only with the usual subtlety of St Thomas and surprising turns of the argument—constituting a denial of the charge that the Doctor merely proved what was already demanded by authority—but also with relatively long reflections on the subject which indicate a wide measure of disagreement, then and always possible among dogmatic theologians. Quite frequently St Thomas is content to weigh up the various possible premises and permissible inferences before he comes down to his own 'I say', qualified even by something like personal preference and grounds of probability.

St Thomas considers quite simply the matters which precede, accompany, and follow the Resurrection. But behind this formal approach there lies the strong conviction that all human actions, as indeed all real things, pursue a rational end and that this end can

---

[1] The *Supplementum* to the *Summa Theologica* was compiled by St Thomas's pupil Reginald of Piperno after the master's death. He made use of St Thomas's Commentary on the Sentences of Peter Lombard. But cf. also the *Compendium Theologiae*, capp. 149–184 and 241–245 (Marietti edn. Turin, 1954), with an English translation by C. Vollert (Herder, 1952). It is of special interest that this late work does not place eschatology at the end, but in the heart, of the great dogmatic summary.

be rationally apprehended. The true end of humanity is that of moral goodness, both in intention and in execution, and this final principle governs man's direction. The human race is therefore destined to unending happiness, for by God's loving purpose men attain to their end in the act of knowing and loving God. Hence man stands within a framework which unites him essentially to the eternal order, for although men may pursue diverse things as last ends they cannot change the goal of all activity. The expanded treatment of man's true Last End (*Summa Theologica* 11, 1, 6) removes all doubts as to St Thomas's positive—one may say, optimistic—estimate of human destiny. Man is meant to be happy because God is God. At the same time the process of consummation is not one of automatic preservation and sublimation and union with God, for man is sinful and is free to miss the Last End.

St Thomas is always aware of the tension which exists between that which Is and that which Ought to Be. He is a traditionalist who consults the masters of the past, but he is also ever-open to the issues raised by State, Church, Humanity as known to him. He knows that in writing he discharges a responsibility which is not merely of private concern, but rather one which must affect the public good. Hence his eschatology must constantly strive to embrace public issues, to buttress the good order, to serve the awakening world of the West, while at the same time he continues to be the Dominican teacher and mystic, who knows that matters of private spirituality and individual perfection equal in importance those of general and social significance. In this respect he deliberately employs an intellectual, almost scientific, and always logical approach and is never prepared to oppose plain common sense and healthy moral feelings, while his arguments and counter-arguments demonstrate that he will not spurn the more fantastical, religious, and extraordinary aspects of the End. No brief summary can do more than give a picture of his closely argued theology and none of the rich dialectic which sustains the same.

The first section deals with questions which arise before the Resurrection, i.e. the Judgement or the Last Day. It is here assumed from previous examinations that the soul is immortal and that it leaves the body upon death. St Thomas therefore makes the empirical, verifiable fact of human death his starting point. This central position accorded to Death has the advantage that we are immediately confronted by a fact, not an idea, and that this fact combines the individual and corporate aspects of humanity.

St Thomas does not wish to deny that the soul may be mobile. The nature of the soul's mobility is governed by its quality, the merit or lack of merit which it had acquired during life on earth.   Merit is said to lift the soul up.   This upward movement agrees, of course, with the general premise[2] namely, that 'above' constitutes a realm of light and beauty, and that conversely the dark places are below. St Thomas defends the view that there are many places which are fittingly proportionate to the states of the souls.   Thus the Holy Fathers are high up in their celestial places, although it must be added that St Thomas sees the difficulty of maintaining a spatial terminology when speaking about souls-without-bodies.   Nevertheless, the principle of congruity helps him here as elsewhere and he postulates objective grounds for the perpetuation of degrees of moral being and merit.

The souls are, in their various degrees, at rest after death, and St Thomas observes that 'Abraham's bosom', which was once identified with Limbo, is now, after Christ's work, a place of rest.   The souls' quality after death shows the essential nature of the soul as such.   Before death the soul is powerfully active, and St Thomas faces the controversial issues arising out of this concept.   The soul retains the sensitive powers after death, but only as a potential force and as a result of its past.   But this does not prevent the soul from physical impressions, such as the fire, which in this respect cannot be called metaphorical or imaginary.   The soul does not only see the fire, or react to it by way of fear and sorrow, or by seeing itself aflame, for, as the Doctor remarks, the mere apprehension of the image is not enough.   Here the realist insists that even a sacramental view of the fire is not enough, for the fire must really hurt, and even torment (as in the case of demons), in order to act upon the souls. Consequently we must conceive of the fire as possessing an incorporeal reality which can act directly upon the soul.

This discussion, despite its theoretical flavour, clearly stresses right from the start the feeling which underlies the medieval logic of eschatology.   The state of the soul is still fraught with dangers and possibilities, and it is the task of St Thomas to address himself now to the great and practical problem of what the living can do for the dead.   It goes without saying that he cannot divorce his analysis from contemporary institutions.   The modern reader must remember in this connection that the thirteenth century is not to be equated with the sixteenth and that the famous abuses of later times do not impinge upon the subject of Prayers for the Dead.

The dogmatic discussion must begin with the reiteration that the ultimate state of the Departed cannot be changed after death. The living can only contribute towards the fulfilments of the satisfac-

---

[2] Cf. U. Simon; *Heaven in the Christian Tradition* and *The Ascent to Heaven*.

tion owed by the soul and herein lies the profit of intercession. But it must not be imagined that St Thomas is only interested in the legal status of the soul, for here (and throughout) he never loses out of sight the overriding factor which is Charity. It is, of course, charity which prompts the living to pray for the dead. They are not forgotten, because they loved and were loved. The dead are not in doubt about their direction, unless they are damned, but they are still on their way as wayfarers, and in this their pilgrimage they are helped by the prayers of the Church. The objective worth of the Prayers of the Church are such that even if they are offered by the unworthy they still retain their value. On the other hand prayers for the wicked are impossible and the Church does not intend to pray for them, for 'guilt cannot be restored to order save by punishment'.

This rule is challenged (among other things) by the legend of Trajan's reprieve, which St Thomas relates here on the authority of St John Damascus. According to this tradition, Gregory, while praying for Trajan in hell, heard a voice from heaven saying to him: 'I have heard thy voice, and I pardon Trajan.' In reply to the objection that prayers do avail for those who are in hell St Thomas replies that Trajan was either recalled to life at the prayers of Gregory and thus obtained pardon and grace in a miraculous fashion, or that his punishment was suspended until the Day of Judgement. The reply does not sound very convincing and leads to the final observation of the infinite qualitative distinction between human limitations and divine power. The legend of Trajan proves, therefore, that the whole system is subject to mitigation. A century later Dante uses the symbol of Trajan in the *Paradiso* of the *Divine Comedy*, where the ex-pagan Emperor reigns in the Heaven of Jupiter as a representative of all the lovers of justice. The baptism of Trajan symbolizes God's acceptance not only of the best of paganism, but of every response to truth. Perhaps it leaves even a loophole for prayers for the damned, although Dante himself bids those in hell to surrender all hope.

St Thomas rejects notions of the possible mitigation of punishment or of deferments of punishment and only unwillingly concedes the possibility of some withdrawal of slight grief. But prayers for the souls in Purgatory are indeed highly profitable, and Eucharist, Prayers, Alms are valid intercessions for the dead and certain indulgences also avail on their behalf. Similarly the Burial of the Dead is not only appropriate, but the rite serves a spiritual purpose. Realist as he is, St Thomas considers the somewhat irritating fact that the rich and well-loved are more likely to be prayed for specifically than the poor and unknown, but he does not scruple to prefer specific to general intercessions, though both types avail. Only the Saints in Heaven and children in limbo neither require nor profit from such works on their behalf.

St Thomas views the signs preceding the Judgement with a great deal of reserve. He summarizes, for example, St Jerome's enumeration of fifteen signs and then contents himself to say that 'When Christ shall come to judge He will appear in the form of glory', which pertains to him. It is, in fact, the Judge's procession which gives the imagery, but little more can be said. There have been wars, fears, etc., from time immemorial and, although these may be more prevalent to foretell the imminence of the Advent, these eschatological signs (which, St Thomas insists, St Jerome did not assert but merely recorded) are of uncertain probability, especially in view of the fact that they are tied up with the original sacking of Jerusalem and Christ's continual coming as Judge. Nor is St Thomas very happy about the predicted astronomical upheavals, though he postulates that at the end the moving intelligences or virtues will cease work among the stars. As regards the final conflagration he stresses again the moral element, as indeed do the Biblical writings. The elements, having been stained with evil by contact, are to be cleansed by the noble, efficacious and transcendent fire, which belongs to the species of fire which we also know. But the fire does not burn up the heavenly bodies. These, on the contrary, will be set at rest. The medieval scientific interest can be discerned in the discussion which asks questions about the final state of the four elements and about the so-called fifth-essence, the quintessence of Heaven for which St Thomas shows no fondness whatsoever. The geocentric outlook of the times naturally confuses the picture of the final conflagration, for how—it is asked—can the fire from below rise high enough considering the height of mountains and waters? But apart from these unscientific-scientific observations we reach the important dogmatic assertion that the fire which precedes the Judgement cleanses the impure, causes no pain to the virtuous, and ultimately engulfs and tortures the wicked. Thus the moral postulate stands cheek by jowl with the logical inferences of an out-of-date science; the presence of the latter derives from the Doctor's deliberate refusal to regard eschatological realities as metaphors or to treat of them as separate ideas.

This realism alone enables the dogmatist to establish the Resurrection as a necessary and universal fact, for he more than anyone else knows how easy is the evasion by metaphors, of loose talk about men surviving in their children, their works, and in their influence on society. We have seen that the Old Testament suggests almost at times such a negative attitude, and St Thomas is not loath to state the arguments on that side. Above all, there remains the greatest of all difficulties, namely the manifest death of the body. But by applying the logic of the great principle that 'the higher governs the lower' St Thomas subjects the body to the spirit, although he is careful to maintain that the process in question is only natural in a restricted sense. It must really be hailed as miraculous, in as much as Christ restores man to life and thus cancels death as the appropriate consequence for sin. But this note of the miraculous does not contradict the profound Augustinian reasoning, which connects happiness with the last end of man; consequently death is to be regarded as an absurdity in the moral universe. St Thomas resumes this theme of universal and 'natural' felicity by paying special regard to the necessity of the resurrection. It might be argued, as indeed it had been, that the soul without the body would achieve much greater happiness than the soul made imperfect by bodily existence. But this heretical view cannot stand the test of Biblical tradition nor the implications of a sound doctrine of God and creation.

The Resurrection, then, is the fulfilment of Man as restored by Christ, and the Resurrection of Christ begins and completes ours. Nevertheless St Thomas is careful to draw a line between Christ as the cause of our resurrection, and Christ as the Lord who as God is, of course, not involved in the effect. Christ by virtue of His indwelling Godhead is the quasi-instrumental cause of our Resurrection.

The subject of the 'sound of trumpets' in connection with the Resurrection seems almost too trivial to merit treatment, but again it matters to the Doctor to steer the course between empty metaphor and literal materialism. We may, if we will, identify the trumpet with Christ's appearing, for 'by the trumpet they were summoned to the council, stirred to the battle, called to the feast'. Similarly we may connect the work of the angels in the Resurrection with the glorification of body and soul.

The time and manner of the Resurrection shows the Doctor in his sober frame of mind which cannot tolerate the fantasies of the apocalyptic visionaries. Joachim of Fiore, he remarks, was partly right and partly wrong, which is another way of saying that all chiliastic speculations, let alone assertions about world-epochs, are to be resisted. Nevertheless the fact remains that, however fantastic, these theories of four, or five, or a thousand years are still worth rebutting. More important remains the statement, which may for a rationalist smack of a lack of rationality, that the Resurrection is both sudden and gradual. Here again a compromise or

6

a synthesis is needed to do justice to two almost incompatible premises, but St Thomas's dialectic succeeds in retaining the dramatic suddenness while obviously favouring a less dramatic gradualness, in which the angels' work also has a place.

Whereas these philosophical problems admit of controversy there can be no shadow of doubt about the more strictly religious aspects of the Resurrection. Man rises from death, i.e. from the dust and ashes, and is directed by the divine Providence in the resumption of the body. The man who rises again is identical with the man who has lived and died on earth. St Thomas reminds one of the extreme position taken up by Tertullian nearly a thousand years earlier. Hence he has no patience with heretical explanations of immortality. The Resurrection is not an instance of a kind of transmigration nor does the soul take up its body as one puts on one's clothes. All these theories lead ultimately to a concept of the pre-existent soul which could get along quite well without the resurrection of the body. The identity of man is vouchsafed precisely by the identity of the body which is brought back from its decomposition. In this matter of the congruity of the resuscitation of the parts of the body nothing is left out, and although the hairs and nails may possibly be exempted from the Resurrection, and the 'humidities', i.e. liquid or near-liquid elements in the body, and the particles of food, are not to be included, the Risen Body is made up of all its members. The Resurrection, in short, raises the whole man in his integrity, and with the whole man there is also raised the whole 'truth' of human nature. Again, as has already been stated in respect of the soul, this culminating event is necessary and universal and irrevocable.

The quality of risen human beings is without any defect; they are young, and even if they died prematurely they now enjoy in their risen state the perfect stature which would have been theirs. The difference of the sexes is not abolished, but there is no room left for shame, if only because all animal functions also cease. St Thomas is very much concerned with the problem whether this perfect humanity may include the possibilities of change or not. On the one hand the enjoyment of God is constant and demands a state of bodies which can neither suffer nor change; on the other hand a modified possibility of transmutation cannot be excluded since the risen still enjoy such sense experiences as touch, sight, hearing, and perhaps smell used to convey on earth.[3] Only the sense of taste

---

[3] Some modern Catholics, e.g. Winklhofer, judge that 'the Fathers, and St Thomas as well, indulged in much unnecessary speculation about the resurrection-body of the just', though they retain the doctrine of the indestructibility of the body.

no longer operates, since food and digestion play no part in the risen state. The risen bodies are not ghosts and St Thomas again rejects the notion of a fifth essence to account for their substance. Their agility is perfect because it is spiritual and they can penetrate space to be in a place which is proportionate to their true being. St Thomas will not forsake the spatial realism, for he insists, among other things, that no two bodies can occupy the same place, except by miracle. Throughout the soul governs the body and moves the body according to its nature. Therefore the risen bodies also share in the temporal processes and experience time by such intervals as would be imperceptible on earth. He arrives at this solution when facing the dilemma of how to reconcile divine simultaneity and experience. Similarly on the equally vexing question of the nature of the risen body he allows that the body is palpable in a restricted sense. It may have the power to be inpalpable. The long discussions which accompany these statements prove not only the difficulty of the subject but also the dogged resistance on the part of the Church dogmatists to yield too much to pure idealism. Even their conception of light does not permit of a mystical doctrine of light emanations. The risen bodies are luminous bodies which are both visible and able to communicate light.

The fate of the damned is accordingly portrayed in non-metaphorical language. Their deformities, which are the result of sin, are real and they are preserved in the resurrection in their complete integrity in order to submit to their punishment. They are therefore exempt from decay, though for a reason sharply different from that which raises the virtuous to incorruption.

After the Resurrection all men are granted an increase in awareness so as to make them intelligent participants in the manifestation of justice, which the General Judgement accomplishes in the finalization of each judgement. As regards this Last Judgement St Thomas is again impatient of such naive questions as to where the Last Judgement is to take place, although he does not object to a localization near the Mountain of Olives. What matters to him, of course, is the fact that each man will know himself in judgement and will recognize the verdict of the court as just. Accordingly men will probably know each other's secrets and even the sinners, ripe for damnation, will know as much as is appropriate. This conception of judgement retains the forensic note and imagery, but it also dwells on the mental processes of giving and accepting judgement. The mind, rather than the word of mouth, registers justice.

'Who will be the judges?' asks the Doctor, and answers: 'Those who will consent with Christ the Judge, by approving His sentence, will be said to judge.' The perfect will be raised to the dignity of assessors and they will take a delight in leading others to the seat of true authority. The privilege of assisting Christ in Judgement is particularly extended to the voluntary poor, whereas angels only approve the sentences and do not judge. All men witness the Judgement at which the merits of the good are brought into the open. Angels are only judged indirectly, i.e. only in so far as they were concerned in men's deeds. A point of great difficulty arises in connection with the wicked: what happens if they are nominally found among the faithful? St Thomas distinguishes between these and unbelievers: the latter are exterminated, the former receive condemnation after discussion. Throughout these proceedings Christ acts as the Judge in his human nature and in his glorified state. His appearance is a cause of infinite joy among the virtuous and even among the wicked it is impossible for him to appear without giving some form of pleasure, for 'it is impossible for the Godhead to be seen without joy'.

After the Judgement the world is renewed. The movements of the heavenly bodies will cease as soon as man is glorified, for it is for Man that the universe was created. Plants, animals and material no longer exist; only Light is not only retained but increased for it is man's paramount privilege to see. Our intellect will be such that it attains to the vision of God, since God infuses his divine essence into us so that we can apprehend the form of the Divine Essence. The matter, however, is very difficult, for it immediately raises the question how the creation can apprehend the Creator without becoming absorbed by God. In Qu. 92 St Thomas engages in a very long discussion which shows the pitfalls of pantheism which must and can be avoided if we think of the union of spirit with God in terms analogous to that of body and soul. We see God not as an object of direct vision but by a kind of indirect vision which corresponds to our knowledge of God. After the judgement a final state of knowledge is gained, and the degrees of beatitude which men are destined to attain are proportionate to their rank in virtue. Therefore the Saints know God as they see him, and see him as they know him, and in this knowledge-vision lies their eternal felicity. The existence of various degrees of blessedness resumes the theme of the 'many mansions'; this differentiation is to be traced to the diversity of merit which in Heaven is the equivalent of divine charity. It goes without saying that the distinctions of rewards and degrees of light do not encourage or stem from base motives but are the suitable fulfilments of inward states and proven virtue.

The Blessed are endowed with eternal gifts (dowries) which

direct them to their beatitude. St Thomas notes in this connection that it is strange for the Father of the Bridegroom to present such dowries, which ultimately correspond to the theological virtues of Faith, Hope, and Charity. The Blessed see what they have believed, enjoy what they have hoped for, and delight in what they love. The Saints are not only crowned with the fruit of their Christlike lives but there is added to their crown of eternal life, the circle of light, which fittingly tells forth in eternity the continence of virginity, the heroism of martyrdom, and the faithfulness of preaching and teaching on earth. Martyrdom is the greatest of all states and deserves the highest reward, though Charity qualifies all. Love is the condition of that glorification, which Christ bestows, himself more excellent than all.

But this state of glory is paralleled by the punishment of the Damned, which the righteous witness and rejoice over without pity. This Eternal Punishment is just; without it justice would remain unvindicated. Therefore the dogmatist rejects belief in a universal restoration, for such a universal *apokatastasis* would make a mockery of God's design and redemption. St Thomas carefully repudiates all diluted theories of Origenist flavour and states explicitly that he rejects not only the salvation of the demons but also that of men who die in mortal sin. Not even Christians are exempt from this punishment if in their role as apostates or heresiarchs they betrayed the truth; nor do works of mercy liberate sinners without faith and charity from their eternal torment. They are all engulfed by the elements for punishment, for their will is always evil and their prison corresponds to their state of being, even if under the stress of pain they would approximate to some sort of sorrow and prefer NOT TO BE. Such a suicidal desire again corresponds to what they are but does not therefore exempt them from the fire, which resembles our fire in its physical effects, nor from the gnawing worm which (in the absence of animal life) may be taken to be spiritual, a figure of the conscience which can regret without being able to repent. The suffering causes real tears out of darkened eyes in a world of utmost unhappiness in the airless darkness. The sufferings are eternal because they make up in endlessness that which they lack in severity, since no one can endure intolerable pain. The pain is only as severe as can be tolerated, and this restriction explains its endlessness.

In Hell envy reigns supreme and the damned grieve for the happiness which they cannot have and which they know others to enjoy. Their knowledge is to them a source of misery and gives rise to the futile wish for all the blessed to be damned. They are tormented by the knowledge of the Bliss which reigns above and hate

God as much as they hate their own punishment. They lack, however, the power to change anything or themselves.

It would be absurd to conclude dogmatic eschatology on this
note unless the *whole* picture in its radiant glory and rationality is
seen to incorporate the terror of damnation. It is a picture of order
and hierarchy, of God and Man and Angels, which is sustained by
the perfect reflection of goodness and happiness. The dogmatic
picture needs the flesh and bones which Dante gave it in the *Divine
Comedy*. Then it lives and the stark colours blend with the subtle
tones of the whole.

This truth, so obvious in poetic genius, also holds good in the
field of theology. As soon as the wonderful wholeness of medieval
scholasticism is lost there remains little incentive to retain its eschatology. As Sertillanges observed in his concluding words about the
future of Thomism, this is not the sort of system which you can
improve by mending or adding here and there. The future of the
old doctrine lies in its openness to new facts. But the question is
whether the modern situation still allows a comprehensive treatment
of any subject. Only a comprehensive treatment can enshrine the
legacy of St Thomas: without aiming at totality of treatment the
little isolated pieces are of little use. His spirituality, his common
sense, his devotion to truth, on all levels, small and great, his cosmic
awareness, his placing of Men in a universe of meaning, under God,
the Lord of Being, and in a hierarchy of graded reality—all this,
and more, is still required in a re-statement of doctrine.

PART II

A FORUM FOR DISCUSSION

CHAIRMAN   *Liberal Protestant,* English
MEMBERS   *Protestant Sectarian,* American
             Catholic Dogmatist, French
             Marxist, Russian
             Psychologist, Swiss

A sanguine temper, though for ever expecting more good than occurs, does not always pay for its hopes by any proportionate depression. It soon flies over the present failure, and begins to hope again.   JANE AUSTEN, *Emma,* Ch. 18.

CHAPTER VI

THE PROBLEM OF ESCHATOLOGY

The Chairman: My friends. I am glad to welcome you here to take part in this discussion. We have all read the preceding chapters on the End, and it is good that we, representing not only different traditions but also different and sometimes hostile countries, should meet and clear the air. For myself, I confess to being a theologian, but I am not bigoted at all and very ready to listen to your arguments. But first let me state the problem for discussion, or, at least, let me state it as I see it, for unless we have a pretty clear and agreed definition we shall all be talking about different things. You will, I hope, share my conviction that if there is a problem it ought to be discussed coolly and rationally. That is what I understand by *Constructive Theology,* to which we are meant to contribute. In other words, we shall depart quite radically from the atavistic style and vocabulary with which the chapters we have just read are weighed down. I hope you will not consign me to Hell and call me damned if I exclude Hell and Damnation.

The Protestant Sectarian: I cannot say that I am happy in the way you introduce the subject. I do not object to what you call cool and rational discussion, but I do object to flippancy. It seems to me highly frivolous to exclude Hell and Damnation. That's exactly what we are here to discuss.

The Psychologist: I think I may be able to help you sort out this little difficulty. It is a question of temperament. As the discussion proceeds you will find, only too often, that your disagreements are really caused by personal opposition. I hope to show later on that there is an apocalyptic temperament which really likes this chosen area of discourse, sometimes even revels in Hell and Damnation. It used to be called Enthusiasm. There is also a temperament which profoundly dislikes the excitement and the fantasies of apocalyptic imagery. This can't be helped and you must put up with your own limitations, but I would ask you to recognize them. Strangely enough you two gentlemen are more likely to be conditioned in this way than our other two friends, for they represent objective views in which they are not particularly engaged.

The Catholic: Oh, quite wrong, we are none of us neutral. As I see it, our subject is meaningless unless it divides people.

The Communist: Unless we accept the scientific proof that it is not a real subject but merely the survival of a particularly dangerous form of oppression.

The Psychologist: Very well, you had better bear in mind the fact that you are involved in a relationship with the subject, whether friendly or hostile. I am so myself, of course.

The Chairman: So am I, I readily admit, but in a special way. You see, I am an old man and I have seen the near eclipse of all this so-called Eschatology, and now suddenly I find that it has come back again into Theology, though in a different way.

The Communist: Please explain. This is a world I know nothing about.

The Chairman: Well, I do not wish to be pompous, but let me return to my promised definition. Eschatology is a word, horrible as it sounds, which was coined only in the nineteenth century. It is really a technical term, which Christendom never knew. It's taken from the Greek, meaning the study or science of the Last Thing or of the End. Heinrich Klee used it in a theological discussion in 1838 in his *Lehrbuch der Dogmengeschichte*; Johann Heinrich Oswald wrote the first monograph *Eschatology* in 1868. G. Bush uses the term in his *Anastasis* in 1844. So much for the history of the term, which having made its bow to the Christian world seems to keep up a continuous performance to this day. But the term only brought into the open doubts and denials which had been felt during the eighteenth century and possibly even before. After all, the French Revolution did not come out of nothing and the guillotine beheaded mythological beliefs which were already outdated.

The Catholic: But what was the problem? Define our problem, please.

The Chairman: That is soon done. But the problem only arises for men who are Christian in outlook and yet modern and without blinkers. The End of the World, the Second Coming of Christ, the Principle of eternal Retribution, the whole concept of the *There* and *Then,* cannot be squared literally with the continuation of the world, the absence of Christ (physically speaking), the principles of modern ethics, and the Christian pre-occupation with the *Here* and *Now.* The eschatological problem, therefore, concerns this tension between tradition and the modern world-view. The question, in short, is, what—if anything—can be retained of the traditional pattern?

The Communist: You surprise me, for your dialectic seems almost related to mine. You argue, if I understand you properly, that as society was organized along feudal lines this thing, which you call eschatology, held together society. The End was the fine point of feudal ideology, and it had its own dialectic, as we have read. For some the End was said to be good, what with immortality and other eternal advantages, and for others bad, what with the assizes, torments, and cosmic upheavals. The feudal system flourished under the aegis of this dialectic, but as feudalism had to yield to capitalism, as trade, technical skills, and education increased and the concentration of capital released new industrial powers, kings and nobles could no longer use the old whip of Heaven and Hell. Now coal, iron, oil, and electricity have replaced the old lumber. I can't see a real problem here. Our only task is to formulate our Socialist ends and then see that they are attained.

The Protestant: Mr Chairman, I rejoice that our enemy defies you, though I would do it rather differently. The problem which you have stated is no problem at all, except the old one of God's People fighting the spirit of the world. You want to mix oil and water, revelation and common sense. That is your problem, but it is of your own invention. I never found, and the previous chapters bear me out, that our Advent message foundered in this age and generation. Take America. Take Africa!

The Catholic: I can see the Chairman's drift, though I do not approve of his entirely pragmatic approach. Can you really discuss such a thing as the End merely from the point of view of experience and whether it works or not? Surely, there is here a metaphysical problem: not whether it works, but whether the doctrines you have stated as outdated are true.

The Chairman: Yes, that is the point, but remember what the great Blumhardt (1805–1880) has said: dogmatics are never worse at any point or at any time than when they concern themselves with the Coming of the Saviour! And his son (1842–1919) remarked: 'First you must fail at the earthly rock before you can comprehend the higher things.'

The Catholic: The real surprise remains that you liberal Protestants do wish to discuss and retain something of the End at all. Why not jettison the whole cargo of uncomfortable doctrines?

The Protestant: Yes, make do with the 'earthly rock'!

The Psychologist: I have already told you: they can't. Take their great patron Schleiermacher (1768–1834) who admitted that the fact of death leaves a thousand unanswered questions. For him, as for our Chairman, the theological problem has become a human question.

The Protestant: Yes, and when he faced the pain of seeing his young son's death he weighed up pathetically the arguments for and against life after death.

The Communist: Too absurd.

The Psychologist: Some of your own people do it, my friend. What is more important, however, Schleiermacher inclined towards a figurative understanding of apocalyptic hopes. He wants the Christian Faith to survive in order to retain the symbolic values of Christ's divine power.

The Catholic: He rather sets a fashion there. Take any of our radical friends. There was Strauss who denounced supernatural deceits and impatiently tossed aside Jewish legacies (to use some of his own phrases), and yet he pleads for the future-in-the-present and the individual's share in eternity. He even thinks of world-history as world-judgement. But resurrection: NO!

The Protestant: You see, they were no longer Biblical. Mr Chairman, your friend Ritschl regarded the New Testament only as an example of a religious hope which is attainable by all. Gone are election and predestination! Instead, certain values make up the Kingdom of God.

The Chairman: I know. I was brought up in that tradition which flourished in Germany. We liberals hailed Troeltsch and put the ethical ideal in the place of the End.

The Communist: And you shut your eyes to Marx who put Hegel upside down and threw out the whole idealistic conception of transcendental ends.

The Catholic: What prevented you?

The Chairman: Well, you must remember that people like myself never wished to depart from the New Testament. The person of Jesus inspired us and we felt, and still feel, that he could somehow be separated from the whole apocalyptic background of his day. Harnack became our prophet and still is the prophet of our position, for he did not deny that the form and substance of the Gospel was apocalyptic, but, as Bultmann has observed, he removed the eschatological emphasis to the point of rendering it harmless. In my young days, about the turn of the century, we had no doubt that the Christian could reconcile his views with his culture.

The Communist: I know, Christ and Goethe, and that sort of rot. Harnack had to please the Kaiser and did so. But then came the explosion, the war, and the proletariat was on the march. Your compromise bled to death in Flanders and at the Somme and, with us, on the plains of Poland. But then our orthodox Church had not moved one inch anyway.

The Chairman: You are wrong there. Not about Russia and

orthodoxy, but about the war and revolutions being the cause of our disenchantment. The great scholars Weiss, Wrede and, last not least, Albert Schweitzer lived and wrote years before 1914 and demolished the liberal Christ more than a decade before political and cultural liberalism ended. No, they were prophets, but not so much by foresight as by a new estimate of the New Testament. They showed that the eschatological element constitutes the heart of the Gospel. The account given in the previous pages largely reproduces their work, showing Jesus as the Coming One who went to his death to usher in the Messianic Kingdom. The Jesus of history, the Jesus of ideals, the Jesus of the Church, the Jesus of evangelical piety— all these and other conceptions miss the essential Kingdom of God which the New Testament conveys to us in its dramatic urgency. Jesus is here, Jesus goes to Jerusalem, Jesus dies: the documents show us one and all on tip-toe of expectation. Since Schweitzer the End is again the focal point, but with a difference, for it is understood by him that Jesus was wrong and that his error belongs as much to the New Testament as to our interpretation of it. The task is now to explain the incredible contradiction that he who died with such high expectations obtained a different end in fact: instead of the end of the world he inaugurated the era of a universal faith.

The Psychologist: This is new to me and agrees with the whole nature of wish-projection. The integration of a mistaken hope renders the negative, the error, into the positive, the faith.

The Communist: Nothing of the kind. Your Schweitzer is no more than the spokesman of declining capitalism. As you say, at about 1900 liberalism, though apparently in power, was already in a state of decline. The moving frontier in the West of the U.S.A. could no longer absorb the stresses of capitalist unrest and the old ideology came crashing down.

The Protestant: What absolute rubbish! My people reached Oregon at that time and we were brought up as good Adventists even later, in the 'twenties of this century.

The Catholic: I fear you are being a little naive if you see theology only through the eyes of politics and regionalism.

The Chairman: Well, I must admit, there was something rather regional about it, for all the real successors to Schweitzer were New Testament scholars in Germany. Dibelius and Bultmann developed Form-Criticism and claimed that nothing could be known about the life of Jesus anyway and very little about what he had actually said. From now on we have to deal with Gospel traditions. Take an important example, from our point of view. Mark 13, which is crucially important, may now be severed from the Gospel context and be treated as a separate little Apocalypse which the infant church cherished before and during the Jewish War. This infant church—so runs the claim—which had turned the prophet Jesus into a heavenly Christ and the supernatural Son of Man now also went one step further and bestowed upon him regal functions to judge the world at the End. The original words of farewell have been altered to explain the break which the Christians carried out with respect to the Jewish People and the Temple. The fall of Jerusalem (A.D. 70) may have influenced this composition which derives from many disparate groups. Some find here a reflection of Roman atrocities, beginning with Caligula's attempt to enforce the worship of himself under the form of a horse (A.D. 40). But whatever hypothesis you prefer, the effect is plainly that you connect the prophecies of the End with some immediate and acute actualities of the period.

The Catholic: In other words, history supervenes and dogma goes.

The Protestant: You sacrifice the integrity of the Scriptures. But what of the Advent itself?

The Chairman: This is very perplexing. The framework of wars, famines, earthquakes, persecutions, signs of doom, sufferings, consummations involving animals, angels, stars, etc., is, after all, traditional. Not so Christ's Return or the so-called Parousia. It has the hallmark of the specifically Christian tradition. This direct, personal, futuristic expectation includes all the other hopes, but it is also the Achilles' heel of all these hopes, if the Christ-Return is a mistake, quite possibly due to the Gentiles misunderstanding Hebrew-Aramaic terminology.

The Psychologist: Mistake: a word I should avoid in your position. We are talking about symptoms and patterns, as I shall show.

The Communist: That's the language of obscurantism. The slaves in Rome bothered their heads about food and freedom, not about patterns.

The Catholic: If you mean they became Christians because of political and economic advantages the whole evidence of history is against you. The Gospel was indeed revolutionary, but not in your sense.

The Protestant: Stick to the Second Coming, then and now!

The Chairman: As you know, strictly this is not the phrase used in the New Testament. But let that pass. What we doubt is whether it ever belonged to the original Preaching after all. Bishop

J. A. T. Robinson, in his book *Jesus and His Coming,* suggests that we have got hold of the wrong end of the stick. Paul's mature thought, he says, centred on being in Christ. John preached the indwelling of Christ by the Spirit in the believer and that this 'I in you' bridged the gap which might be felt to exist between promise and fulfilment. But, although Pauline and Johannine Christianity triumphed, the pressure of events created a belief in a second Advent. Thus 'a second focus of Christian hope' brought a re-orientation, almost as if Christ were an absentee Lord inoperative in Heaven. Jesus had never looked 'to a second act in history after an interval, a "part two" of his coming'. But the damage was done and Christianity lived again between two ages, between the times. Indeed such an attitude even pushed the Pentecostal fulfilment back again, thereby removing the End from immediate experience. Small wonder that by the time the second century was under way many Christians nearly apostatized with the plea: 'Where is the promise of his Coming? . . . all things continue as before.'

The Protestant: I have read this thesis and find it utterly arbitrary. The Bishop arranges the New Testament according to his own bias.

The Chairman: His view is extreme, I admit. But people like Bultmann also think that the eschatological despair was great, though they claim that it was tamed by the sacramental institutions. Baptism and Eucharist, when developed by the Church along lines unknown to Jesus, were vehicles to provide a union with Christ. Here the Church wins, so to speak, over the eschatological Kingdom of God and paves a way for Christianity in history.

The Catholic: Pray, have you any more of these engaging permutations? Liberal Church history of Christian origins seems abundantly provided with them.

The Chairman: I think we have good reason to be proud that we have so many people working at this subject. It shows vitality. Come to think of it, some of your own co-religionists have not been exactly slack in that respect.

The Psychologist: This interests me enormously, for it shows that what you call the eschatological is a deep-rooted, almost archetypal—if you like—way of experience. Tell us about some of your people.

The Chairman: Before I mention names let me make clear the principle, which is not difficult to grasp. It is that the End has already begun in some way. The End has been realized, the End has been inaugurated.

The Communist: When? And which End?

The Chairman: This view is simple and associated with the name of C. H. Dodd. The End coincides with the Resurrection and the Coming of the Holy Spirit. All promises were then fulfilled and from now on history becomes the arena where the New Creation marches forward in realization of God's Presence. This is Biblical and it still makes full allowance of historical stages of development. T. W. Manson liked to think in such terms of graded eschatology. Or again we have O. Cullmann who while retaining the Day of final victory sees this victory within our grasp: D-Day points to V-Day. Our space-time experience leads up to eternal significance—time: *chronos* to *kairos*. Put it this way: events in duration-time are caught up in God's own time.

The Communist: This obscurantism is almost too ludicrous to deserve comment. Now if you had said that the New Age dawned with early Christian Communism and that it was betrayed later on there would be some sense in discussing 'inaugurated Eschatology'.

The Protestant: The term is a lie, it's as simple as that. What we have read in this book shows, if it shows anything, that Evil increases in history and moves on to a climax of fulfilment. The Gospel came into the world, the Spirit was poured out, the Church grew; but all this happened in a world hastening towards its doom.

The Psychologist: If you are not careful this discussion will get bogged down in history and I distrust nothing more than generalizations about history and empty value-judgements.

The Chairman: I am afraid you, as a psychologist, fail to understand our difficulties. You say 'Damn to history', but we can't follow you, for, whether we are Christians or Communists, it is within history that we claim to experience reality. That is why Christian Theology can never get away from the problem of history. If we were not embedded in the historical process our debate would certainly lose its controversial sting. But, as you see, I defend the thesis that the End-hope is being realized in history, in the experience of time, while my Protestant friend denies this realization, because history increases the accumulation of evil, and our Communist friend in his turn opposes my claim of realizing Eschatology because his pursuit of the Millennium coincides with the dictatorship of the Proletariat. Thus it is plainly on the level of history that we are forced to discuss our problem.

The Catholic: Yes, up to a point I agree, but I do think you are all apt to overdo this historical business. True, we are not Gnostics and we do not live in the realm of ideas only, but the Psychologist is not to be ruled out of order when he protests against the overdose of history in Theology. Take R. Bultmann's Gifford

Lectures for 1955, entitled *History and Eschatology*. Do they really get you anywhere?

The Chairman: They seem to me to give us an excellent idea of an existentialist interpretation of our problem. Man is crushed in his historical existence, says Bultmann, but 'the new people of God has no real history, for it is the community of the end-time, an eschatological phenomenon'. The decisive event has already happened: 'the real life is the life confirmed by God, the forfeited life is the life condemned by God.' Give up the myth of future cosmic events, like John, and enter 'the dialectic of indicative and imperative': you are, do this! History, thus understood, is not only the objective sequence of events, documented and interpreted, but also the subjective perspective: every present moment in the historical process shares the fullness of the whole of history (Croce). Therefore man encounters reality in the present situation and 'the relativity of every historical situation is understood as having a positive meaning'. In every decision I grow, I become, I am free. Thus, for me, Jesus Christ is the eschatological event, not a cosmic catastrophe, but happening within history in preaching and in faith. The meaning of history lies in the present: 'you must awaken the eschatological moment.'

The Protestant: If you can swallow this you are in fact 'swallowing up Christian theology in a unique style of anthropology', as D. M. Mackinnon[1] put it in his review in 1958. Yes, this Jesus Christ is just a formula for radical subjectivism.

The Catholic: And, if I am permitted to add, this is not as new as it sounds. For example, my friend M. Schmaus, writing about the Last Things in 1948, said: 'Our subject is not concerned with matters beyond or after this world and age but rather with this world and age, only with regard to its reason and goal, its becoming and its being', and he goes on to show that Christ's Realm is not only of the future but also present, though here Christ is of course concealed and the future offers greater nearness of Christ. But, and this is the point, for Catholic dogmatists there is nothing new in the thesis that the present, with its personal, moral decisions, forms the future, and that Hope embraces the consummation, in history and in the universe as well as in the individual, of all that has preceded the future. My friend Winklhofer unites every stage of life with Christ's Coming. But Bultmann divorces the individual from the objective institutions, from the real forces of history, and from the Church and the Sacraments.

The Communist: This individualism really does not deserve

[1] *Journal of Theological Studies*, 1958, pp. 205–208.

the attention you would give it, for man does not encounter a mythical Christ somewhere but class struggle here and now. There is nothing free about it. As regards Bultmann I take all this talk with more than the customary grains of salt. I happened to have looked at his Marburg sermons and I would like you to read one preached in June 1941, on the Sunday after the invasion of Russia. Well, the Christ encountered in that Preaching shows singularly little awareness of the political crime and the military madness involved in Hitlerite aggression. No. This is just evasion of responsibility.

The Chairman: And yet the intention of all contemporary theologians who endeavour to state the truth of Realizing Eschatology is precisely to harness morality to religion. They would oust the Myth of the Return in order to gain a responsible attitude to political decisions. Take Hodgson in his Gifford Lectures for 1957, where he battles *For Faith and Freedom.* We must make sense of our existence, we cannot wait aimlessly for the Last Event, we must work for the End if we would discover the nature of the Last End, a share in God's Life. Hodgson agrees we cannot say much about tht Beyond, dismisses Hell and Purgatory, and despises the 'reconstitution of dried eggs' as a desirable end. Instead he holds up our active and free Christ-like actions as meaningful ends.

The Protestant: I cannot tell you how tired I am of these superficial cancellations of the End-hope. For that is what they are. We in America simply abound with theologians who talk of the irrelevance of future time (Grant). They go much further than Dodd. For them Eschatology really is Ethics, even though they grant that it represents more than a high moral capacity (Wilder). We hear a lot about 'living out the future in the concrete moment of history': dates are of no concern, only persons who live into a future. Now what is so marvellous about that? You don't have to be a Christian to live into the future. We all do that. A very limited future, namely from the cradle to the grave. How one can talk along these lines, like W. G. Kümmel, of *Promise and Fulfilment* is a mystery to me. You can, as he does, say that the Kingdom is 'imminent', that its 'imminence' brings out the 'has come near' of the New Testament, but surely this is just a matter of words. I agree that Promise and Fulfilment are inseparably united and depend on each other, but I do not agree that fulfilment lies outside the orbit of history and of the objective Act of God in the specific Christ Return, which is heralded by stages.

The Catholic: One of your Protestant theologians takes Kümmel to task, and that in an interesting way. E. Fuchs examined his argument in 1947, especially his thesis that the New Testament gave an 'eschatological promise', as distinct from an apocalyptic doctrine, that Jesus predicted neither future eschatological events nor merely present fulfilment, in as much as he connected the present and the future with its continuum of eschatological content. But, as Fuchs stresses: what kind of history is being fulfilled? Can one speak of the history of salvation as being fulfilled? Or of ethics? Or of the Kingdom? Can one speak of fulfilment apart from Grace? Is not the central problem this: how did it come about that Jesus himself, and not just the Reign of God only, became the subject of the Gospel message? Christ is the End of history, and no modernistic verbiage can modify the problem which, as I now see it, is a matter of doctrine and not of speculation about history.

The Communist: That's how you would like to get out of it, I see. You can't really seriously face the challenge of historical fact and so you would reduce the whole thing to an abstraction of your own making.

The Protestant: Don't be absurd! If you really want to find out how we feel about it read the whole of the *Evanston Report.* Some looked to *Christ—the Hope of the World* as a direct spur to practical action and peace (Hammarskjöld). Others had to fight back against the disproportionate emphasis on the present reality of the Christian Hope as against the ultimate hope. And over Israel there was a great controversy, if not a split.

The Chairman: Yes, it is the pressure of history which causes us to ask questions. We could just glibly content ourselves and say: 'Well, there is hope in the future', and leave it at that. But we don't, and instead we insist that 'only those who know the Presence can hope for the Parousia, and only those who hope for the Parousia can know the Presence', to use the words of J. E. Fison in *The Christian Hope.* That means we must take experience in history seriously, which is more than making doctrinal statements. Indeed, the propositional alone will never do justice to the truly religious, just because we see this End-hope not only as an event but also as a relationship, an act of Love between God and his creation. That's why I side with Bishop J. A. T. Robinson, who takes us away from an interest in the End as such, such as the final state of this planet, and fixes our attention on God: *In the End, God . . . ,* seemed to me not only a good title, for, instead of objectivizing Hell and Heaven in propositional form, we are drawn to our God as the End.

The Communist: Satisfactory as long as you believe in God, but quite meaningless if you don't.

The Protestant: Meaningless, because utterly distorted. No wonder this leaves you cold, but if I tell you that he who is the present

Lord and now the absent King will come to be your judge with power then the abstraction yields to fear, because you and yours are in fact the dragon and would destroy our hope. I agree to that extent with P. S. Minehar, *Christian Hope and the Second Coming*, a fellow-American, who ends on this note: 'We must recapture the same level of existence' which the Bible speaks of. I find this quite easy and what he calls the images of the Second Coming are to me a reality. But I quarrel with him when he speaks of symbolism, for to me these images—of the defeat of the dragon, the shaking of the world, the keys, the trumpet—are literally true.

The Chairman: And the clouds of Heaven?

The Psychologist: There is the rub at last. All your arguments from and against historical event have proved moribund, but now at last you are on the right track. The question surely is, here as everywhere, what is the relationship of our images to our unconscious state. To me the problem of eschatology should be re-stated: How can these related images illumine our treatment of nervous diseases and further the integration of personality? That's my definition, and I stick to it.

The Communist: And to me, on the contrary, the problem may be condensed simply to this: How can this lie, a delusion of the future which does not exist, be exposed in all its craftiness and futility?

The Catholic: To me the problem is that of all theology: how can supernatural revelation, such as Christian Eschatology, be stated in reasonable terms and what is its precise place in the rational order of things. If you like, to me the problem is one of metaphysics; in other words, I do not acknowledge the existence of a problem of faith but only one of articulation or systematization.

The Protestant: I cannot detach the problem from real life and faith. For me systematization means abstraction; dogma becomes a kind of pigeon-hole for antiquarian inessentials, thus rendering our subject impotent. For me the problem is to recover the spirit of our forefathers who lived by the Bible and hastened the End by Preaching and Practice. Or, putting it differently, my problem is why, if we no longer believe in these things, we should not simply declare: 'The End of the End' has come, instead of watering down to meaningless trickeries that which cannot be explained away: The Second Coming, Judgement, and the End.

The Chairman: Obviously then, we cannot discuss our problem as one, for we disagree even as to the exact location of our problem. For me, as you have seen, it is the problem of reconciling New Testament language with historical facts and contemporary experience. My problem is frankly that of modernism. But I will not press my position to the exclusion of yours. Let us first discuss why we should retain the notion of the End in any shape whatsoever.

The Communist: Free from religious bias?

The Psychologist: And not confined to historical issues?

The Chairman: Yes, by all means. No bias whatsoever.

The Protestant: Which will condemn me to silence, I suppose.

The Catholic: I shall note the analogies and venture to connect them with their true order.

CHAPTER VII

COMMON INTIMATIONS OF THE END

The Chairman: We have agreed then to leave behind us for the moment the peculiar Christian nature of the problem and build up a picture of the End as it is commonly conceived by men.

The Communist: Not conceived: I will have none of your ideal abstractions. Let me give you a list of phenomena which have certain ends in view. I would follow here Ernst Bloch's magisterial *Prinzip Hoffnung,* one of the greatest treasures of Marxist philosophy, written during the second World War in the U.S.A., but first published in Eastern Germany, where he was a professor at Leipzig.

The Catholic: And from where he had to flee to Western Germany. I mention this only to warn you in advance that what you are about to tell us may not be hall-marked Marxism after all. It may be deviationist, for all you know. Remember Ernst Bloch!

The Communist: His work remains great, if only because he takes seriously the dictum of Marx: 'The world is possessed of a dream of which it must only become conscious in order to put it into effective action.' Bloch shows that 'we dream FORWARDS' in negation of tradition and its mournful interest in the past. The principle of Hope reaches out to that which has never been, which has not yet been known and which overtakes the normal order of things. This anticipation is not fantasy but evokes social determination: the dream is to be made concrete. The bourgeoisie has in fact reduced this dream by making of it a middle-class morality, with talk of natural rights and decency. But since industrialists hardly ever man the barricades, and bankers never, you can be sure that their defence will crumble. Again quoting Marx: 'Until the victorious revolution the last word of social science is quite simply "Struggle or death, bloody war or nothing"', for since the day of Marx we have overcome the abstract character of Utopia.

The Catholic: Which entitles you to Gautier's slogan: *La barbarie vous vaut mieux que la platitude.*

The Communist: Because instead of throwing a light upon our chaos we have determined to change it. This, if you like, is the proper Chiliastic Utopianism, because we have both the will and the competence for power.

The Catholic: Ubi Lenin, ibi Jerusalem!

The Communist: Precisely. As Bloch says: 'Zionism leads up to Socialism or it leads nowhere at all', and whether we apply this to the Jews and their state of Israel or to Jerusalem in the wider, idealist sense, the truth remains that only the materialized ideal has any meaning. The Hierarchy of Hope, as Bloch calls it, culminates in the reign of freedom and order, and that is Communism.

The Chairman: I thought you were going to give us phenomena which imply ends: instead you are broadcasting propaganda.

The Communist: Not propaganda, but the necessary thread upon which the pearls of forward-looking actions and thoughts are to be arranged. Granted the basic materialization of the ideal we propose to include everything: the baby gropes in anticipation of all later desires to have what it has not. It loves dirt, even excrements, in the first stage. Brothers fight endlessly in the nursery. Then comes the passion for collecting, the keeping of pet animals, the building of the secret hide-out, the formation of the gang, the fantasies of heroic conquests, the first erotic dreams, the shy passion, the fiery lust, the romance of freedom, the escape from parental control: in short, the child presages the future. Here are your phenomena of human behaviour. They are all meaningless apart from what is yet to come.

The Catholic: Now you are speaking my language. Here I am in my element, for I detect sound teleology: the potential craves to be actualized. You need not go to Bloch for this. Aristotle as the first great biologist has already given to the world this empirical principle of life, and I am prepared to view our problem of the End through the analysis of commonly held ends.

The Protestant: I see what is happening. The supernatural, divine, unique Christ-event is now being drawn into the orbit of natural science. Woe unto the deceits of false analogies!

The Psychologist: I am not so worried about false analogies as superficial assessments of nursery behaviour and adolescent patterns of development. I grant you the facts: what of their interpretation?

The Communist: This is not difficult. The childhood pattern anticipates human needs: food above all, security, family, social coherence. But all these serve an even greater need, the attack on the New, the invention of the Never-Before. Man wants to have and to be, in order to make.

The Catholic: Is man's creativity then part of his entelechy? Show us how you work it out.

The Communist: Matter is self-moving and self-creating and man is matter. His possibilities are enormous. Nothing human is strange, everything strange is also human. We build up from those simple beginnings: sucking the breast and making love. Our passions increase, we strive and seek and desire, always implying activity forward towards something unknown. It is our fundamental urge to envisage a state when things could be better and other than they are. We dream of perfect health and beauty, pushing back sickness, old age, and even death. We transform nature, we build cities, we explore at last unknown regions of space, for we have, given in those early instincts, perspectives of an ideal world, of which Utopian commonwealths in the past have only been shadows. You Christians have forged the blue-prints, have eternalized them, so that no one would think of carrying them into practice. But even you could not obliterate the desire, not only for change, but for transformation. The technical revolution has lifted humanity out of this gloomy trough of passive endurance and idle day-dreaming. You see, Utopia until now seems to have led either to brain-fever of the kind which Don Quixote stands for, or to those little adjustments of bourgeois culture which led to the abdication of hope.

The Chairman: Are you not guilty here of a little forgery? Take concrete expressions of the instinctive hope: did not men navigate the seven seas and build perfect shrines, colonize in the swamps and reclaim deserts, years before Marx?

The Communist: You confirm my thesis, for I mean to include all these concrete expressions of the Principle of Hope in my mapping of ends. Of course, a great deal was achieved in the past and I call upon architecture, painting, sculpture, music, poetry, drama as my witnesses that the possible is also within our grasp of execution. At the same time I have to account for the hopelessness which has overtaken us, for this is still our problem. Our instincts guide us towards the sun of socialist achievement, but instead disillusionment overtakes our best intentions. I exonerate Anti-Christ, who does not exist, and I accuse Capitalism as the source of our Principle of Despair.

The Chairman: So that the progress has been interrupted by the organization of man going astray. Now I am as devoted as anyone to the conception of evolutionary process, would in fact explain the Person of Christ, and this business of the End, along those lines, but for the life of me I cannot understand why you should pick on capitalism as holding up this trend towards perfection.

The Communist: Let me explain: the capitalism of the bourgeoisie is the antithesis to true progress, and it is the task of the working-class to push it over so as to establish the synthesis of socialism. The creation of capital and industry is not to be faulted and agrees with the principle of the forward Hope, for only the new technical inventions enable us to break out of the closed circle of the known world, which is to be left behind. But the bourgeoisie as a class stands in the way: it is a social malformation, a cancerous growth. By creating private property and the exploitation of the means of production as well as the exploitation of man by man, the Have-class stands in the way of the implementation of the Principle of Life. Hence it adjusts its hopes and betrays the Hope: gangster-romance replaces true exploration and the 'happy end' turns everything into a frivolous lie. I could give you scores of examples how, as a consequence of this great layer of lies, the bourgeoisie has not only given up the loyalty to its true Fatherland—i.e. certain moral and aesthetic convictions—, but also the pursuit of the True Patria, this Eden-Paradise, or eschatological destiny. Hence you heirs of the End-hope really no longer believe in it and talk instead of defensive action: to mend broken marriages, to deal with delinquents, to reduce the birth-rate, to overhaul hospitals, to aid the aged, etc. You see, your whole social purpose is now on the wane, altogether negative: you wish to patch up the cracks. But these cracks appear because the whole building is rotten, and the whole building is rotten because you have no longer any ideas which could attract a united enthusiasm, even a sacrificial response. Your religion is a last, and on the whole unwanted, coverlet to hide the nakedness of your dead society. This death can only end with death, but out of the ashes of your remains there will arise the Socialist state of workers who will go forward to build up that which hitherto has only been a dream. So I repeat: the common intimations of the End are implanted in our nature and if they are not heeded then all members of society must perish. The process itself is life, and the End of the process lies within our grasp, though its exact destination cannot yet be defined. Largely, it is cultural and scientific.

The Protestant: Strangely enough I find myself in greater agreement with you than I should have thought possible. Politics apart, we are at one: what you call 'the process' has gone unutterably wrong. But you get the date wrong: it happened before the word Capitalism was invented. The angels sinned, the first man fell, sin enslaved mankind, brother killed brother, every man went his own way, society existed only to kill and fight, there was and is war in heaven and on earth. Christ came not into the process, but he was sent to stop it and transform the human species so that the first Adam who had lost the divine image, freedom, and immortality, should be succeeded by the God-Man who ended the slavery and puts before us an end Glorious and Eternal. Without such an end, I agree, mankind is lost and a sad illusory plight prevails on earth. Like you I repudiate this endless normalcy, but unlike you I detect a different cause for the disease and certainly a different cure. Not action, but faith; not revolution, but repentance.

The Psychologist: No wonder you find yourself somehow akin in words and feelings, for although you seem to be poles apart you are in the same Utopian camp for the same reason. You seek therapy in this forward-dream, and what a perilous dream it is! It is my job to explain it and to integrate its elements with your personalities, lest the dream devour you, as it does with neurotics and, to a worse degree, with psychopaths.

The Catholic: But do you deny the empirical basis of the Utopian dream? Never mind the more fantastic side of their interpretations. Are they right, or nearly right, when they claim to have discovered a common ground for the End-hope? Is it proper to speak of the intimation of a human eschatology, evidenced by instincts, attitudes, hopes and fears? Are they reasonable when they analyse the undoubted breakdown of our society by calling in question those adjustments which most of us affirm as signs of civilized moderation? For myself, I prefer reasonable normalcy and sound institutions and codes of morality, however frail and liable to be offended against, to the somewhat chaotic, ruthless, and highly immoral advance to an undefined End. This seems to be a dangerous distortion of the Christian hope, if it is put in such radical terms.

The Communist: It is the Christian hope which I denounce as a dangerous distortion. Let me state it again: the End-hope is nourished by human instincts which create political needs. We have taken over the theme that the End ends oppression. We proclaim the THEN of the triumph of the cause, but we say that the THERE is here, not in Heaven or Paradise. Marx comprehended that our industrial existence made such a foreshortening possible and desirable. He took the dream out of the indistinct future and transplanted it into the conscious here and now. And he changed the nature of the dream: instead of recalling a golden age we look forward to the new world. We make it, precisely, by denying Utopian Messianism. The collective determination of the working class ends the reign of private property and now the abstract character of Utopia can be overcome for the first time.

The Chairman: What impresses me is that in the realization of your ends you do reproduce the features of traditional eschatology. War and violence marks your progress and until the day of complete victory you prefer catastrophe and destructiveness to compromise and collaboration. You are historical realists and nail the ideal to your banner in what is a campaign against the enemy. This is genuine apocalyptic.

The Communist: But in doing so we free the hope from its apocalyptic vagueness and other-worldliness. We break with the eschatological tradition, because we detach from our hope that 'other' hope: there is, for us, no inner meaning, no metaphysical connection, pattern, analogy, or goal, to which the Communist Revolution can or should correspond. As soon as the proletariat has lost its chains and the class-enemy has been liquidated the new classless society is itself the end in its political power and economic existence.

The Chairman: Deny the correspondence as much as you like: it is there, shouting at us. Just because Lenin defines your system in terms of atheism he could and did incorporate all the old millenarian ideas within the new framework. Look at your Messiah: admittedly no longer heavenly, nor indeed, royal, but the party secretary or commissar now fulfils the role of the protector of the people. The cult of the individual leader, whose portraits appear everywhere, is taken straight from the original imagery. Your classless society—if only it were classless!—looks up for authority to a face which embodies this hope.

The Protestant: It is the pagan parody of the truth. You embalm your dead and show the corpse in public to exact homage. Pilgrims come from distant lands to worship at the shrine of the relics of power. As in death so in life a ladder of ascending power distinguishes the different layers of the Communist hierarchy, for your society is strictly graded: monolithically one in power, but within that unity there are degrees of rank. Yes, your imperium reflects unconsciously the Truth-turned-into-lie.

The Catholic: With that charge I also agree, only for me it makes for hope, for despite your repudiations, Tovarich, I too cannot help detecting those very analogies of the Paradise mythology. You may abuse the features of antiquity: the Messiah, the hierarchy, the life after death, the pilgrimage, but you cannot get away from them. So in common with my great doctor, St Thomas Aquinas, I discern the *Analogia Entis.*

The Psychologist: But because you will see things from outside. You look at these eschatological features as if they were real. For me they are symptoms.

The Chairman: But more than symptoms, surely! Consider how their eschatology continues the classical dialectic of war and peace: Peace is the theme of all their pronouncements, the final goal, still far off owing to the wicked machinations of the enemy. Thus war is a necessity too and you have the lurid background of gathering clouds. They prepare for and support violence, acclaim heroic glories and promise final rewards. Thus they create a volcano which may blow up at any time while they hold out the hope of bliss, contrary to all evidence. But this war-peace dialectic enables the echelons of power to maintain their rigid order. They even live by peculiar ethics, the so-called interim-ethics which an impending clash would appear to justify. The manner of life, therefore, is one of an extreme and enforced austerity which stands in direct contradiction to the blessings vouchsafed in the future. It is the ancient calculus all right, for despite Marx the future puts its heavy grip on the present. The Here and Now are mortgaged against the Day.

The Psychologist: The Coming of the Day is an integral part of the expectation. It provides an emotional fuel which sustains the fires of fanatical devotion. 'Soon', they sing, 'comes the Day', and that indicates that devotion to a person is not a sufficiently lasting bond on which to erect the gigantic structure of immense social forces. The human condition under the stress from within also requires the Day.

The Chairman: This business of the Day jarred in ancient eschatologies as it does in modern totalitarianism, Communist or Radical. The Messiah alone was not enough then, and so the Messianic figure of the Leader does not suffice now. If he is too familiar a figure, who appears among the people or on television screens, he loses that numinous quality which enjoys supernatural authority and unquestioned infallibility. Both Hitler and Stalin knew this and abstained from courting popularity. They were in fact less accessible than any king of old. But the disadvantage of the supernatural aura is also plain: it leads to a form of isolation which can be politically disastrous; it invites assassination and wars of succession. Accordingly some dictators are content to sacrifice the holiness of their sacred person in favour of a broader and even more human basis for their power. They mingle among the people and denounce the cult of personality. This is the old Messianic dialectic which stresses now the supreme authority of the divine leader and then again exalts the State or Kingdom at his expense.

The Protestant: I fail to discern the ancient pattern in these modern monstrosities of tyranny and power-inflated upstarts. Surely, the Day and the Messiah in *our* language stand in direct opposition to these men and their lies.

The Communist: I can set your mind at rest there. These analogies exist only in your minds, not in reality. For, before you interrupted me, I made it perfectly clear that our ends are not only political but also scientific.   Now the application of scientific methods rules out such categories as Messiah and the Day.   What you seem to forget is that we have already entered upon such a state of scientific perfection as gives a foretaste of future blessings.   We need neither Messiah nor the Day when we survey our building projects and fire manned rockets into orbit.   Indeed, when we penetrate the universe and carry out experiments under the earth and under the sea we show that the myth of the blue sky was nonsense and the fear of Hell rubbish.   We plan and control our world without a Messiah.   We bring the future to bear upon the present.   Every scientific success belongs to the members of the party without whose sacrifices and work nothing could be achieved.   We give homage to them, we hail their instalments of further successes.   We believe in Science.

The Psychologist: Yes, and thereby establish another myth of the End.   Even in the past they saw the connection between the will to power and the possibilities of science.   Do you remember the book of Enoch, for example, where the writer links science to war? Science is only another intimation of the End and just as frightening in scope as anything pictured in the ancient writings.   No wonder your enthusiasm carries with it an apocalyptic fervour, a feverish excitement which would not be warranted by rational enquiry and ordinary research.   No, your spirit of scientific expectations envisages higher measures of control and an ascent to further knowledge and greater power.   You measure the time by scientific milestones on the long road towards the End and do not know that you are playing out a psychological drama.

The Chairman: The note of despair which goes alongside this newly harnessed power also reminds me of ancient eschatology. I could never quite understand why the ancients portrayed the future with such horrors as the battle at the mount of Megiddo and the struggle against Gog and Magog.   They betokened a horror which no weapons of destruction then extant could possibly bring about. So they judged that supernatural forces would act on a grand scale. Now the anticipation of horrors sheds the supernatural and is linked with forseeable methods of extermination.

The Protestant: And yet, while noting all this, you still shy away from identifying our situation with that predicted in the Bible. In fact, you would rather not be heirs of the End-hope, though all the signs point towards the great Day.

The Chairman: I do shy away from it because I do not believe a catastrophe to be the destiny of Mankind.   Just because the

apocalyptic danger seems so great now and may realistically overtake us I am against it and would confound these radical intimations
of the End.   Who, I ask you, could pray 'Make an End!', if this
means the end of civilization as we know it?

The Catholic: I have found some who suffer innocently and
outrageously at the hands of the Communists, who would, in fact,
pray for such an end.   I do not approve of it, I merely state the fact.

The Communist: These are your warmongers, but they cannot
hold up our final victory.

The Protestant: Your victory!   The victory of Antichrist if
that could be.   But do not forget that at Armaggeddon you will be
beaten.   You merely exploit our morality and our war-weariness.
In our century too many battles have been fought, apparently for
nothing, and there are some among us who are pacifists because of
the End-hope.   But do not misinterpret our good-will as cowardice!
People like our Chairman may give you the impression that you only
are heirs to the military End-hope, paying lip-service to peace and
co-existence while you plan to blot us out.   How can you hope to
defeat God?

The Psychologist: And so you both reiterate another feature
of ancient eschatology in our own day, which suits my book: the
enduring conflict.   You simplify it, of course, and you take over
into modern conditions that determinism which is so typical: conflict is inevitable, the enemy must be defeated, therefore be prepared
for the final battle.   Little do you realize that the battle rages in
yourselves.

The Chairman: This note of finality is so ridiculous that it
ought to be dropped.   You are playing with an illusion of the End.
The 'for the last time' motif angers me.   Dou you remember Hitler's
troops and their *Zum letzten Mal*?   Well, it was NOT.

The Communist: Because we happened to defeat Germany.

The Psychologist: Finality is an ambiguous counter.   It appeals
to the ordinary, non-hysterical, because it promises in war a speedy
release from danger and a safe return home to enjoy the fruits of
victory.   But, on the contrary, to the young and emotional it sounds
the heroic note, an ultimate break with everything that has ever been.
Hence the revolutionary *Jour de Gloire*—atmosphere kindles a flame.

The Catholic: And the ensuing absence of finality is never
sufficiently noticed.   After all, even the most revolutionary régime
settles down.

The Chairman: But not without claims to near-permanence
and therefore finality.

The Protestant: The forces of Antichrist uncannily fulfil the role assigned to them in our ancient prophecies. Note how their rulers claim to be free from all moral obligations. They act under an evil authority and employ others who carry out their orders. They intimidate, they terrorize. They cause physical suffering, mental fear, and spiritual desolation, as it is written in the predictions of the pangs of the Messianic age. Their political oppression has an almost demonic character. Cannot you discern the equivalent of the dark powers in these unknown tormentors who are themselves tools of a greater power? Note how they coerce one another in a network of suspicion, for here hatred has ousted love for ever. They arrest innocent persons, condemn them without a fair trial, torture them before and after sentence, degrade them and strip them of honour and personality. Why do you not acknowledge that these are the signs of the End?

The Chairman: I am still an incorrigible optimist, for I see signs of improvement on the horizon. After the worst excesses men generally settle down. We must adopt a wider view and not be carried away. What is one century in a world such as ours?

The Protestant: You do not wish to sample the evil. I could almost wish that you were made to experience the apocalyptic terror: treated worse than a beast and denied all human rights, regarded as worse than vermin or dirt, hence to be dealt with as a thing, with complete indifference.

The Psychologist: Ah, but far more significant: they want *you*. They exact confessions of imaginary crimes, even before they put you to death, for unconsciously they are head- or soul-hunters.

The Catholic: Another analogy here: they would wash away your true self. The purges almost suggest that the state desires the conversion of personality and even the victim's consent. This dialectic reproduces again the apocalyptic pattern, in which impersonal powers act personally.

The Protestant: The last infamy, namely to induce the faithful to apostatize. And you have only to read in recorded memoirs how this is done. In the revolution of Antichrist judges, camp commandants and executioners inflict suffering and death and they ENJOY doing this. They beat the prisoners, they squash the babes, they gas the children, they starve whole communities, and yet these organizers of human misery express no regrets. Their invincible administration of death causes them as much satisfaction as it causes despair among the victims. These devils fulfil the apocalyptic role, for they enjoy evil for its own sake. The victims too fulfil the sombre prediction that only a few can endure the onslaughts of the signs of the End without ruin.

The Chairman: Please do not think that I feel less passionately than you the appalling nature of what has happened. But in order to better the human lot I will not greet these things as having anything to do with religion. God had given us eternity to outgrow these aberrations. We must circumvent the final catastrophe and we must not give a welcome to nuclear destruction. We may even commit a grievous wrong if we make room for any kind of eschatological determinism. These horrible things only happen if we allow them to. It is like the dreaded chain-reaction of nuclear explosions of which none of us know where they may end. And consider that we have no right to condemn to death not only our children but also all plant and animal life. It does not belong to the Christian hope to turn this fruit-bearing earth into a sterile planet. No, the end of the world is unthinkable, except in millions of millions of years, and even then the universe will survive. This should give us courage to take up our stand against all misguided Utopian ends and means.

The Psychologist: Of course you are absolutely right. Yet you tend to underestimate the cogency of some of the Utopian phenomena which our friends here seem to espouse quite happily, partly for themselves, partly for what they lead up to. Your trouble is that, like our friends here, you will externalize these phenomena and consequently you shrink back in some horror of what has been done in the name of apocalyptic Utopias. You sense the sadism, for example, which brutalizes man. But the right way is not to condemn this without understanding its motivation. All your phenomena are facts, I have no doubt. But you, Mr Chairman, will circumvent them, while Monsieur le Père Catholique would systematize them in an analogical theology, and while our extreme friends are actually locked in battle. Let me now at last give a new edge to the argument. Let me explain WHY men should think and act according to the pattern of the final expectation. The forward dream, the ensuing conflict, the determinism, victory, sufferings, and defeat; in short, all your eschatological data, are meaningless unless they are understood from within.

CHAPTER VIII

MOTIVES OF ESCHATOLOGY

The Psychologist: The 'Pursuit of the Millennium' is admittedly enmeshed in the turmoils of history, as Norman Cohn shows in his excellent book.[1] But he claims that 'least of all is this a history of social revolt as such'. The quasi-religious salvationism of Cohn's *Prophetae* is of a peculiar kind. Like the Nazis and the Communists your Millenarianist endows social conflicts and aspirations with transcendental significance. Fantasies, which are downright archaic, link your Müntzers to your modern fanatics. Cohn diagnoses the uprooted surplus populations as the seed-bed, which can and does receive the magnetic seed of eschatological doctrines. He knows that the personality of the sower is at least as important as the seed. But when he concludes that 'A boundless millennial promise made with boundless, prophet-like conviction to a number of rootless and desperate men in the midst of a society where traditional norms and relationships are disintegrating—here, it would seem, lay the source of that peculiar subterranean fanaticism which subsisted as a perpetual menace to the structure of medieval society', I would go much further and pinpoint the disturbance in the Psyche. You see, he talks of fantasies and the atavism of the Nazis, but he does not, to my mind, state with sufficient emphasis that we deal here with a sickness. Eschatology is a neurosis, *tout court*. I agree with Cohn that the Pursuit of the Millennium is a bad thing which produces a wholesale crop of horrible manifestations, but I think he dwells, as a historian, too exclusively upon the manifestations. The particulars derive from the universal: the malady is the central thing and causes the observable and recorded irrationalities of apocalyptic behaviour.

The Catholic: I agree with the sentiment of Cohn's book which in condemning Millenarianism also shows up the enormous work of the Church in taming the rough chiliastic instinct. We civilized successfully the atavistic; but Cohn errs, I submit, when he more or less assumes that our own other-worldliness was among other things only a device to get these gangsters to remain quiet and respectable and to keep the medieval world from harm. Our institutions, too, must be considered in their own right and not as a defence mechanism.

The Protestant: I would go much further in my opposition to

[1] Norman Cohn: *The Pursuit of the Millennium.*

8   95

Cohn's book.   Bloch at least recognized the virtue of the Principle of Hope; Cohn takes the worst disfigurements of apocalyptic hope and then condemns the lot.

The Chairman: In other words, he judges from the particular to the universal, as I am afraid you, Sir, are bent on doing now.

The Psychologist: I?   Well, as a medical man I must argue from the particular patient, his symptoms and, we hope, his cure, to the more general field of mental sickness.   For us this is perfectly legitimate, as long as, like all scientists, we are willing to change our presuppositions when experience demands it.   I have no reason, however, to question Freud's basic concepts of neurosis.

The Protestant: For the life of me I cannot see the connection between your Freudian Pan-sexualism, which incidentally I abhor, and our subject which concerns the End of Man and the End of the World.   This reminder seems to me necessary.

The Psychologist: Not at all.   I am wholly aware of our subject. To put it quite plainly, the motivation of all eschatology is frustration.

The Communist: This is nothing new.   Bloch not only admits but highlights this frustration which is basic to human existence: it begins at birth and grows with every minute of a life spent in a capitalist society.

The Catholic: This so-called frustration is not primarily economic but organic, and Bloch actually acknowledges this un-Marxist fact.   He traces the frustrations of the mature man who cannot reach his goal.

The Psychologist: Man then compensates for what he has not got.   He cannot stand reality, so he tells lies and dreams up vengeance and triumph.   He keeps the demon of self-disapproval at bay, and as old age approaches he tries new measures.   New mines have to be excavated.   Wine and wealth replace the purer passions.

The Protestant: Again this is as old as the hills.   Read what the Preacher says about the Vanity of Vanities and the cracking of the Golden Bowl.   He scorned the ends of life, the play of the child, the enthusiasm of youth, the respectability of the householder, and the final decay.   All must come in its due time, but there is no hope. Thus the Preacher prepares men for the supernatural Hope of the Gospel which begins where human hopes end.

The Chairman: Such pessimism goes against the facts of life. There are those, like Cicero in *De Senectute,* who regard old age as the time of harvest when the good vintage shows its quality.

The Catholic: It depends on the goodness of the vintage, the result of Grace crowning nature.

The Protestant: Not nature! In nature we move forward to lose everything. As Bloch says humorously, the first realization of the end, in personal terms, comes to the man when a young girl offers him her place in the bus, when the woman ceases to be capable of child-bearing. The tides of the sea cannot be arrested. The decreasing faculties bring less light, deafness, absence of taste, want of touch: the old desire tranquillity and of that they get often more than their share.

The Psychologist: And the frustration continues, for no man is willing to abdicate. He struggles to the end for his place in society.

The Communist: Which he gets as long as he can pay for it. The capitalist society prepares a nice stew for the toothless lion . . . if he can afford it.

The Catholic: What an affront to the aged who reach serenity by sheer force of character!

The Protestant: And by the hope which lies beyond.

The Psychologist: What you have all missed is the really important feature in frustration. First, it is the outcome of innate desires and only indirectly the result of external pressure. Secondly, frustration is itself active and leads to the transmutation of desires and the build-up of complexes. That is why I regard your eschatological passions as symptoms of a neurotic complex. I am only interested in its different nuances as parts of the whole. For me it is idle to discuss whether you believe in the End of the world as such, but I am prepared to investigate *why* you should ever come to believe such a thing at all. For the believer is the cause of the belief. Just as the patient is more important than his library so the neurosis of eschatology is more illuminating than its documents in literature and creeds.

The Chairman: But what possesses your patient to make up this myth of the End?

The Psychologist: I am glad you use the word 'myth'. Freud discovered that the Pleasure Principle reigns supreme and is mirrored specially in religious myth: 'The doctrine of reward in a future life for the—voluntary or enforced—renunciation of earthly lusts is nothing but a mythical projection of this revolution in the mind'.[2]

The Catholic: But then Freud's anti-religious bias is in itself an obsession.

The Psychologist: I would not grant you this. In any case, the compensation principle is central in the making of the eschatological myth. What we have not got we would have by other means. Our Communist friend recognizes the force of hunger and thirst, but

---

[2] Freud: *Collected Papers*, Vol. iv, p. 18.

the sexual urge is greater for it dominates both. In childhood the given libido receives its first decisive shocks and the neurotic sets in motion a censorship of wanted but forbidden sexual satisfactions. Thus the pleasure principle also gives birth to the urge towards killing and destruction. Observe now how the millenarianists are obsessed by the images of death. For them the libido now acts in reverse. Killing, often with associations cruel and perverse, discredits their theme of the End, and thus eschatology becomes a clinical subject in analytical psychology.

The Protestant: It seems to me that you invent experiences in order to associate our pure hope with your dirt.

The Psychologist: This has nothing to do with dirt. I am trying to show you how your passions for the End stem from a complex whole. The whole thing begins with your relationship with parents. In 1928 Freud was taken to task by a young American doctor for his indifference to the subject of survival after death. The 'infidel Jew' (Freud's self-descriptive term) thanked his brother physician for his solicitude but dismissed his intercessions as useless. Instead he showed how this doctor had deceived himself about religious conversion. You see, that young man had in a dream seen a 'sweet-faced dear old woman' brought into the dissecting-room, and had nearly lost his faith in God who allowed this to happen. He wanted to destroy God and give up faith, but he heard a voice from Heaven and thereupon made his peace with God. Freud points out that this is an almost classic case of tension and a conflict resolved, for what he really saw in this woman, naked or about to be stripped, was his own mother. He was still in love with her and wanted to destroy his father, God. It was a typical Oedipus situation.[3]

The Chairman: You go, or rather Freud goes, too far. This story alone shows that his method precludes him from ever arriving at a conclusion at variance with his presuppositions.

The Catholic: Precisely. The reduction of all human urges to one denominator is difficult to maintain. The desire for power, for example, is known to be very strong and would explain the eschatological trend much better: real power can only be absolute if it be permanent. Your ancient Kings and Pharaohs deemed themselves immortal, not because of sexuality but because of the divine power attached to them. We fear an end which may terminate life; despite anguish and adversity we wish to go on. Here on earth everything is partial and the human soul, knowing itself to be immortal, must look to the End because of its inherent nature. I agree that there

[3] Op. cit., Vol. v, p. 244.

is an innate desire for future felicity, but I deny that it derives from frustrated sex.

The Psychologist: Freud realized that you would not wish to see the facts. It is our own censorship which prevents us from acknowledging the cause of our destructive nature. Your talk of future felicity hardly harmonizes with the dread of death which most people nurse. Now Freud's death-wish, very different from consolation in death, really gets to the bottom to our relationship with death. It is based upon the Pleasure Principle defeated and distorted into destructive channels.

The Communist: Permit me to comment that what makes this analysis so ludicrous is that it is based on childhood experiences. The whole of life is made dependent upon the past. The future is governed by Mum and Dad. Well, this may be true of Capitalist neurotics; it is nothing to do with working-class life.

The Psychologist: Your Communist censorship is militant and works its own defence-mechanism. In point of fact class-membership is quite irrelevant to our analysis.

The Chairman: Still, in view of our objectors, would you tell us what evidence you have for your thesis? After all, you claim that the whole of the End-drama, both in tradition and in individual faith, owes its existence to a perilous replacement of healthy sexual needs.

The Psychologist: Our evidence, by the very nature of it, must come from case-histories. Or, if you like, visit our various mental hospitals and attend clinics! The evidence is always the patient. He supplies evidence which can be put into words and into images. He is invited to paint spontaneously, he submits to spontaneous word-associations, and, above all, he gives a report of his dreams.

The Protestant: I am glad you mention dreams, that famous repository of analytical material. Now I have taken the trouble to peruse Freud's own Papers and to my astonishment I find that there is plenty of Phallus and Castration, and the like, but nothing at all about the End. In fact, if Freud accuses the dreamer that 'he does not know what he knows' I would extend this to him and say: 'the good doctor does not know what he does not know.' In other words, he does not realize—and you yourself do not realize—that this End-hope is precisely the one thing that lies entirely outside your orbit. Nor does this surprise me, for considering, as has already been pointed out, that the whole Freudian method goes back to the beginnings it is impossible to see how that, which is essentially of the future, can be comprehended in the past. We do not *dream* of the Kingdom of God, of the Return of Christ, of the Judgement, and of Life Everlasting. You may motivate dreams of self-destruction but not of Christ-fulfilment. The former may be due to sex-frustration but do not concern us here; the latter cannot be brought within your clinical compass.

The Chairman: And yet would you deny that there are raving lunatics who have especially shown eschatological signs of madness?[4]

The Protestant: Without a doubt. The possessed and their madness derive from Satan and not from sex-frustration. Naturally, I repudiate their dreams and fantasies.

The Catholic: I would part company with you here. Not that I deny the phenomenon of possession, but I would affirm the evidence of eschatological dreams, though not in the Freudian sense.

The Communist: To me you seem to be giving your whole position away if you call upon dream-material as evidence. Do you seriously believe that in this age of science we are allowing ourselves to be duped by dreams? Surely the bourgeoisie must be near its collapse when they must forsake the arena of rational arguments and scientific processes.

The Protestant: I repudiate the dream-material on altogether different grounds. The prophet Jeremiah and the book of Deuteronomy make it plain enough that dreamers are nothing better than sorcerers and are not to be heeded unless their dreams are in agreement with the will of God.

The Chairman: Don't be too harsh in your condemnations. The books of the Bible approve of some, and not of other, dream-material. Anyhow, modern psychology cannot proceed if you disallow the witness of dreams and that of other fantasies. I don't like it, but I accept it.

The Catholic: Dreams are essentially a protection of sleep, and the desires and fears which may keep us awake assume concrete shape in dreams. Dreams of the End are therefore not rare, if you can detect the meaning of the symbol. The extravagant world of these dreams we know from the imagery in apocalyptic literature: wild beasts, valleys, hills, trees, stars, shapes of light, oceans, caves, etc., adumbrate our somewhat confused theme. Without the interpreter we may recognize nothing. Take one of the commonest symbols: water. For some it is just that, but if you are steeped in our subject you identify the floods of the dream with the myth of the Flood, at the beginning and at the end, and also with the deep unconscious. You have to remove the mask from these End-dreams.

The Psychologist: Do it, by all means, and you will find there the castration phobia and connected problems.

---

[4] Dryden seems particularly apposite here:
  'Great wits are sure to madness near allied
  And thin partitions do their bounds divide.'

The Catholic: And something else which is the common possession of all mankind and which comes from the common pool of human experience: Jung's famous archetypes, of which our subject is a notable one. Jung takes you out of the sphere of merely unfulfilled wishes and the treatment of dreams as indicative of the past only. He uses the dream for future integration. Thus the End is really in the Psyche and balance is unthinkable without awareness of it.

The Communist: Well, at least that lets us out of the Freudian Mum-and-Dad centredness. What have you instead?

The Catholic: Meaningful symbols. As Christ signifies the self-ruler of the inner world—where light and darkness are locked in conflict until the moment of integration—so Antichrist is the symbol of enmity. The dragon is not artificial, as the rationalists hold, but the cosmic aspect of this Antichrist. Note that the libido-symbols do not stop at sun, light, fire, etc., but have a whole range of other expressions at their disposal to bring out the conflict, e.g. the snake, itself both symbol of fall and destruction as well as of healing and integration. All these archetypes enable the neophyte in his religious ecstasy to aim at the stars, to immortalize himself, and this concept of the 'heavenly journey' is a deep inner necessity. To it correspond the heroic representations of apotheosis, the pilgrimages in alchemy, and not least the Second Coming. The love for the 'heavenly bridegroom' or for Wisdom, Sophia, the Bride, is a phenomenon by no means confined to the sphere of Christianity. You see, eschatology is universal because it answers to a universal need.[5]

The Protestant: I am shocked that you, as a Christian, can accept this pagan mumbo-jumbo and connect it with our Lord Jesus Christ.

The Catholic: Analogically, not literally. These heavenly myths suggest the truth while he is the Truth. So it is also with Jung's interpretation of New Testament Eschatology which he evaluates as symbolic of the conflict of the Psyche and our own situation today. In the individuation process, he claims, the end looks to the beginning and contrariwise: 'Unless ye become like children' evokes for him the *satori* of Zen Buddhism ('show me your original face!').

The Psychologist: This little extract proves how Jung has perverted his master's teaching. Does not the arbitrariness alone

---

[5] Cf. Jung: *Symbols of Transformation*, pp. 87ff., 368, 396. The speaker would have referred to the chapter on 'Life after Death', if C. G. Jung's *Memories, Dreams, Reflections* had not appeared since the debate (E.T. 1963).

frighten you?   Can you not say anything if you detect analogies here, there, and everywhere?   The real flaw in his profusion and learning is the archetype.

The Chairman: A curiously Platonic thing, really an 'idea' I should have thought.

The Catholic: No more than an idea, for it is not transcendent but always latent in the Psyche, a hypothesis evoked by clinical therapy.   This aspect indeed leaves us Catholics dissatisfied.   First of all, if we followed Jung altogether we would have to abandon ontological statements.   We could not say, for example, 'This is Antichrist', but only 'this is Antichrist in this clinical case'.   Nothing is metaphysical, everything is therapeutic.   For example, on Life after death Jung seems very positive as compared with Freud.   Although 'we do not know any more about Life after death than about life on Mars', he yet says: 'as a doctor I am convinced that it is hygienic . . . to discover in death a goal towards which one can strive. . . .'   A supramundane goal is reasonable, because from the standpoint of psychotherapy it would be desirable to think of death as only a transition within many stages of life.[6]   But there is a world of difference between hygiene and truth, between 'desirable' and 'existent'.   But even more unacceptable is Jung's principle of individuation when applied to Satan and Judgement and related eschatology.   For him Satan-Serpent-Evil, though perfectly real, must not be crushed, but the dark Son of God must be brought within the framework of integration.   No wonder Jung must, from our point of view, be heretical and his citation of other religions, in the same breath as quotations from Christian Scriptures and Liturgy, makes him highly suspect.   Yet, we greet him as a step on the long ladder of analogies just as cordially as he acclaims us for our vital symbolism.

The Communist: In fact, birds of one feather politically.

The Psychologist: His religious partisanship discredits his psychological insights.   You mentioned the snake: I leave it to you to judge which interpretation is nearer the truth.   For us Freudians the snake is the typical repression of phallic concern; the sexual interpretation is inevitable.   But Jung, while knowing all this, fastens other-worldly, supernatural, mythological associations upon it, and lo, eternity replaces the penis.   Can your systems of analogical reasoning defend so monstrous a jump?

The Chairman: You move in different worlds.   The weakness of all symbolism is inescapable, but especially in psychology.   But there is a further drastic weakness, from which neither Jung nor

---

[6] Jung: *The Structure and Dynamics of the Psyche*, pp. 401, 404.

Freud seem to escape.   They deal with the pathological; hence the
dreams and the symbols are never free from the taint of sickness.
Now how can you make that other jump: from the sick to the
healthy?   Or to apply this to our problem: is all eschatology motiv-
ated by neurosis?

  The Psychologist: Yes, I suppose it is.   But the dividing line
between the healthy and the sick is not as firmly drawn as you would
seem to believe.

  The Communist: But the Chairman reminds us in this connection of the really decisive flaw in the evidence.   Whether sick or
healthy, case histories can never get beyond the individual.   How can
you draw general conclusions from such premises?

  The Psychologist: Well, all science does it up to a point.   Where
should we be without inductive reasoning?   In medicine above all
every advance is carried out by an analysis of case histories.

  The Catholic: Yes.   Hence if the analogical material suggests
in individual cases what we know to be held dogmatically by all,
everywhere, and at all times, we may draw upon the particulars to
explain to ourselves the universals.   Thus eschatology in therapy is
related to eschatology in dogma.   Indeed, the connection is a close
one, for otherwise how could we picture to ourselves the future and
exchange despair with eager expectation?   Don't imagine that I
would confine my analogies only to the dream-world and the Psyche.
No, mankind is endowed by God with the anticipation of his work.
Again I turn to the natural universe: the bud promises the bloom,
the maiden grows into a woman, the boy into the man.   So youth
serves as the allegory of a purposeful advance.   Everything is in
preparation and in pursuit of its end.   Dante expresses well the keen
experience of such progress in his age, and many of his contemporaries would have echoed this sentiment: 'L'acqua che io predo
giammai non si corse' (no one has yet cruised on the waters which
I take).

  The Chairman: And so would I echo this.   Progress then on
all levels towards a goal, but not literally an end with a capital E.

  The Protestant: Thus you sum up the human hope of ends as
against the End to be manifested by God.   But how strange: you
can accept your search for progress despite the whole succession of
fiascos.   You in fact project your hopes as inexperienced young
lovers project themselves into the beloved only to find disappointment.   In human terms alone the End is meaningless and negatived
by experience.   Perfection is never found here.   But the End-hope
is not concerned with isolated hopes but with the Whole, created
and ended by God.   It is transcendent and therefore inaccessible to

psychological insights.   It is not the result of dreams: consider how the God-given dreams in the Bible (Jacob, Joseph, Daniel, St Joseph), never lead to symbolical interpretation but to practical action. Eschatology is not the projection of the inner self but a point in time when God's redemptive work is complete.   Therefore we must distinguish between false Messianism—your notions of projected power—and Jesus Christ who hands over his Kingdom to the Father. You cannot apply psychological categories to such an act of transcendent Grace.   Human speech can only speak of the impossible: the desert becomes the garden, mountains are made low, valleys exalted, and God reigns.   But this language is also the Word of God, so that when we consider the End we know nothing, unless we are inspired by the Spirit of God which declares how the summer-fruit betokens the harvest, the crooked wall the collapse of the house, the shaking earth and the fire announcing that the end is nigh.   Admittedly, the broken heart (what you call the Psyche) recognizes its plight in this revelation, just as the fear of bombs and social chaos reflect already something of the things that are to come.   But only faith can recognize the truth.   It is the Spirit which manifests the End, not the Psyche which revels in ends.

The Chairman: Our disagreements are now in the open.   Perhaps you are right that the failure of Utopian hopes should serve as a corrective to our thinking, just as our criticisms would invalidate some of the absurdities so often associated with the End.   However divine the End-hope it must be contained in human terms.   Outside the limits of moral and rational coherence it becomes not only meaningless but also reprehensible.   The End which awaited the swine which rushed down the steep cliff, according to the Gospel, is hardly what we expect for the Universe.   Let us now turn from the origins to the criteria which should govern a sound eschatology.

CHAPTER IX

CRITERIA OF THE END-HOPE

The Communist: I am relieved that you acknowledge that our subject stands in danger of becoming meaningless. We have disagreed on the definition of our problem because we have now found that we discern quite different causes in the making of this End-hope. I stood out for the social conditioning and, in the words of Marx, I regard the working-class as the midwife in the birth of the new Age. But now I can go further than this. The criterion for the End-hope is that it involves political action. Therefore, I submit, the contents of the hope are this-worldly and capable of implementation on a tangible scale. Granted the fulfilment of this social hope I next postulate scientific criteria: I envisage an enormous advance in practical and theoretic knowledge. As we employ new techniques we build up new models in our explanation of the physical universe. Thus you will find that our development in electronics will go hand in hand, as it were, with our discoveries in space and our control of space. Thus I would say all my criteria in planning for the future are governed by scientific means and ends. Or, putting it differently, anything unscientific and outside the compass of mathematical-physical representation I reject as irrelevant and misleading.

The Chairman: But you would admit that your nineteenth-century materialism is now somewhat out of date?

The Communist: Not really, for it was never that caricature of a theory which identified matter with solid materials. The discoveries of our century enable us to reword our theories but the main tenet remains unshaken: we repudiate a meaning, ideal, or anything behind the given universe of facts which we comprehend by scientific means.

The Chairman: I still cannot see how this approach can have anything to do with our subject, namely the End-hope.

The Communist: To be precise, it denies the validity of the term End. There is no such thing, but there is a future before man which every generation penetrates further. The scientific approach warrants the soundness of this penetration and its continuity. We proceed from less to more. There is a kind of ascent in knowledge, but no End is in sight.

The Psychologist: Thereby you also depersonalize your Hope. It is the Hope appropriate for a computer, not for a human being. I don't mean this sentimentally, but scientifically. Every human being has a beginning and an end. Hope is a meaningless term outside this context. I would postulate a man's Hope is nothing if not a personal expectation. In the first place it is to get satisfaction, then to sublimate his appetites, and finally to come to terms with himself and the world. As regards the End a man's Hope is that in the school of life he has learnt to face it without qualms. Having resolved the conflict of life he has also come to terms with death. My criterion of the End-hope is entirely to be found in individual behaviour. It is a pragmatic criterion: health, ability to balance. I also disparage the End as a valid concept, but I would harness the neurotic illusions about the future to the present task of living.

The Chairman: As I see it you are both limiting the field too severely. Thereby you gain coherence, but you lose richness. The scientist accepts ultimately only the world of phenomena and therefore, like you Tovarich, he dismisses everything outside the realm of, what Kant called, Pure Reason. But remember that, according to Kant, you bring to it your own spectacles: you digest the phenomena as you select and devour them. Clearly, therefore, Hope and End are not on your plate. The scientific criterion helps in as much as it keeps out pure speculations, mere fantasies; but it cuts off too much. Now the Psychologist also errs, for he keeps the plate empty for too long. His Hope as well as his ends are only human, all-too-human. He accepts only the spectacles and the effect of what is seen and disclaims the objective itself. Impersonal reality does not interest him. This again is surgery of a kind which may kill the patient. No, I would have the phenomena of science, the moral will of practical Reason, and the judgements of our aesthetic sense to guide us in our pursuit. Let the End-hope, then, be hemmed in by what it finds in the outer world as conveyed to us in scientific terms, by the dictates of our conscience, by the universal Law, and let it also be informed by our whole culture, by the admittedly vast treatment given to it in Art, especially Western, European, Christian Art and Literature. Can you quarrel with my criterion? The End-hope must not contradict the conclusions of Science, nor offend the dictates of the informed conscience, nor ignore our cultural tradition.

The Catholic: The True, the Good, the Beautiful as general criteria are indeed very acceptable, although I feel that the clear-cut Kantian division is in many ways unfortunate, because it is, of course, an abstraction. Man is a whole and even the dualistic world of Buber—I and It, I and Thou—is an artifice rather than reality. But on the whole I accept your criterion of Science, Conscience, and Tradition, as long as you permit me to point out that here we move merely on the level of Natural Theology. Now the End-hope is more specifically contained in our tradition and I would therefore add as a Catholic criterion that the scientific, moral, and aesthetic sanction, which we bestow upon the End-hope, must be informed by, and not contradict, Church tradition. To be more precise: The Third Part of St Thomas's *Summa Theologica* is still in all essentials a criterion of the reasonable character of our hope.

The Protestant: I am not opposed to reasonableness nor indeed to science, conscience, and aesthetic judgement, but I doubt whether these apply a criterion to our quest. I sympathize strangely with our Swiss friend, for to me the personal experience within is of far more importance than, say, what St Thomas has to say. Institutionalism is apt to obscure this subject, for it is not in the interest of any institution, including the Church, to confront a future as depicted in the Bible. I would like you to read Paul Schütz. He argues with prophetic voice against the 'objectivization' of this unique expectation, which cannot thrive in 'neutral' ground. The very terms 'eschatological', 'apocalyptic', etc., are dangerous for they 'historize' the whole expectation. But prophecy stands above—though also in—history. You see, for Schütz, as for me, the criterion is our Inspiration. We are talking about the more-than-visible, and who but the Spirit can plumb the depth of that? Hope is a charisma, not a scientific principle, as with Bloch. Without the Spirit of God there is no possible nexus with the End, for 'the time of history ends against a blank wall'. Our trouble is that Christian truth is no longer an event resting in eternity, but has become an object of discussion. Without regaining the Messianic heights of command, there is no criterion in sight. Only the prophet sees, for he is a partisan of the future, and this future *is* his reality. Therefore eschatology is not beyond but coming with the Coming One. My criterion then is: God's future known prophetically.

The Communist: In other words, your criterion is the exact opposite of mine. Anything that is irrational, unscientific, and religious. . . .

The Chairman: Ignoring his jeering note, would you say that you favour the wildly incoherent, that you actually establish the criterion of irrationality?

The Protestant: We have often been accused of this. There is, in fact, something to be said for the Irrational as a criterion of religious truth. You said yourself that we ought to consult the past.

Well, there have never been wanting those who suspected the wisdom of this world—i.e. the evidence from the senses, the cool, detached reason—as being diametrically opposed to the wisdom of God. What the world could not know by its own wisdom God revealed to the uneducated. If this goes for earthly things, how much more for the future with its celestial note. 'I believe because it is absurd', concluded Tertullian, and near our own day Kierkegaard condemned the scientific approach in his unscientific postscript. But let me hasten to add, that ultimately the Wisdom of God is the only wisdom and that His Word is the true Reason, the Principle of Order. I would not have you believe that my criterion is one of mental anarchy. I hate and abhor disorder, as indeed all the prophets did, and my criterion in Eschatology is the agreement with this prophetic rule of order, 'the rightness', which is of God.

The Psychologist: Even so I cannot see how you can dissociate yourself from all the different brands of ranters and enthusiasts who manifestly believed they were 'right', especially in their eschatology, and yet to us now in retrospect appear to be rather silly.

The Protestant: This superior attitude to enthusiasts in the past is very unfair. R. Knox in his *Enthusiasm* shows not only his own prejudice but also displays a profound misunderstanding of the prophets whom he ridicules.

The Chairman: His was an interesting Love-Hate relationship with regard to Pascal, Wesley and kindred spirits. I would have thought he was very fair in his evaluation.

The Catholic: Yes, Knox shows precisely where the spirit of prophecy errs and must err, especially when it espouses the irrational, free from the bridle of tradition.

The Protestant: Your strictures on a genius like Pascal seem so ludicrous as to condemn themselves. Was Pascal not the scientist before all scientists? Was not he a pious Catholic in a godless age? Was not he a true prophet? What would the European tradition be without its Pascals? No, let us have Pascal as a yardstick by all means of what I mean by the prophetic criterion.

The Communist: Your Pascal reminds me of all the kindred spirits like Tolstoy, Soloviev and others, whom Lenin branded as 'crazy landlords intoxicated with Christ'. How can I accept this criterion?

The Chairman: But if a scientist is also prophetic, how do you then proceed? Do you dismiss Newton's calculus because he is also the expositor of the books of Daniel and the Apocalypse?

The Communist: Newton still had one foot in alchemy. We accept the science, not the rest.

The Catholic: I would not have you think that we disown the prophetic altogether but we would guard against its extravagances and refuse to admit them as criteria of Christian hope. The Second Coming has always been distorted by the so-called illuminists, who spoke in tongues, were possessed, foamed at the mouth, swelling in their bodies, trembling violently, and worse. In our view the Pentecostal manifestations discredit eschatology. No wonder your prophetically inspired leaders often looked forward to their deliverance from Church and moral authority altogether. In France the prophets of the Cévennes and Port Royal come to stand for a revolt against decency and pleasure; theirs was an intolerable, arrogant self-righteousness, a quasi-mystic anti-naturalism, from which Pascal was not free. If Knox brands him as a 'Christian pessimist', who had the makings of an embittered atheist, you can hardly quarrel with that estimate. Therefore I would set up as my criterion of a valid eschatology: freedom from the prophetic spirit, its contempt for the intellect, the perils of enthusiasm. Pascal must serve for my reservation against the division of truth; I repudiate the playing out of religion against science, or of private intuition against tradition.

The Psychologist: Pascal's case is an interesting one of near-schizophrenia. His so-called vision, the famous Memorial of his conversion of November 23rd, 1654, 'Dieu d'Abraham etc.'—indicates a fearful strain. Like you, I would suspect all 'prophetic' or 'spiritual' criteria, here and everywhere.

The Protestant: Because you know so little about the subject. Let me tell you that your little simperings about the abuses of prophecy are as nothing compared with the prophets' own repudiation of pagan ecstasies. If only you knew your Bible! From Elijah to Malachi, nay from Moses to Christ, God reveals himself by *his* prophets: they are not possessed, they suffer from no split minds, they are healthier than the rest, and they predict the future more accurately than the scientists of the age. Moreover, they curb the professional aspects of prophecy: no incubation for them, no drugs or liquor, no orgies. They drew for ever the demarcation line between true and false prophecy. It had to be non-induced, free of charge, in the name of God, and confirmed by God in history. Therefore, freed from all the dross of pagan mantic, they speak God's Word. It is the Word, incarnate in Christ, and the Spirit proceeding from God, which authorizes tradition, not the other way round. And if you push the example of Pascal I do not object at all to such company.

The Chairman: Very well, then. We grant you your prophetic privileges so as to remain Biblicist throughout. The others will measure by their declared yardsticks. What you now have to prove is that your criteria are meaningful. Can we, for example, speak of a scientific Hope, or a hope with scientific ends in view? Can we discuss usefully perfection or the attainment of the good as a real expectation? Can we enrol aesthetics too as part of our forward-looking activity?

CHAPTER X

SCIENCE AND ESCHATOLOGY

The Catholic: I am very glad that we may now turn to more objective considerations. Being by training a scientist I am averse to discussions which fall outside the orbit of empirical observation. Always remember that we derive our cherished principles of causality from what we have seen throughout centuries of trial and error. We had to learn to sift reality from mere appearance. We had to strip off prejudices and outworn concepts. We had to accept the new and revise the old. So my first thesis is that modern science was rendered possible by the futuristic outlook. If Christianity looks towards the End in history it also introduced to the world confidence in the future and thereby an affirmation of scientific research.

The Chairman: I would have thought Greek science started centuries before the spread of Christianity. We owe to it the search for the simple explanation.

The Catholic: The spirit of scientific enquiry was alive, but it was tied to the cyclical pessimism of the age. As long as all things are believed to return to their origin the incentive to new discoveries is thin. It lacks the forward drive, and this it obtained in the Christian age.

The Protestant: An additional factor, not to be forgotten, was the demolition of the pagan gods, above all of astrology.

The Catholic: Yes, science had to be liberated from the gods and the stars, in short, from mythology.

The Psychologist: You speak of science, as men often do, in such a personalized way which strikes me as quite unscientific. After all, there never was a Mr Science nor a Family Science, and the term 'spirit of Science' is blissfully vague.

The Catholic: Very well, I accept this. Let us speak of the men-of-science. But do not let us underrate the significance of the objective, impersonal element in science, for this is my second point. I would assert that the Christian culture welcomed the pursuit of truth for its own sake. The scholastic tradition, in particular, handed on to Europe the spirit and the tools of free enquiry. This self-assurance was based on the conviction that truth exists and that it will be vindicated at the end. Just because the Church had tamed the wild eschatological impulse and had, in a sense, put off the Day or the Hour, men were encouraged to look around and work towards the End. The great scientists of the eighteenth century, you feel, stand in the tradition of Christian expectation. 'Our physics', they would say, 'agree with metaphysical truth', therefore our theories point towards a common consummation of truth.

The Protestant: I am not sure that this identification was not the cause of great harm, exalting science as God.

The Chairman: It is true, I suppose, that the doctrine of this so-called correspondence derives from the Greeks rather than the Hebrews. I don't think the worse of it for that reason, but I observe that 'correspondence' is almost antagonistic to the concept of the End. You see, if you take Leibnitz's Monads, for example, which, in the classical tradition, mirror the whole universe it seems to me that you postulate a non-ending universe.

The Catholic: Not necessarily, for, as we shall see, the termination of things is a constituent factor in science. The Monad may very well mirror a universal factor.

The Communist: I am not quite clear what you mean by that. Are you discussing now objective physical facts or metaphysical speculations?

The Catholic: Your question provides my thesis. I hold that the Christian religion, by virtue of its integrated futurism, favoured the study of objective physical facts and received these data positively because in its philosophy provision had been made for New Things. The fact that motion within the universe, design of the whole, contingency of being, and purpose of becoming had already been built into our way of thinking enabled us to digest all reasonable evidence without upsetting the universal structure.

The Communist: Except when the evidence became uncomfortable and you had to burn your Galileos and Brunos.

The Catholic: I am sorry you should think that, for it is historically simply untrue. Copernicus was a Christian priest, the Jesuits were the makers of modern science, Galileo was not burnt. The Church guarded herself against such pantheistic or heretical interpretations, arising out of the heliocentric hypothesis, as were unwarranted and in fact opposed to the findings of science. The pantheistic notions, which, if true, would break with the eschatological tradition by identifying God with his creation, cannot possibly be read out of the empirical laws of nature.

The Chairman: To what extent do you actually observe terminations—as you call them—and the coming of New Things?

The Catholic: I think we have to distinguish here sharply between empirical data of the past and of the present, although you may well say that what happened in the past is also applicable now.

The Communist: But is it not a contradiction to speak of the past and empirical data?

The Catholic: Not at all. I should have thought astronomy provided clear data through our biggest and most powerful telescopes. We may state it as a simple fact that certain stars still appear to exist, but do so no longer. We still receive their light after several light-years, after the cessation of these stars. The nature of their end does not concern us here: it is enough to know that in the stellar universe we have a constant process of ending and becoming. The heat-death of the universe is already being answered, we think, by the continual creation of matter which fills up 'vacancies to let'.

The Protestant: But surely not in the sense of the Christian Gospel.

The Catholic: Analogically there is a link. But let us stay on the earth. There again we have the evidence from pre-historical times and the study of fossils, and other remains, takes us back quite a considerable time, though on the scale of astronomy all earthly evidence must seem very parochial. Here again we witness the process of ending and becoming, in short, the evolutionary ladder. Now here the lower orders vanish or adapt themselves; but, more important: higher orders are not merely the result of adaptation of what went before but we have to reckon with new things, genuine qualitative novelties.

The Communist: The world will come to an end if you start pleading Darwin for your cause; surely, evolution spelt death for religion.

The Catholic: Only when interpreted with atheistic blinkers. For myself, trained in palaeontology and biology, the evolutionary scale pleads the cause of a rational eschatology, i.e. a coherent system of development towards ends within a universal process. The climax is represented by Homo Sapiens who brings consciousness to living organism. Man not only knows, but he knows what and that he knows. Nor is there at present any telling of how he may develop this amazing gift of reflection.

The Protestant: This means that you virtually put off the End into infinity.

The Chairman: I should not mind about that, but I can't see how you can escape from the pantheistic conclusion. If you accept the premise of emergent evolution how can you fail to follow Alexander's conception of emergent deity: 'in the end heaven and earth will create God', and the world may be called God by anticipation. This is certainly eschatology, but God stands at the end of the process, a concept rather than the God of the Christian tradition.

The Communist: I suspect that is the reason why your authorities were troubled about Teilhard de Chardin. Your scientific Jesuits parted company with his assessment of Man as a real breakthrough in creation. I myself also distrust the mixture of science and mysticism.

The Catholic: Let me make it clear that what I stand for here is a scientific analogy to the universal End-hope, a modern teleology. I do not see that this must necessarily lead to pantheism or mysticism. I do agree that our conception of Time leads to a revision of the Biblical metaphor. We have declared the millennium a heresy and we extend Last-ness to where it belongs: to the as-yet-unknown End. Meanwhile we observe stages of *Eschaton* in various branches of Science, especially in physics and in the study of organisms past and present. In both realms we have to deal with a wholly new situation, if only because the equation: matter=energy has forced upon us a re-thinking of first principles. If Einstein once said: 'You can't scratch if you don't itch', no one can go through our present-day universe without a collossal itch. 'Where men feel the itch, there let them scratch', writes Dante.[1] Science gives the itch.

The Protestant: But the scientists themselves do not agree on any point. How can you induce from their disagreements anything which corroborates our faith? For example, some astronomers believe in a steady-state, others in a 'once-with-a-bang' universe: how can their conflicts and uncertainties help us in any way?

The Catholic: A great deal. The wealth of divergent models should not in any way discourage us from their use, always subject to revision in the light of further facts. In the natural universe we have activity which is interrelated in high complexity. But the resultant changes are more than bare activity for they operate in a pattern of unity, which we call the physical universe and which we apprehend in laws. These explicate the relevant phenomenon of discontinuity-in-continuity, the dynamic process of reality.

The Communist: Are you not guilty here of one of those abstractions for which there is no necessary, and therefore no legitimate reason?

The Catholic: I do not think so, for you must have realized from modern techniques that you can no longer evade logical constructions arising out of events. The laws of physics imply symbolic relations. Drop them, i.e. do without mathematical physics, and you invite bankruptcy. In other words, the phenomena in a way do not exist for us apart from the pattern in which we endeavour to apprehend them.

[1] *Paradiso*, xvii, 129.

The Chairman: But this is epistemology, not Science. In other words, you think of discontinuity-in-continuity and foist this model of thought upon your observations.

The Catholic: This is a charge from which we are never exempt, as Kant has shown once and for all. But it would be stupid to conclude that we are reading what we like into the facts. Take the Law of the conservation of energy which is derived from the facts and not read into them. It serves my purpose admirably, because it establishes a dynamic principle in the universe which accounts both for eschaton and newness. Again the whole contemporary world-view, which embraces the least and the greatest, in the atomic theory of modern physics, is the result of phenomenal research. Global theories vie with ultra-microscopic hypotheses, and from these we infer discontinuity and continuity in the universe.

The Protestant: Let us not lose ourselves in philosophical subtleties. Show us, if you can, how the last-named theories connect with our theme.

The Catholic: The theme of eschatology and science finds its connecting link obviously in time, the problem of time. We accept the axiom that space-time are correlatives, not empty substances in themselves. Thus the ancient picture of Heaven and Hell, both in its temporal and spatial aspects, is filled with new meaning. Time has simply become enormously expanded, just as the cosmos is no longer one's little parish. But not only expansion enriches the old imagery. A new reality is supplied by the relativity of Time.

The Chairman: So if we ask nowadays 'Where?' and 'When?', what sort of answer may we expect?

The Communist: And if there is an answer given by Science are you willing to incorporate it?

The Catholic: Certainly. I think we may safely say that the 'where?' is no longer describable in spatial terms at all. Space is only perceived as the framework of an event. In some experiments the same atom behaves like a spatially concentrated particle, in others like a wave filling the whole space. One may say that we experience the spatio-temporal measurements of the atom. Thus we regard space no longer as an absolute but as a system of measurements relative to the velocity and energy of the observing and the observed. In astronomy this relativity of space is not just a theory but a necessary basis of method. For the purpose of our discussion, too, we may postulate dogmatically that absolute space must yield to a concept far more flexible; for space is no longer to be considered an empty house or giant bell but rather as an infinitely finite structure which 'matter' determines. I do not wish here to enlarge what is meant by 'matter', for we have already seen that matter=energy and beyond this we need not go.   But let us first agree that this conception of 'finite' space agrees more readily with our religious tradition than the somewhat fantastic models of the past.

The Chairman: It marks an enormous step forward, to be sure.

The Protestant: Considering these modern dimensions we may even adhere to our apocalyptic language, if only the cosmos appears so much more worthy of divine intervention than before.   Here science finds in me a ready listener for once.

The Communist: But time surely is far more significant?

The Catholic: I do think so, if only our conceptions of event are unthinkable outside a temporal process.   In particular the discontinuous event in the continuum implies a temporal category which is more than just 'spectacles of time'.   We have already learnt to abandon the sterile concept of absolute, empty time in favour of a much richer conception of the universe.   It is not eternal, for according to the Second Law of Thermo-Dynamics it is conceivable that a catastrophe initiated it, perhaps some three billion years ago. What matters is that time does not exist 'in itself' but comes into being with eventful physical existence.

The Chairman: Do you mean to say then that creation and end-of-creation is proved by physical existence?   What about other theories?   Continuous evolution, for example?

The Catholic: It would be nonsense to speak of proof.   All I would say is that the event-patterns determine the nature of time.

The Protestant: So that we, who believe in the Bible, may view time from the Biblical point of view?   I have read, in authors such as Marsh, Robinson and Cullmann, that there is already in the Bible a distinction between 'chronological' and 'real' time and that the New Testament reflects Hebraic feeling in as much as it has no or little interest in 'chronological' time.   The whole emphasis in the Bible, then, is on significant time, the time that matters for redemption.   Leaving the cyclical calculations to the Greeks, the Hebrews espoused a linear concept of time.   Hence what you call the 'event patterns' in the Bible are spiritually conceived patterns, purposeful shapings of ordinary time into eternal-time.   It seems to me remarkable how Cullman, for example, uses this concept to good advantage, showing how the whole Biblical drama of redemption is already on the way towards the consummation.

The Chairman: I should not be too sanguine about this *chronos-kairos* division and so-called Biblical concepts of time. J. Barr has shown to my satisfaction that the etymological basis of 'Biblical Words for Time', and certain so-called Hebrew insights,

are really quite spurious. Barr has demolished all these generaliza-
tions and advises us to hook our space-ship for the exploration of
Time to Genesis Chapter I. If we want to be Biblical there it is:
Time began with creation.

The Communist: This begs the question again. If you say
'Time began with creation', and proceed to 'Time ceases with the
end of creation', we are precisely where we were before.

The Catholic: Not quite, I think; for Time, let me repeat, is
the linchpin of our problem. It is agreed that we can no longer look
to a 'Time must have a stop' kind of end, after which another era
begins, and that pretty soon. Science, not the Bible, forbids such
a naive foreshortening of the temporal perspective. We are dealing
with a span of billions of years. 'Very well, then', you may say, 'let
us add a few or even endless noughts to our measurements of Time!'
But this gets you nowhere, for Time is not a commodity to be increased. It is a relationship. In an experiment on earth the observer
measures Time in observing the observable. Yet, unlike a relationship, Time appears to be irreversible, so that it is probably right
to speak of Time as 'having an arrow', a conclusion reached by
G. J. Whitrow on the basis of evidence taken from the natural
universe. Now eschatology, I take it, deals with the target which
this arrow will hit, namely the removal of the limitation of Time in
our experience of God.

The Chairman: Modern Science, you would seem to suggest,
really teaches us a new Time-scale by revising our notions of the
continuum. There is no Time continuum, there is only what
'happens'. If and when we think that we know what 'happens' in
one molecule of hydrogen we register the limitation and thus impose
a temporal framework upon the event. But from thence you wish
us to go on, towards unlimited Time, to Eternity.

The Communist: Mystical concepts again, I fear.

The Catholic: Even you will have to come to terms with the
facts of relativity.

The Protestant: Karl Heim's work points the way here. The
future of the world as foreseen by natural science, following the laws
of entropy and/or radiation, gives something like fifty million years
as a 'date' for the annihilation of life on earth. That's one date. But
the future of the world, in the light of the Gospel of the Resurrection,
stands beyond the realms of the objective and personal world: it is
the new creation in which the irreconcilable poles are restored in
the supra-polar realm. The transition from the unredeemed to the
redeemed has already begun, but of the consummation only Faith
can speak, not natural science.

The Catholic: But Science has enlarged our perspective decisively. We are no longer confined to meaningless temporal concepts, such as three-and-a-half, or six hundred and sixty-six, or a thousand years. Instead the 'final event' is the event beyond temporal limitations.

The Communist: I suspect you are about to abolish clock-time altogether, and yet it is basic to our understanding of observed and experienced facts.

The Catholic: Here lies a problem which will probably always defy solution. The time-concept is governed by so many clocks.

The Chairman: Would you approve then of speaking of clock-time and real-time, or duration and time, or *chronos* and *kairos*?

The Catholic: Such a distinction has its uses, for it really stresses that there is a difference between 'time', as conceived of before 1905, and 'time' after the approval of Einstein's theories of relativity. But we must always bear in mind that these theories are not just theories but the result of calculations arising out of the observation of the velocity of light. If the velocity of light were not finite these theories could not have been verified; as it is, the facts demand them.

The Protestant: But what is this difference and how does it affect us?

The Catholic: There used to be time stretching indefinitely into the past and into the future. There used to be a concept of simultaneity, of an absolute overlapping of events, regardless of the observer's state of motion. Instead of these outdated concepts we now look upon time as a fourth dimension. Just as space co-ordinates matter/energy, so time co-ordinates matter/energy.

The Chairman: This does seem to me to warrant the chronos-kairos distinction. I see it like this: a countless series of events happen and each one against a four-dimensional time-chronos duration; but the transcendent event which has taken place, or may or will take place, escapes from that dimension and can be seen from an eternity-kairos point of view.

The Catholic: I am not sure that the evidence allows us to go so far. I can hear our friend Tovarich protest that this smacks of mysticism. On the other hand I agree that the materialist will have a lot of explaining to do if he wishes to face the implications of relativity without blinkers.

The Psychologist: Two things stand out for me: the ancient Myth of the 'there and then' has departed, and the new four-dimensional reality opens astonishing perspectives.

The Communist: Yes, and perspectives which leave your man-centred philosophy far behind. Do not your theories of King Oedipus sound even more ridiculous when, as you say, we have overcome mythology?

The Psychologist: Remember that mine is no philosophy, only a means of therapy. But did I not hear that the role of the observer matters greatly in our concepts of relativity? May we not say that matter/energy in temporal events depends upon us who measure them?

The Catholic: True. It is we who always do the counting.

The Protestant: But may we not go further than that and say that, since man only measures a tiny fraction of the universe and therefore controls hardly anything at all, we may look beyond ourselves to God who measures reality, dividing—as it says in the account of the creation—all things according to his will? And may not God, who was the maker of the beginning, be also the God who makes an end?

The Chairman: But outside the duration-process which we have now discarded.

The Catholic: You indicate the shift of emphasis which eschatology must in my opinion derive from such scientific insights as we have.

The Chairman: It is a shift of emphasis, as you call it, which began centuries ago, when St Augustine pondered on the problem of Time. He wrote down in his *Confessions*[2]: 'We measure times as they pass . . . I perceive time to be a certain extension, yet I do not know what time is . . . we measure from some beginning to some end, etc.'—You must read these chapters, for out of his tremendous struggle he comes to the realization that the end of time lies with the eternal Creator of all times. I wish he were alive today to interpret the data of relativity, for I have no doubt that for him Science and Eschatology would point to the same thing: they suggest that space and time are relative to Beginning and End. Though they cannot prove Eternity they seem at least to suggest it.

[2] Chapters xi, xii.

CHAPTER XI

THE HOPE OF PERFECTION

The Chairman: We have seen that the future of Science involves Man the scientist and that therefore it leads directly up to what is in my opinion the central issue: how is human conduct governed by the End-hope? We are not concerned with competing systems of Ethics now. I want you to tell me what you envisage to be your destiny in the light of what we are and yet may become. I want you to distinguish between what actually exists and what ought to be. For us Christians this is always the real problem, for we believe in an ideal man and speak of an ideal kingdom, Church, or society, while we know ourselves always to be falling short of this ideal. Most of my friends consider eschatology and ethics to belong indissolubly together, for what we believe about the beyond and the hereafter is only genuine if it be made effective here and now. My previous survey has shown you that we may vary in details but hardly in principle. We seriously believe that the New Testament injunctions 'Be ye perfect', 'Seek ye first the Kingdom of God', are not pointers to another world but to present-day responsibility. As A. N. Wilder has shown in his *Eschatology and Ethics in the Teaching of Jesus* once we get rid of the entirely misleading 'Last-ness' and apocalyptic notions we can really get to work and make God's deed operative in human existence. Thus Jesus sanctions all our ethical ideals; indeed, without them destruction is inevitable. Wilder relegates the eschatological conceptions to the periphery and stresses the ethical centre. The former rouse the imaginative quality and enhance the hearers' free responsiveness. This remains basically the same with us. We need not really know nor greatly care about the unknowable future, but we must bring to the existent situation an inner vigour which can change this situation. Thus the element of Hope infuses into us that self-same energy which changed men and the world and will continue to change them. We are open to the future if we use our freedom.

The Protestant: With due respect, Sir, this point of view owes nothing to the New Testament. Do you think that St Paul for example was joking when he asked what was the good of fighting with beasts at Ephesus if that was the end? No, he insists—the climax of 1 Corinthians—without the Resurrection, 'let us eat and drink', for tomorrow we die: all effort is unprofitable. The world was hopeless without God and Christ. Behaviour becomes irrelevant apart from the 'afterwards'.

The Communist: When I hear of Life after death I reach for my gun. How can anyone go on with that dope, not hope, in our age? A serious discussion ought not to touch on a subject which, as has been shown previously, is as confusing as it is trite. Marx and Lenin have abolished this bourgeois trickery.

The Psychologist: Your venomous attack proves that you are not free from passion. To bear out your attitude you ought to behave quietly, say like Charles II, who—in Winston Churchill's words —'did not wish to distract this world for the sake of the next'. Moreover, my dear fellow, before Marx and Lenin were heard of, there were men, like Frederick the Great, who would let everyone go to Heaven in their own way—which includes also those who do not go. It was in fact the aristocracy in every age who began the tradition of not caring a damn about the Life to come. Now this apathy is common ground, of course.

The Chairman: I am not so sure about all this. Cicero represents for me the aristocratic feeling about the After-Life, as given in the last chapter of *De Senectute*. 'The wisest people', he argues, 'die with greatest equanimity, and the most stupid are the least resigned'. Here is a great Roman who adapts the Greek doctrine of the immortality of the soul to himself and the deserving great ones of his age. All this is a long way from modern vulgar indifference. However, don't we now revel in the fruits of Psychical Research, not to mention spiritualism?

The Psychologist: And what have the various societies' researches shown, except that—fraud apart—communications from the so-called Beyond are always indirect and trivial? Their evidence cannot suggest more than that survival is dependent upon the groups who want it. Medium-control conditions every apparition.

The Protestant: The failure of necromancy has nothing to do with eternal life, if only because this kind of survival is by its own definition impermanent.

The Chairman: Agreed. It is just a 'little mountain' in the high region of the mountains of truly religious belief. Thus W. H. Salter summarizes himself the evidence taken from his Society's annals which deal with psychic research.

The Protestant: Yes, he calls it Zoar, the little place to which Lot wished to flee to preserve his life.

The Catholic: And yet, without breaking a lance for necromancy, you are, if I may say so, too superior. Aristocrats and Communists may be above mere survival, but ordinary people do want to live on. This desire is natural, and the songs and poetry of many races back up the desire. 'Get ready for the judgement day!', sing the negroes, 'it's peaceful on the other side, shout Allelujah, you'll be so happy'.

The Communist: Fancy you quoting this typical stuff emanating from a suppressed class.

The Chairman: I confess I am rather repelled by the 'Watch the coffin lids fly open!' kind of expectation.

The Catholic: Not at all. It is engaging in its naiveté. Take the Grandmother in Gorki's *Mother*. She paints as attractive an Hereafter as any Elysian Fields.

The Chairman: I know what you mean. There is something engaging in that simplicity, most familiar to me from the country-folk portrayed by Thomas Hardy. Do you remember Coggan in *Far from the Madding Crowd*? He has some nice things to say while he sits with his cronies, drinking before the burial of the poor girl who died from exhaustion. 'Churchmen', he insists, 'must have it all printed beforehand, otherwise dang it all, we should no more know what to say to a great gaffer like the Lord than babes unborn.'

The Communist: That's only half the story, mark it well! Why does your friend Coggan stick to his 'old ancient doctrines', as he puts it? Why, he tells you so himself: because the parson supplied him with seed potatoes at a time when his own were frosted. He dares not offend the parson. The appalling poverty of the country people is at the bottom of it all.

The Protestant: Nonsense. Coggan explains that he sticks like a plaster to the old faith he was born in, but he has no illusions about mere conformism. 'Chapel-folk', he admits, 'may be more hand-in-glove with the above than we . . . if anybody go to heaven, they will, they've worked for it, and they deserve to have it, such as 'tis. I baint such a fool to pretend that we who stick to the Church have the same chance as they.'

The Chairman: Let us exclude the rivalry of the different denominations, if you please. We don't want more complications.

The Protestant: But the hope of Perfection is tied up with it.

The Catholic: It is, but there is a common denominator of that Hope. There must be some merit here, there must be some continuity there. They hope here because they feel confident that their virtue will be rewarded there in a manner foreshadowed here.

The Communist: Let me call this your 'Jam and tarts' eschatology, after the grave of a lady at Bloemfontein who expected, following the hope expressed on her tombstone, to go on baking the cakes for which she had been famous.

The Chairman: Ah, these simple things do not worry me at all. No, what makes me unhappy is the implied sequence of cause and effect. I am not against Everlasting Life as a concept of philosophers, but I am totally out of sympathy with Death as an ordeal and the associated fears and torments of the damned. I was horrified by what was recapitulated as traditional doctrine. How can we even begin to speak of perfection, when the enjoyment of other men's torments is part of it?

The Protestant: I can see because of your revulsion you would like to cheat Death. But Death, like Sin, is horrible. We must retain the sense of dread, the solemnity of Death. Both are appropriate, as Blake recognized:

> 'Our doom decreed demands a mournful scene,
> Why not a dungeon dark, for the condemned?
> Why not the Dragon's subterranean Den,
> For Man to howl in?'

The Chairman: Why not? Because God cannot tolerate the state of eternal punishment in which Satan and his legions would have to act as punishing officers. We know too much nowadays of criminal prison guards. No, let us pair Eternal Life with annihilation, but not with eternal punishment. Or, if you must have pain, accept the stings of man's conscience as adequate.

The Psychologist: No, that loophole won't serve, much as I should like it to. Conscience is but a sloppy invention devised to replace the ancient fire. Decent people have a conscience, are proud of it, and suffer for it. But those who have no conscience, how can they be tortured by what they have not got? Dostoevski deals with this admirably in *The Brothers Karamazov.*[1]

The Protestant: Clearly, retribution remains indispensable if we are to rely upon an absolute and objective sanction for right. There can be no morality without the Hereafter.

The Communist: Your honesty is commendable. You deny the possibility of social behaviour except on a cash-basis. Only *your* pay-off expects bonuses from the God-bank. Apart from that I am with you, for the sanction of morality is not in an ideal but in wages.

The Catholic: Our tradition does not deny the incentive of rewards in moral conduct. I am not for the moment concerned with the nature of these rewards, but it is clear that the Gospel and Tradition firmly unite in the award of consequences which are

[1] Book XI, Ch. 9

proportionate to, and commensurate with, the virtues and vices which we intentionally acquire during our lifetime. The expectation of the future is, therefore, the basis of all moral theology, for the demands which are made upon us here are sanctioned by the eternal Law, which is immutably operative from the beginning. We should perhaps say that what we experience as the hereafter is an ever-present fact. The task of the Church is to enable men to reach that perfection which lies within their competence on earth. As we see it, the future is determined by our obedience to these demands. To put it very simply, we must avoid mortal and venial sins, be punctilious in religious observances, such as attendance at Mass, Confession and Prayer, give our support to the Church, extend her work, give alms, show mercy. We believe, in the words of Deuteronomy, that the task of the good life is not beyond our strength, nor is it a hidden mystery. The task is near, and so is the help which God appoints through his accredited channels. In all this hope is really part of the life itself, just as charity is perfect itself and yet reaps an eternal reward. Of course, we do not deny the existence of moral problems; both socially and individually there are the so-called hard cases. These matters concern our theologians and their findings you can look up for yourselves. In principle we always believe in the lawful and the possible. We accept mortifications but we reject fanaticism and puritanical negations. For us the right faith and right conduct go together.

The Psychologist: I cannot bring myself to withhold my unstinted admiration of your Church's deft mixture of opportunism and moral principle. On the whole it works well, because you have been sane enough to retain in the Confessional a safety valve for the repressed. Nevertheless, you must admit that you are now a bit out of date. I mean no one could now easily swallow all that hell-fire stuff, and it is just as well that this is so, for we know that fear is a poor stimulant. When you read examples of Jesuit preaching you may well doubt their efficacy, for the expectation of eternal torment —as for instance, brought out by James Joyce in his Autobiography —is more likely to turn a man away from virtue. We know too much nowadays of the sadistic-masochistic symptoms of neurosis to be happily impressed by such incentives.

The Chairman: I would go further than that. If you condemn the whole system of after-life rewards as psychologically dangerous I would repudiate it as a moral principle. It is intolerable for the wholly Good Will, the categorical universal Imperative, the basis of Practical Reason, to be sustained by anything outside itself. Why, by linking virtue and love to anything outside virtue and love you imply that in themselves they are not good enough. As I said at

the beginning I can just about swallow the eschatological language
as the cradle of responsiveness from which good intentions will spring
in due time. I can tolerate futuristic notions in morality, e.g. 'I do
this in order that this may happen'—as stages in personal development, as signs of growing maturity, but further than that I cannot go.
It seems to me self-evident that the introduction of the End—in this
case, a final reward—destroys the pure ends of human behaviour.
I would enumerate all the virtues listed in Stoic or Christian lists and
top them with supernatural graces; but unless they are freely
achieved without afterthoughts they cease to have any value.   I
therefore challenge you to free ethics from eschatology, after the
manner of St Francis Xavier (1506–52) who said: 'Love would
remain even if Hell and Heaven, Reward and Punishment, were to
disappear.'

The Catholic: Ah yes, but whose love? Can you discuss the
fruit apart from its seed and cultivation? Virtues cause joys, just
as vices cause sufferings. You must not overlook the connection.

The Psychologist: This is not quite what we mean. Fear is
not the fruit of anything, but its anticipation. What we question is
whether an act of blackmail can authorize a moral system.

The Catholic: Anticipation is incumbent upon the prudent
man. It is enjoined upon us in the Gospels where the simile of the
harvest endorses our tradition. It does not spoil a good harvest to
know that you can avoid a bad one.

The Protestant: But this is precisely where your tradition has
gone wrong. Not that you have made too much of the End! You
have bent it to your own ecclesiastical purposes, so much so that you
now consider yourselves competent and authorized to direct the lives
of men. This leads directly to the dreaded justification by works,
the raising up of Adam to a celestial status, a second Lucifer ready
to rebel against God. Instead of 'Down Peacock's Feathers!', you
shout 'Do these things and you will live!' As long as a minimum
code is observed you leave man with the notion that he can raise
himself to Heaven by good works. You use the End-Dread as a
lever, but it is not really your personal Hope, the consummation of
all things. The Return of the Son of Man almost clashes with your
infinitely delicate structure of a moral calculus. You will still be
busy with hard cases, special clauses, exceptions, annulments, dis-
pensations, in short, the whole fabric of Canon Law, when the
Trumpet sounds and our righteousness appears as mere rags. In
your tradition the lawyers have beaten the prophets. It is the
spirit which counts, and your spirit is that of Law rather than
Grace.

The Chairman: This may partly explain why Rome is nearer reality and also more successful than Geneva. If you are right, Rome uses eschatology as a convention.

The Psychologist: Surely more than that, for I can see how Catholic imagery remains in touch with the needs of the Psyche, whereas Protestant literalism is really a way of despair, as we have already seen in connection with Pascal. For you thoroughgoing eschatologists Perfection is not to be attempted here: it will be given to the elect after this life. You simply . . . wait.

The Communist: A parody of living results. Remember Samuel Beckett's great play *Waiting for Godot*! The tramps, who wait under a tree for the mysterious Godot, know perfectly well that Godot will never come. 'Time will show', goes the refrain, but nobody comes, except the fat Pozzo who draws the miserable Lucky on a rope and feeds on chicken. The bones he throws to the tramps. Lucky recites a speech in celebration of the absurdity of everything: in spite of the tennis and a few other things there is nothing. The two boys, who announce Godot's postponed advent poignantly, return to the same theme: nothing happens, life is absurd. The waiting is boredom, and the boredom is the end. Mr Beckett seems to have anticipated our dialogue by exposing the farcical nature of this 'waiting for God'. In his *End-Game* he demonstrates the world already dead. Only a few are left alive to die presently. A man looks out of the window; his employer, whose parents occasionally pop up from their dustbins, bids him do this and that. The time for the pain-killer, he is told, has not yet come; when the time does come there is no pain-killer left. Slowly death creeps in. Nothing more. Full-stop, for no reason, no purpose. The active principle has run out. No tears, no laughter.

The Chairman: It is odd that you should treat us to this résumé of Beckett's strange plays which may not be more than a typically Irish *jeu d' esprit*. I can't see that we can discuss the categorical imperative and perfection in his terms.

The Communist: I was anxious to show how your society really cannot believe in itself, and therefore in perfection, because it expects nothing.

The Psychologist: Whereas in your society the individual is not even encouraged to wait for anything but must be submerged in the mass. You wait corporately for the classless brotherhood and the withering away of the state and the exaltation of Science. They wait individually for wealth, security, recognition, advancement and so forth. 'Godot' is just a symbol of whatever you wait for passively, of the great illusion of what you will never obtain. If you happen to be religious then Godot again stands for after-life and rewards. I think the plays are very relevant to our discussion for they throw into relief, first the power of an illusion, and secondly that a cure of the illusion comes either through death or, better, through a realization of the seat of the disease. 'Godot' is really a psychological morality play which lampoons the illusion of perfection and help from outside, be it from the state or religion.

The Protestant: Could misinterpretation go further? I, too, believe in the relevance of these two plays, for in them Beckett portrays our faithless world. All his characters are despicable. The tramps are the heirs to the Christian hope who no longer believe. They have no purpose in life; therefore they are left in the lurch of unbelief. Absurdity and death, as shown here, form the Gospel-before-the-Gospel, the despair and darkness which precede the dawn of hope. Pozzo and the tramps, Ham and his entourage, proclaim the necessity of an End-hope, without which Perfection really is death.

The Catholic: Only a Catholic renegade could have written thus. The whole thing reminds us of a black Mass. The ingredients are Christian, but perverted in their use. Now this deliberate distortion should not blind us to the absurdity of what the plays convey to some, but we should also have the courage to resist the message. The trouble with Beckett's creatures is not the absence of an End but their inner decay. They live in complete isolation, and in that respect much modern writing bears witness to the same thing: man in industrial society, non-rooted and without purpose, is in danger of obliterating the divine image. On Saturday night he drinks and makes love and fights, on Sunday morning he sleeps. If he reaches the Room at the Top he finds it empty because he is empty himself. Our French novelists and playwrights similarly bring out the nausea of a life that is meaningless and absurd.

The Chairman: We lack the time to survey all our contemporary literature in order to analyse the enemy of perfection, nor is it necessary to do so. We all agree that human greed, brute selfishness, sordid conditions, famines, and wars engulf us in a vicious circle. But the question is whether we can still maintain the 'Be ye perfect' injunction, apart from the myth of the End?

The Psychologist: I must really take issue with you over this. Your either-or is superficial and to me wholly unacceptable. You merely use clichés to conceal the sickness of the Psyche. Let me repeat that the imperfections are as much part of us as are the so-called perfections. You abhor destruction, crime, cruelty; you exalt construction, virtue, generosity. Very well, but you cannot

10

have one without the other. The 'Be ye perfect' injunction is as
unsound as are the discredited rewards. If I started a case with
Perfection in view I should almost certainly do my patient a great
deal of harm. As for the End, he and I share the hope that he will
sublimate the destructive rages and find happiness in his cure.

The Protestant: Out of your own mouth: you make happiness
the End. Perfection equals happiness.

The Chairman: As the result of knowledge obtained through
treatment here and with no hope of another future. But what if
this happiness is grounded on immoral things, e.g. adultery?

The Psychologist: How wonderfully naive can one be? Really,
do you expect Perfection to be such a simple art? Perhaps you could
learn more from modern literature than you are prepared to expect.
It will be best to start at the beginning in order to learn how our
world has changed. Take, then, the classical tragedy, itself heir to
the cult of religion. There the hero-victim reaches perfection
through suffering. You may say the end rounds off the whole, and
perfection may be equated with the climax, the terrible *dénouement.*
Perfection, according to Aeschylus and Sophocles and that whole
tradition, lies in resignation, for we can do nothing except submit
to the destiny which decrees for us the humbling of self. Nor is there
any circumventing of this hard path, which moves the onlooker to be
purged by terror and pity. Oedipus is elected by Fate to initiate the
disasters for the house of Atreus. There is no reprieve except the
End. In resignation he finds reconciliation. Or take the tragedy
of Antigone in which the very concept of public duty, i.e. the concept
of perfection, must lead King Creon to bring death to daughter
and wife before his own submission in death. The gods and the
cosmos provide a tragic canvas to given situations, and the hero
reaches perfection only in the logic of defeat.

The Communist: Why do you take us back to that slave-ridden
society?

The Psychologist: I want you to see as clearly as possible that
once upon a time perfection, morality, suffering, and eschatology
were felt to go together. This was not a Christian prerogative. The
ancient world projected its experience to the stage in this way. But
just as in science you revealed a new world I hold that we can no
longer accept this world, however enchanting it may have been.
Perfection, as we now portray it, is not a necessary process of purgation in which we are made to become good through ordeals imposed
upon us from outside. We look to no such *dénouement,* we barely
entertain the idea of a final solution. Above all, we have abolished
the tragic wonder and, in its place, we look for therapy.

The Chairman: So instead of Oedipus and his tragedy you treat of the Oedipus complex. How then do you view perfection-without-an-end? Have you any work of literary merit to dramatize your method? I say 'method', for it appears that for you perfection is no longer an ethical ideal nor a final goal, but only a cure of complexes. You put treatment for *catharsis.*

The Psychologist: My textbook here is not Freud but Proust. His *À la Recherche du Temps Perdu* is the outstanding literary work of our century which deals with our problem. First, it exposes your fears that our 'treatment' is inferior to the past as groundless, for this masterpiece stands beyond the niceties of criticism. Here is a really great work, a dissection of the human Psyche. Secondly, as you can recollect from the title we assist at the retrieving of lost time. We must catch up with the past in order to establish reality. Proust is a tragedian without eschatology. Therefore he is a psychologist. Whereas his great predecessors, such as Stendhal and Flaubert, had already penetrated to the inner depth of human motivation, they could not yet conceive of the unconscious-in-action. Their universe was mainly rational, their action a continual forward drive. You could still see the moral problems on a conveyor-belt, the future untying the knots of the past, very much as in Dickens and other authors of the nineteenth century. But Proust departs from the narrator's narrative, dispenses with chronological sequence, builds up no plot, and moves in a world which does not move from one end to another. The events have happened and have now to be re-lived without an end in view. The only end is to bring back the beginning. Memory holds the door to the past. The absence of a climax underlines the absence of an organized action. The intensity of feelings and reactions stands outside a framework of moral development. Proust is the precursor of the next generation of writers, such as Kafka, who rely upon something else than the flow of events in time and space. Unlike Thomas Hardy, who organizes events to leave their tragic imprint upon men, these writers find castles, prisons, etc., in their own given condition. You get the same approach in your flash-back novels and films, where the end is shown first and you then disentangle the man's life to find an answer to the question: 'Why was this so at the end and why did it have to be so?' Orson Welles in his famous *Citizen Kane* set the fashion of the recovery of the past in visual terms. On the stage, Ibsen too used the revivification of past skeletons which ordain what is and is yet to be.

The Protestant: I know little of these things; so please go back to Proust and tell me what this discovery of the past shows and how the hero wins through without a future, without the end of Redemption.

The Communist: I may as well leave you, because I am honestly not interested in the recovery of the lone bourgeois. Why should I bother about the past? I know his future does not exist, and furthermore I also know that perfection comes as a by-product of the classless society. What you call evil, or original sin, disappears with its cause.

The Psychologist: And yet stay, for Proust's recovery opens the stage for the whole of society, including even a few members of the lower strata. After all, the 'I' of the story is not really the hero, for as some critics have pointed out with ironic satisfaction, Marcel (the author) alone seems exempt from the terrible forces of crushing, disintegrating corruption. The other members of the cast abuse others and themselves until love is swallowed up of perversity. But this evolvement of corruption out of innocence and gradual display of loss on every level of existence, the endless self-deceptions, the corrosion of nobility, the pathetic worship at the shrine of grandeur and money—all these make up the picture of our problem: how can time be regained out of a chaos so frightful and so—amusing? In a sense the puzzle invites comparison with Bunyan's *Pilgrim's Progress*: Christian, too, never seems to get to the end of his journey. He is ambushed and frightened. At the end when he does reach the celestial city Bunyan knows no more than to quote Scripture, almost word for word lifted from the Apocalypse. Then, in a weaker effort, his Christian goes back to bring up the family, and the whole picnic starts all over again and less convincingly. Now Proust does the exact oposite: the celestial city is the beginning. The early boyhood experience of the imaginary Combray, the grandmother and the mother, the maid, the friends, the walks and vistas, the exquisite little tune, the unique smell of the *madeleine* at tea-time, these are things which restate love and joy, humanity in the broadest, loving, hopeful sense. Life is always a mistake, but to revert to our origins is to revert to what we really are. Perfection is to see the endless terror, from the vantage-point of experience, and thus to return to the true self in knowledge and detachment. You, Mr Chairman, misconceive the value of psychological insight when you imagine that such a survey and recovery of the Psyche is only a 'method' of perfecting happiness. Perfection is disillusionment, the termination of self-deception. It is a finding of oneself.

The Communist: Was I not right when I threatened to leave you? What is the point of the 'perfecting of self'? It is exactly opposed to my social hope.

The Chairman: Not quite. At least you would have the satisfaction of seeing your enemies, the pseudo-aristocracy and the
bourgeoisie, beaten down, if not by the working-class at least by
their own hands: by what Marx called their inner contradictions.
You must admit, mein Herr, that the recovery of Marcel Proust
implies the condemnation of the rest. In other words, while I find
my salvation in my beginnings I also find total perdition in the
course of events. There seems to me still a sort of eschatology.
After all, Proust's men and women are largely bad, they suffer, they
receive their due reward in their disintegration.

The Psychologist: You are reading that into Proust. He is the
complete Amoralist and non-Eschatologist, as I have tried to show.

The Catholic: That may be true, but you have not shown
enough. You suppress the fact that the time retrieved is altogether
peopled with symbols and that recovery—actually there is none (it
has been called a great hoax in that respect)—is at least as 'Christian'
as Bunyan's *Pilgrim's Progress*, though the hero seems to regress.

The Protestant: How could this be? Surely, Christian really
reaches the celestial city! I altogether deplore your attempted comparison. Bunyan's Christian faces evil within and without, fights with
both, wins through, not by good works but by his acceptance of the
Grace of God, and thus he enters upon a state of perfection not of
his own making. Surely this lies completely outside the realm of
literature, pagan and contemporary. Perfection is God's work in
man, the fruit of Grace abounding. Moral perfection and faithful
love flow from the soul in communion with God in Christ. How
can you even consider Oedipus or Proust in the same breath?

The Catholic: I think we can and must. Otherwise we stop in
the seventeenth century, but the struggles of the human soul are
timeless and ever to be seen in a new light. Let us agree, that perfection cannot be stated in terms apart from God's redemptive activity.
But the symbols in the human soul are surely imprinted by God's
spirit so that we may grasp even here the milestones on the road.
Now here it seems to me that Proust serves better than Bunyan.
Instead of viewing Christian's Progress through Bedfordshire we are
ourselves mirrored in Proust's images of Combray. It does not
matter in the least that we remember rather than that we anticipate.
After all, the creation stories do not contradict the oracles of the End.

The Protestant: This means that you reintroduce the old pagan
notion of the circle, that all things return to where they had been,
that 'in the end is my beginning'.

The Catholic: Symbolism has that effect, possibly. But, really,
in Proust's work it does not matter at all what comes first and what

comes last. The point is, as with Bunyan, the redemption of the soul, the regaining of life. Now our friend in his summary has already told us of the great Mother and Father imagery there, but he has omitted the Church. Proust, half-catholic and half-Jew, places the Church at Combray at the very heart of things, not doctrinally but in the active remembrance. His description is unequalled in world-literature. The spires, the emerald-studded windows, the light, but, above all, the feeling of belonging. Here is the sense of *Patria*. This Church in his *Recherche*, together with the countryside, the hawthorn in flower, the sea-shore, in short, traditional France, provide the counterpart to the highly personalized account. Here is the fount of health. Now this seems to me immensely important because Proust breaks through the doleful isolation of excessive individualism and brings healing through the memory of this past which endures also into the future. He still stands in the classical tradition which, despite tragedy and pessimism, looks into a future, for this world endures: call it the natural-spiritual universe. The moral is not difficult to draw: if we conceive of perfection in terms of eschatology, we must not isolate the soul from its deep springs and attachments to nature and religion. There is more than psychological treatment, yes, more than the recovery of the Psyche, for the integration of personality brings perfect adjustment also to the outside world, past and future. Put it differently: subjective and objective lines of perfection merge into one.

The Chairman: But even your improvement on the merely psychological estimate of perfection leaves much to be desired, for although you make provision for the future, and at that an objective future, you fail too clear the air morally. Presumably your pilgrim is still pretty fallible, if not outright bad?

The Catholic: He has been forgiven and learnt to live with himself. He has mastered the destructive and brought it under control. Jung uses the example of the serpent, which, as you know, was in antiquity (even in the Bible) a highly ambivalent, not to say ambiguous, symbol, namely of death and of healing. Now how is Leviathan to be tamed? Jung shows on coloured plates, made from a patient's dream experience, how the serpent is bent on biting and poisoning during the neurotic state. As the therapy proceeds, the serpent gradually becomes part of the pattern, coils round the whole picture, and ultimately encloses it in decorative circular fashion: the destroyer has become protector. This is, as you must admit, highly suggestive.

The Protestant: And terribly dangerous. The serpent is to be trodden down underfoot, the dragon is to be slain. Even as a symbol

I do not like a tamed serpent, if only because the symbol of the circle denies the forward movement in the defeat of evil.

The Chairman: And yet it says: 'They shall take up serpents'?

The Communist: Leaving aside your symbolism and circular or elliptical ornamentations, let me say that if you must go to literature for 'redemptive activity', how can you ignore Tolstoy? Take the end of the *Anna Karenina* and *War and Peace*—and they are ends, after the climaxes!—and the lesson is clear: perfection is found in the social duty, on the land, in the home, in work. It is so simple and requires no symbols.

The Chairman: And this echoes Goethe's approval of the reclamation of land, as when Faust would acclaim that moment, when work has started in the damming of the sea, as one to which he might say: Remain! Stay! For this the hero would even give his soul.

The Psychologist: Ah, you forget: Faust, whom you call the hero, is blind and mistakes the digging of his grave for public works of great merit! Observe the wonderful irony. He *thinks* that salvation lies that way and dies with that illusion still in his heart. And as to Tolstoy, does not the anti-climax of normalcy prove that housekeeping and work are *not* enough? Where is Anna? Dead! Where is Vronsky? Also Dead! Again, where is Prince Andrew? Dead. I could go on for ever. No, if you take Tolstoy as your guide, you must confess bluntly: the end of man is passion and death.

The Communist: I don't agree with you. Now Dostoevsky might be said to approximate that ludicrous thesis.

The Chairman: Hence no *persona grata* with his beloved Slavs.

The Psychologist: Well, no wonder, for in Dostoevsky all the psychopathic complexes reach an almost transcendental dimension.

The Communist: Yes, but at least he has a social hope as the great End. I don't agree with it in his form—holy Russia and all that mystique of the land and the Orthodox Church—but at least his universe is not a private clinic but the vast world of the oppressed. At least he writes as one who views the problem of perfection not from the salons of the privileged, but from the scaffold, the exile, hungry and consumptive. That he became a morose, sadistic, masochistic reactionary is another matter.

The Chairman: I have always greatly disliked Dostoevsky, the anti-liberal par excellence, and, with Thomas Mann, I would say: 'Dostoevsky to be taken only in moderation!' I admire the pathos and the strength of the narrative, I do not commend the teaching.

The Protestant: What would you say is his conception of Perfection in the light of the End?

The Psychologist: I suppose it must be called mystical, for he identifies all his heroes with Christ, though in a way strange to Western ears. *The Idiot,* for example, is the Christ-character who ennobles all the fallen by contact with him. This Prince really bears the sin of sinners by what he is. Again in the *Karamasovs* salvation comes through suffering and mystical understanding culminating in love. But underlying all this is the old cause-and-effect thread: crime must lead to punishment, but this punishment is ultimately self-chosen, for without retribution there can be no restitution which is the basis of justice. Oh yes, you Christians ought to like your Dostoevsky for he also retains a cosmic note. The world is peopled with devils and saints, and the end is always one of catastrophe and purgation, however wild the scene.

The Chairman: It is this violent extremism which antagonizes me. For him the whole world is apocalyptic, as if there were nothing but possessed swine rushing down cliffs to be drowned. It is intolerable, for such a distortion allows nothing for education, growth, and social progress. It is near hysterical.

The Catholic: His hatred of Catholics, Jews, Socialists is also very distasteful and bodes no good as a universal maxim.

The Protestant: And yet, though I see the force of your criticism and do not share by any means the chauvinistic pan-Slavism, I cannot help detecting in Dostoevsky's work the genuine stamp of the Gospel. In fact, in *Crime and Punishment* the Raising of Lazarus is central to the understanding of the novel, as in the Devils we have those accursed swine you dislike so much. *Karamasovs* is altogether a thoroughly apocalyptic book in the Biblical sense. Can you call the author or the work hysterical? I doubt it. He himself caricatures the abuses of extremist monks and the aberrations of miracle-workers. He is far too realistic to assume that perfection is reached by mortifications in the desert.

The Communist: But he never quite frees himself from the monastic smell. Even Tolstoy, who caricatured all eschatology in that amusing episode when Pierre tries to persuade himself that he is the chosen instrument to kill Napoleon by manipulating the famous 6–6–6 into the spelling of his name . . . well, even Tolstoy retains a mystical flavour, even in *War and Peace.*

The Chairman: Surely the vision of the wounded Prince Andrew—of the blue sky and its attendant peace—remains unsurpassed, whether you label it mystical or not.

The Psychologist: How all these characters live! I rejoice to see that you can identify your eschatological ideas with those great characters of fiction. But are you not going astray just the same?

Surely, all these famous characters still portray men in search of their soul, in search of integration and healing.

The Communist: You mean that once again your dogma must win? That our and their first years determine every condition?

The Chairman: I fear we all cling to our dogmas, though modern literature helps us to see one another's point of view. I appreciate the therapy-only approach, but I deplore its narrowness; I endorse the social-hope futurism, though I cannot share its political bias; I profit from the Catholic interpretation of symbolism, though it seems to me arbitrary; I sympathize with the Biblical outlook, though I cannot reduce all writing to a Christo-centred finality. I admit, however, that you have shown that ethics-and-eschatology cannot be banished from modern thought. You have converted me to the continued existence of this connection. But is it as yet too vague to matter. Have you any more evidence?

CHAPTER XII

ART AND THE END

The Catholic: I would now turn to the argument from beauty to sustain the case for my interpretation of the End. Aesthetic evidence is as suggestive as it is subtle. I hope you will not refuse to admit it altogether.

The Chairman: Not at all. Since Kant himself acknowledged aesthetic judgements, beside scientific inferences and moral postulates, I cannot see that we can exclude the evidence from art. My only trouble is where to draw the line. We shall spend years together if we discuss literature and poetry, music, sculpture, painting, architecture of all races and of all ages. So please confine yourselves to general principles.

The Psychologist: Except that general principles are almost always wrong, especially in this field of aesthetics. How can you discuss Beethoven, Shakespeare, or Michelangelo in terms of general principles? Are we not primarily concerned with the peculiarity of genius, the unique and unrepeatable?

The Communist: No, I second the chairman's ruling; for our purpose it is enough to establish a definition of art. This will show that art is social phenomenon which owes nothing to transcendental sources. As Croce insisted, art serves no ulterior metaphysical purpose. There is no need to differentiate between the various displays of human skill. As society moulds man it enables him to progress in the use of his hands, and it is with his fingers most of all that he produces buildings, pictures, sculptures, books and even music. Ability is always there, but the social conditions must be such as to promote its application. In the socialist state there is no division between work and play, for our socialist culture unites productive and aesthetic activity. Work, sport, recreation are inseparable. Thus a corporate culture arises which has absolutely no connection whatever with what you call the End-hope. On the contrary, art exhibits the intention of life (as Bergson observed) and excludes a reference to the future, let alone the End.

The Chairman: You do not have to be a Socialist to endorse this point of view. As I see it, from a liberal point of view, art is the human endeavour best fitted to circumvent fears and hopes of the End. I do not now mean so much the passing show of ephemeral works, which are obviously produced to satisfy a market and then vanish from the scene. No, the great and lasting works of art, which have outlived their makers and their customers, prove even more cogently that the way of the genius powerfully abolishes the narrow notions of religion and eschatology. Consciously or unconsciously, the genius produces something of permanent worth. 'All flesh is grass', says the eschatologist with his End-hope in view. But art is not flesh, and works of art are not like the flower of the field. This is the marvellous thing about art, that the creator is dead but his works outlive him and his generation. That is why the Socialist definition of art does not go far enough for me, for it knits the artist too closely to the life of society. Art, however, transcends society as it transcends nations. It also transcends the notions of the End. Let me give an example, against my own ruling: you enter the ancient Egyptian temples and you know that the religion of these temples is dead; the priests have gone, the builders are unknown, the cultus is lost. But the work remains and touches you, for it is immortal, without end.

The Communist: A bad example, for these temples will for the most part be flooded by the new hydro-electric schemes. Nothing is immortal unless society cares for it and transmits it as a living culture to future generations. But I agree that the problem of an End does not arise in connection with art, whether it survives or not.

The Chairman: Even so art is more than environmental furniture and to that extent it transcends society. No doubt, we must deplore the loss of many treasures. Even so, our museums and galleries are full of untold treasures which have no social relevance now except their inherent beauty. For in art 'beauty is the infinite finitely presented', as Schelling put it once. We have a presentation of forms which, visibly or audibly, communicates to us the highest that is open to man. Hence we may put art above religion, for whereas the latter always requires this End, beyond and above, art puts you here in the beyond and above. Perhaps I may put it this way: the aesthetic way liberates religion from its myth of the End by enshrining the End in forms which we can apprehend with pleasure and profit.

The Protestant: Your definition has made it very clear why men of my tradition are basically opposed to art and view man's worship of the works of his own hands with suspicion. Just because you would get round man's sinful condition and God's redeeming activity by means of artistic finesse I am persuaded that you are reviving the old pagan life. As you say, art is not only an end in itself, but it acts as a substitute for religion and abolishes the expectation of the End. We are often accused of silly Puritan bias because we would, like the Jews and primitive Christians, ban from our midst all the representations of God and the complications of so-called aesthetic achievements.   Now perhaps you can appreciate our position.   Just because ornamentations and decorations, precious stones, grandiose designs, and enchanting tunes, can so easily entice our senses so that we forget what we are, our mortality and our sinfulness, and what God is and has done for us and will do for us in the End, we repudiate art as a means of salvation.   The Jews did not portray the Lord and they ridiculed the arts of man, unless they were severely disciplined and dedicated to the sacred cause.   They were right, for, as you said yourselves, there is no connection between art and eschatology.   Therefore, I say: eschew art as a beguiling instrument, and hold fast to eschatology as the true Gospel.

The Chairman: But surely this is fanaticism beyond the fringe of reason and history?

The Protestant: Not at all. I need not labour Biblical texts to make my point.   You all know how Jeremiah lashed out against his enemies who shouted 'The Temple of the Lord', how the book of Isaiah disowns the makers of figures and likenesses, how Jesus warned his disciples against aesthetic assurance.   In fact, it is in the New Testament that the campaign against man-made salvation reaches its peak.   You must understand that even the wildest iconoclasm has its rights, for it protests precisely against this aesthetic substitute for apocalyptic religion.   Can't you see how mosaics, pictures, reliefs and the like take the place of the living God, and consequently aesthetic pleasure here and now pushes aside the expectation of the not-yet?   Once you own earthen treasures you do not even want celestial consolations.   After all, even outside the Biblical tradition you have your opponents to artistic stimulation and satisfaction.   Why is Plato so sceptical in his approach to art and poetry?   Because of their danger to morality.   There is a deceit, such as the song of the sirens, which obscures the human condition and the challenge of the truth.   Kierkegaard knew this when he analysed the temptations of aesthetic enjoyment.   And Tolstoy, greatest novelist perhaps of all times, preached against the almost inevitable perversions implicit in art, for he recognized that the aesthetic always follows the worst paths of human desire.   It arouses sexual passion, evokes patriotic aggression, distorts religious faith. Art tends to be immoral and is always of this earth.

The Psychologist: Though you did not intend this, you have given the argument the right twist.   You formulate an indictment against art, and in so doing you are rightly stressing the personal aspect of artistic activity.   Art as such does not exist: the artist does.

Your dislike of art merely brings to light your suspicion of the artistic motive. This is grounded in the pleasure principle. Art is not simply pleasure, but, in the words of Santayana 'pleasure objectified'. Very well, then, what sets the creative impulse going? At the risk of generalizing, we may postulate that the artistic endeavour derives from deep-rooted frustration. The simple fulfilment of pleasures may for many reasons lie outside the reach of the defeated ego which thereupon builds up a super-ego. The artist is born when frustration is turned into an asset by the development of the imagination. What your poet, musician, painter, could not achieve in the realm of real life he now achieves on his own chosen ground. No wonder sexual passion and aggressive traits abound in artistic creation, for here the creator imprints his marks of compensating deeds. They are not immoral at all. Rather, I should call them therapeutic.

The Chairman: But does your aesthetic theory never rise above the level of neurosis and its compensation? Do you really wish to bracket your little defeated men, who go in for a bit of art, with the giants of our culture? Are Dante and Michelangelo, Beethoven, and Cézanne no more than frustrated creators of displaced libido?

The Psychologist: There are nuances of neurosis and there are masters of sublimation. My plea is for no more than the recognition of the psychological necessity of artistic creation. We need no aesthetic theory to show that the artist gives the clue to art. Therefore, I conclude, the evidence from art cannot point to anything but human content.

The Protestant: Well spoken, you confirm my thesis.

The Chairman: This strikes me as excessively naive. The trouble is that Freud, who confessed himself defeated by the specific characteristics of the artistic activity, understood practically nothing of art. Of music he had no understanding at all. And yet you take him as your guide to an experience to which he was blind and deaf. I should be much happier if you followed that school of psychology which did try to do justice to the wholeness of artistic experience. This *Gestalt*-psychology really sympathizes with the forms of art and infers meaning from the work.

The Catholic: 'Meaning from the work'! This is my clue and my justification for using aesthetic evidence. Unless you are prepared to look at human culture and artistic genius in a manner which transcends social environment and personal neurosis, you must imprison all beauty in your man-made categories. But once let go your doctrinaire limitations and you will be made to see the connection between art and true eschatology. The connection lies both in form and content, for to use Malraux's dictum, 'the world of art is not an idealized world but another world'. That's the rub, for art expresses man's hope that he harbours the source of eternity. Here the divine image shines, or at least its lustre radiates and lures man on to further revelation, both of the world and himself. Hence, as E. Cassirer so rightly observed, art invariably retains and transmits the divine. The former longing, expressed in ancient mythologies, is now fulfilled and still vibrates in Christian art. Hence I leap to the defence of art and I would vindicate the Church's patronage of the arts, for these things made by human hands and meant for human ears and eyes are not pagan devices, as my friend here maintains, but rather their form and contents enunciate eternal truths, and among these the things pertaining to the End. Indeed, the transmutation of bizarre, fanatical, useless eschatologies, the right utilization of the apocalyptic temper, occur precisely on the level of artistic creation. The great discovery of Christian culture was the marrying of the unbridled savagery of apocalyptic hopes with the rational canons of art. Thus the prophetic spirit came into direct contact with Hellenic order and restraint. Do not speak to me about pagan art, for paganism is nature-worship and orgiastic abandonment of reason. In Christian art the whole setting presupposes a moral end and a purification of the senses: it stands above nature in the great design of divine salvation. Art is made a sacrament, ancillary to worship. It follows the pattern of divine perfection, is modelled after it, and if it arouses pleasure—through 'noble simplicity and quiet grandeur'—it is a universal and necessary pleasure which we derive from its harmony. As Kant saw it, we come to appreciate the sublime experience: we are shocked at our own smallness and yet we are exalted with the greatness of our moral nature. Now grant me this, and I will elaborate further the place of the End in this sublime experience.

The Communist: This is no more than the old idealistic twaddle.

The Chairman: I would not say that. But would you claim that all Christian art blends the apocalyptic and the rational, fuses passion with restraint?

The Catholic: Of course not. Plainly a great deal, probably the greater part of artistic creation (but what are quantitative statements worth in this respect?), is irrelevant to my thesis. We can leave aside the comedies and operas and genre paintings of previous centuries, and I will be content; for how does Molière, for example, tally with the Apocalypse, or Boucher with Jeremiah's portrayal of the desolate world? I would not deny for a moment that our heritage contains a host of masterpieces—e.g. your Jane Austen's novels—which need not even eschew the apocalyptic and eschatological, for they never come near the periphery of our present concern. At the same time there is more of the mysterious and near-apocalyptic in the pattern of some artistic creations than some spectators are likely to discern. Take Mozart's *Cosi fan tutte*, one example among many. Here is an erotic opera, which our Herr Psychologist will probably claim for himself as evidence for the frustrated sex-instinct. But, no, how wrong! This light *opera buffa*, with its ridiculous deceptions and disguises, always hovers near that other world, of which Malraux speaks. The music transforms the simple eighteenth-century plot, so that the lovers enter a world beyond themselves. Listen to their 'Adio', when the two officers pretend to leave their loves. It is all great fun and mere pretence, but Mozart transforms the fun into the pain which was felt from the beginning of the world when love parts from love. The comedy remains, but the comedy continues the long tradition which Jesus epitomized when he also bade farewell to his disciples. Indeed, it is this light-hearted note of farewell—the ordeal of parting, the test of faithfulness implicit in separation—which connects so much of our apparently un-Biblical, non-religious art with the deep theme of the End.

The Protestant: Do you seriously maintain, then, that the Lord's departure as well as his Second Coming is in some measure contained in art?

The Catholic: Without a doubt. It would be easy for me to prove this by taking you to all the famous representations of Christ in Majesty, the mosaics of Christos Pantokrator in the apses of our great ancient Churches, where the Alpha and the Omega are united in the exalted Son of Man, surrounded by the celestial company and facing the faithful. Nor could any of you avert your eyes from the great pictures of the Judgement. Where words fail Michelangelo's Last Judgement in the Sistine Chapel will not fail to persuade. Here the Eschaton has become fact: the books have been opened, the trumpets have sounded, the damned are on their way to perdition, the glorified break into the songs of the final triumph, and the Mother of God is supreme witness of the new creation. You have asked for proof: go and see for yourselves.

The Psychologist: The case of Michelangelo also happens to prove my thesis. I do not deny for a moment the supreme worth of his genius, but it is a genius born out of complex neuroses, as any good biography on the master will show.

The Communist: I see him as a victim of economic necessity and a rebel against the Pope and the Florentine lords.

The Protestant: And of his indecent nudities the shock was such that they had to be draped. You see, the sensuality which is thoroughly pagan quite distorts the Second Coming.

The Catholic: Let me then leave the individual work and revert to the general pattern, for I will not so lightly give up the aesthetic restatement of apocalyptic truths.

The Chairman: In what way, then, do you think that art can illumine our subject more effectively than any other approach?

The Catholic: Art equips us with that superb, and apparently contradictory, detachment-cum-involvement which we do not find elsewhere, or never to the same extent. As we look and listen we know ourselves to be spectators: thus we can adopt a detached, critical attitude. This favours restraint and coolness of temper. But if the impression made upon us is tremendous then we enter into the artistic emotion as if we were identified with it. Form and content engage us and we become part of it. Now this dual role, of observer and of participant, is particularly profitable when applied to our subject of the End-hope. We have seen that we need the critical detachment, lest we be overcome by fanatical millenarianism; but we also need to share in the hope in order to understand our subject.

The Chairman: In other words you hope to display for our benefit a symbolism of eschatology. The real thing being inaccessible you supply the language of communicating signs.

The Protestant: When the divine promise is relegated to symbolism we become untrue to the Bible, and therefore we cease our concern with the Christian End-hope. Symbolism belongs to abstract thought; symbolism is un-hebraic. If the aesthetic activity requires symbolic interpretation it is a sure sign that it is irrelevant to the revelation of God.

The Communist: And to the needs of the people, who have a healthy dislike of abstract painting and symbolic poetry. Here I side with my Protestant colleague. Symbolism is no more than a way of tricking us into accepting propositions which we would never dream of sustaining in broad daylight.

The Psychologist: Hence your art never rises above the level of the 'Tractor Driver's Lunch Hour' or, rather, your true artists have to work in secret. No, on the contrary, if you can link eschatology with symbolism I shall see much promise in this. At least it will move these odd notions out of their stuffy corner. A common symbolic language unites different cultures. I shall be glad to see eschatology removed from its limited Biblical appeal.

The Catholic: Your opposing voices put me in a dilemma. I repeat that the form and content of our culture displays certain patterns which suggest, perhaps even urge, a common apocalyptic-eschatological trend. Call this symbolism, if you like, for if it makes sense of 'these antique fables' it serves its purpose.

The Chairman: I follow you, or rather Shakespeare:

> 'the lunatic, the lover and the poet
> Are of imagination all compact:
> One sees more devils than vast hell can hold,
> That is, the madman: the lover, all as frantic,
> Sees Helen's beauty in a brow of Egypt:
> The poet's eye in a fine frenzy rolling,
> Doth glance from heaven to earth, from earth to heaven;
> And as imagination bodies forth
> The forms of things unknown, the poet's pen
> Turns them to shapes, and gives to airy nothing
> a local habitation and a name.'

The Protestant: A Midsummer Night's Dream bestows authority on fancy for the duration of the night. It does not authorize the symbolical interpretation of the Bible.

The Psychologist: Why so humourless and uncompromising still?

The Protestant: Because symbolism dilutes facts into fiction.

The Chairman: Oh hardly that! It is the poetic imagination, the creative experience, which turns mere words into reality. What is all this apocalyptic in propositional form? Nothing, until it is reshaped thus:

> 'Th' infernal Serpent: he it was, whose guile
> Stir'd up with Envy and Revenge, deceiv'd
> The Mother of Mankind, what time his Pride
> Had cast him out from Heav'n, with all his Host
> Of Rebel Angels, by whose aid aspiring
> To set himself in Glory above his Peers,
> He trusted to have equal'd the most High,
> If he oppos'd; and with ambitious aim
> Against the Throne and Monarchy of God
> Rais'd impious war in Heav'n and Battle proud
> With vain attempt. Him the Almighty Power
> Hurl'd headlong flaming from th' Ethereal skie
> With hideous ruine and combustion down
> To bottomless perdition, there to dwell
> In Adamantine Chains and penal Fire. . . .'

The Communist: Stop! We like Milton for his revolutionary propaganda, not for all this mythological nonsense.

The Protestant: Milton I accept, for he does not imagine but restates Biblical apocalyptic with prophetic inspiration: 'For what concerns my knowledge God reveals.'

The Catholic: Precisely: 'For though that seat of earthly bliss be fail'd, A fairer Paradise is founded now for Adam and his chosen sons.' Thus you help me to establish my first principle of apocalyptic in art: Its form is dramatic. I would not confine this principle merely to what we call drama, but even to the realms of music and the visual arts. The artist shapes his material in such a way that it exhibits an inner dynamism which leads up to the crisis or climax of the work. Everything is conceived in terms of this climax, the point of no return. Paradise is lost in order to be regained, just as man is condemned in order to be saved. This is the pattern or symbolism which I commend to you now. It is a reality without which mankind cannot live, but it is in the realm of aesthetics that this drama is lived out. In artistic realization the End is therefore anticipated.

The Communist: What are you talking about?

The Catholic: Let me restate my thesis: all the arts testify to the presence of the End in their form. Observe the rhythm of such compositions you know best. They are conceived in terms of crisis, climax, and final reconciliation. You may say that this is merely the old pattern of tragedy warmed up. However that may be, the Hebrew-Christian belief in Christ suffering, vindicated, ascended and coming, has baptized the classical form into our cultural heritage. I am here concerned with the form which contains the action.

The Communist: I begin to follow you. But some of our own writers, such as Brecht, pursue the same form.

The Psychologist: The point I was going to make. It is not confined to any one camp. Would you exclude Homer and Virgil from your scheme of things?

The Catholic: Not at all, though I would observe that the Eastern world, with its many virtues of contemplative piety, does not seem to know this peculiar dynamic. Eastern forms know nothing like, say, Beethoven's Eroica, where the heroic tragedy is governed by the climax of finality. Beethoven's compositions altogether epitomize what I mean by apocalyptic art at its highest. All themes are subservient to the ecstatic End, the redeeming End, the Finale which alone justifies the beginning. The form itself is action, the whole artistic concept establishes the apocalyptic in music. Yet there is here nothing hysterical, for the action is tamed, so that restraint blends with ecstasy, a blend which I have already proffered you as the hall-mark of valid End-hoping.

The Chairman: Even the visual arts seem to add to your argument, although here the wholeness of the design cannot depend upon time-sequences. Yet the eye apprehends a climax apart from before-and-after events. How the design of cathedrals draws us to the centre, how the economy of light and darkness, even in small paintings, reveals the same apocalyptic art-form, borne up by the identical powers of restraint and passion! Indeed, we discern the presence of the climacteric against the background of the merely decorative. How do you account for this dramatic element? Is it mere contrivance? A formality?

The Catholic: A mere convention? Oh, not at all! Art realizes the things pertaining to the End only when the creator has in his imagination perceived the total revelation. He has cancelled time, distance means nothing to him. He has fed on that celestial honey-dew, visited that other world, and adapts the dramatic form accordingly. And here I must warn you that not everything that has an apocalyptic flavour rings true, at least not to my senses. Indeed the more openly apocalyptic the less acceptable the result. Take Blake: both his poems and paintings are modelled on Apocalyptic themes, but are you any the wiser after the event?

The Communist: A great deal wiser about the society in which he lived and the protests he wished to utter against it in the name of all the oppressed.

The Psychologist: He elucidates the almost incurable tensions of his and kindred psyches.

The Catholic: Precisely, we meet our Blakes in the confessional, but they tell us nothing authentic about the End. Their contrived eschatology kills their and our desire.

The Chairman: You surprise me. If Blake will not do, who does? What are the criteria of genuine apocalyptic creativity?

The Catholic: It lies in the nature of the conflict. The drama depends upon an inner necessity; the action springs out of a necessary conflict, which stands in direct contrast to chance and absurdity.

The Protestant: Do you mean that the conflict mirrors that between Christ and Satan?

The Catholic: Yes. Life is dramatized as an ordeal in which two sides build up their resources; intrigues, deceits—such as the Trojan horse—delay the final outcome and enhance the tension to breaking point. At length, however, parleys must end and the battle begin. Thus the masters from Homer to Pasternak incorporate the violent conflict by foreshortening the horizon. Violence is set in the context of beginning and end and elevated to a moral level. The historical is personalized. The conflict is apprehended as inevitable and full of eternal meaning.

The Psychologist: If you make the conflict central to apocalyptic creativeness will you not be accused of elevating aggressiveness at a high degree to an artistic principle? We also acknowledge the importance of the aggressive-destructive in the psyche but we would rather it could be cured.

The Chairman: As indeed Oriental religions aim at peace and tranquillity and suspect all passions of lower motives.

The Catholic: This is true and may explain why the Christian tradition differs so sharply from the East. But don't misunderstand me: I am not trying to glorify the aggressive-destructive in man. The achievement of apocalyptic art is to portray conflict in a meaningful manner. Examples abound: Take the sack of Troy which becomes in this interpretation more than a war of aggression. Or think of Tolstoy's portrayal of Napoleon in *War and Peace*. The battle-scenes are there, but behind the galloping horsemen and the armour there is spread out before you the whole tapestry of the causes and of the ends of the conflict.

The Chairman: A diagnosis of power, in fact?

The Catholic: Yes, but more than that, for in this classical tradition the universal conflict belongs to a sphere beyond human control. Men are responsible for their struggles, but ultimately they do not initiate them. They cannot help siding with a power which is greater than themselves and which may intentionally conceal itself; only as the action unfolds do men gain their sight and see the origins of their wars.

The Protestant: Thus you bring in the cosmic note of the warfare.

The Catholic: Certainly. Cosmic and yet also ethical, for in the artistic creation the combatants stand for a way of life. Good triumphs over evil, and the end coincides with the moral satisfaction that right has been done.

The Communist: Your optimism surprises me.

The Catholic: No, the tragic predicament remains in the eschatological drama, for it shows the good man defeated; only in his failure can he be said to conquer. The tragic hero is in a sense the final meaning of the End-drama, for his part in the ordeal is more enduring than the clash of military sides.

The Protestant: The Suffering Servant in Isaiah, the figure of Christ in the New.

The Psychologist: Our old friend Gilgamesh too. In fact, the man who is divided in himself and who brings upon himself the catastrophe, for the tragic person is a split person whose mistakes are a necessary part of his living.

The Protestant: This is too narrow a definition of the conflict of the soul. St Paul stands for the man who does not do what he would do and who does what he would not do. But this conflict, seen in Moses, Elijah, Jeremiah, and the martyrs, is only apocalyptic if it involves more than an inner division. These men overcome by sacrifice. They imitate Jesus.

The Chairman: But the creative artist cannot be tied down to one type of conflict only. Surely, if we are to accept the evidence from art at all, we must cast our net very wide and accept all the classical tragedies, not to mention the endless multiplicity of Shakespeare.

The Catholic: We do well to do so, although we shall discern the peculiar End characteristics more fully in certain plays. These are the necessary ingredients: intensity of feeling, as in *King Lear*, derived from innocence and weakness. Next the inevitability of the conflict which stems from the human situation.

The Protestant: The motif of the 'Must Suffer', as in the Gospel.

The Chairman: The Greeks knew this. Fate and chance bring even the best to humiliation. I suppose *Antigone* moves us to this day because it is the dutiful King Creon who, while warding off lawlessness and civil war by his stern conduct, causes the death of the whole royal household. Only this universal death can solve the impasse made by law and private duty and affection.

The Communist: Rather the impasse of the political system.

The Catholic: You still fail to understand. These heroes transcend their systems. Hence the genuine resolution of the conflict does not lie in political reforms nor in supernatural miracles (the *Deus ex machina* who puts everything right for a happy ending), but in the redeeming end, in death. The stage strewn with dead bodies is, therefore, not a picture of despair; death, the simple physical fact, contains the complex spiritual answer. To see life from beyond, to resolve the conflict from that other side, that, in my opinion, links human art and feeling with the eschatology of the Christian tradition.

The Psychologist: An interesting connection, but not really sustained. Take *Hamlet*, possibly the most controversial example. The Prince of Denmark, who at first cannot bring himself to avenge his father's death and prevaricates endlessly, surely comes out of the textbook of the psychologist's experience rather than from the stable of theology. This non-hero only suffers death in the end because the rapier's points are poisoned. Nor is this the solution, for, as

Shakespeare seems to insist, the hero is Fortinbras, the man of action, who claims his due.   He solves the enigma of life, not the Prince and the corpses.

The Communist: Exactly.   The victory goes to political and military competence.

The Chairman: Is that your interpretation?   It reminds me of those producers who stage Mozart's *Figaro* as a documentary of the class-struggle and not as the sublime victory of love and forgiveness over faithlessness.

The Catholic: I am glad you mention these emotions, for unless we see the eschatological conflict as caused by the tragic division of love and hatred we shall never get beyond stock figures.   But Hamlet is not a dressed-up doll; he is a man.   His duel with Laertes is a necessity to which the poisoned weapons are accidental only.   I repeat, the transmutation of death in dying is the important feature, not suffering in itself.   Dostoevsky distinguishes between his suicides (Kirilov, Stavrogin), whose ends are unredeemed, and the deaths and sufferings which are redemptive because they introduce the humble, Christ-like characters to the new age.   Indeed, they need not even die a physical death, for the murderer Raskolnikov and Dimitri Karamasov, for example, are both reprieved and find life in the suffering of exile and prison.   How is this possible?

The Psychologist: As you say, the solution lies in the individual soul, which is re-made for love, for love and hatred are the powers which drive all towards their consummation.   Love and hatred, attraction and repugnance, tenderness and cruelty, fidelity and promiscuity: these place men in their respective heavens and hells.   That is why the drama of love is perhaps the modern equivalent to the apocalyptic frenzy of antique drama.

The Chairman: So that for you Romeo and Juliet distil in their death-union the perennial tragedy, for they must die in order to be free to love.

The Communist: But can you ignore the political and social background?   Is not Verona rent with the strife of the Montagues and the Capulets?

The Protestant: I find that play condemns sin: the unfaithfulness of Romeo to Rosalind, Juliet's disobedience, the nurse's corruptibility, the friar's dubious conduct.

The Catholic: Precisely: the tragic condition of love draws upon the whole canvas of corporate guilt, and even chance is not to be excluded.   Remember that in Thomas Hardy's novels the tragic impact comes from the uncontrollable hostility, the archetype of the enemy.   This anonymous foe is no longer He, but It.

The Protestant: So that what Satan is in the Bible becomes, in modern art, the hard core of destructive evil?

The Catholic: You could put it this way. Love destroys itself, as when Othello is entrapped in an image of love so vulnerable that it must lead to all-consuming jealousy.

The Communist: Not at all, that's the race-conflict pure and simple.

The Chairman: Ah, now, you are wrong. Black and white are united in harmony, but it is the evil principle which speeds Othello on to his doom. Critics are apt to ridicule the machinations of Iago, but they only show their lack of experience of real passion. I accept *Othello* as a tragic drama where the beginning points to the end, and only the end brings release to all, for Desdemona is a meaningful sacrifice to love, Othello dies to love's ambiguities, Iago to its abuse.

The Psychologist: Better and better, for in this mood you may include all love stories in your list of transmuted eschatologies. Whose love could be more intense and destructive than that of Anna Karenina, who despises her husband, forgets her son, and on seeing Vronsky at the station in Moscow is already lost and as good as dead? I suppose you would call the train, which crushes her to death, a symbol of modernized eschatology.

The Protestant: But we have moved a long way now from the innocent tragic hero, who enters the new age in Christ-like humility, to the sinful suicide. In your liberal approach you fail to do justice to the most essential requirement of apocalyptic religion: the vindication of the right, the exposure of the wrong.

The Chairman: The modern world despairs, I think, of this vision. It no longer believes in it. Ivan Karamazov is made to say: 'In the world's finale, at the moment of eternal harmony, something so precious will come to pass that it will suffice for all hearts, for the comforting of all resentments, for the atonement of all the crimes of humanity, of all the blood they have shed; that it will make it not only possible to forgive but to justify all that has happened with men.' But he goes on significantly: 'Though all that may come to pass, I don't accept it.' Hence the modern tragedy is no longer apocalyptic: only a delineation of despair without reconciliation. Take Ibsen's tragic characters! What do they solve? Nothing. Hedda Gabler, the frustrated wife, fulfils her wishes best when she kills herself, flouting the accepted convention that 'such things are not done'.

The Catholic: Yes, modern despair is not tragic because it dispenses with the supernatural and discards moral judgement. Hence even love and death lose their revelatory power. In this respect the classical comedy is more revelatory than the modern tragedy. Consider in particular the work of Mozart, who composed, as has been said, from the other side, with the experience of death already imbibed.

The Communist: Because at the far end of the table of the servants of the feudal lord he never got enough to eat and died from exhaustion at the age of thirty-five.

The Chairman: That may be so, but his music rises above social conditions, though I must confess that for me his elegance and delicacy seem to have little to do with the supernatural.

The Catholic: His is the humour of Dante and of the classical tradition, which takes the moral and supernatural structure of the universe for granted. I would acclaim his musical eschatology as my trump-card in this aesthetic argument.

The Psychologist: I admit that this is partly borne out by his letters. The anticipation of death and bliss is never far away from his highly erotic sensitivity. You would not deny that the eroticism is quite basic to his work?

The Catholic: On the contrary, but the eroticism is controlled by the end.

The Chairman: You mean, for example, the inevitable doom of the profligate Don Giovanni? The fires of hell and the triumph of virtue?

The Catholic: Yes, but the important thing is that Mozart goes beyond mere morality. If this were not so, boredom would defeat the composer. Observe how Mozart raises the Don to the heights of a tragic hero, although he is in reality no more that the perennial libertine whose virility becomes even slightly ridiculous. He has conquered 'a thousand and three' in Spain, we are told. But he is in truth a demonic character and Mozart uses his d-minor trombones to acquaint us with a *mysterium tremendum*, namely the Judgement which is eschatological through and through. Do you recall the great scene in the cemetery when he asks his servant Leporello to invite the newly erected statue of the murdered Commendatore to dinner? The servant falters and the Don repeats the invitation. There is a reply: Yes! The ghostly voice confirms it: he will come.

The Chairman: Kierkegaard discerned the awfulness of the Don's perdition. I suppose a modern school of theology ought to teach eschatology quite simply by attending a performance of this opera.

The Catholic: Yes, but my point is that so much of European culture is unthinkable apart from this artistic motif of the Last

Judgement. Whether you find it over the porches of medieval churches (think of Bourges!) or on the stage, the fall of the damned is a tremendous theme without which our tradition is unthinkable. This Judgement is the corollary of love abused. Mozart, like Michelangelo, shows, that the tragic lies not in the fearful winding-up, but in the inevitable approach. Man sinks into eternal torment because of what he is. The contest between the condemned and the devil is itself eschatological. The flames and the smoke attend upon the guilty for the Judgement is no longer a myth of the future: it is here.

The Psychologist: I absolutely agree with you, as long as you permit me to identify the psychopathic, suicidal sadist or masochist with the Damned. What you call the Judgement is for the medical practitioner the final break-up of the personality. Dostoevsky portrays this last stage of disintegration in the mysterious Stavrogin in his 'Demons', for whom there is no healing.

The Chairman: The final destruction then, derives from habitual self-delusion and wickedness. Stavrogin has seduced a child, 'married' a cripple to defy love, assented to mass destruction. No wonder he cannot be reclaimed.

The Communist: I dare say in our camps even your villains could be brought to reason and be made to lead a useful life, This whole business of damnation rests upon an individualism which we have outlawed. In our society a Stavrogin would be arrested after his first crime.

The Protestant: But surely damnation is only one side of the coin?

The Catholic: Precisely. There is another aspect of Judge-ment in the Christian tradition and no one felt it more deeply and expressed it more movingly than Mozart. I mean the motif of farewell and reunion. Idomeneo and Idamante, father and son, separate in the shadow of threatening death; again the lovers in *Cosi fan tutte* part to solemn Adios; in the *Magic Flute* Tamino and Pamina endure the ordeal of separation. Here is a unique emotion, for only in separation can man comprehend the joy of love-to-be. The edge of this joy comes from the anxiety and even despair which precede it. For when the lovers meet in the end and all mis-understandings and jealousies depart an ecstatic wonder overtakes the patient, purged, waiting souls: at last they can embrace and remain together. Here then eschatology loses its terrible aspect and salvation is set forth in terms of personal union.

The Protestant: But if you thus get rid of doom and punish-ment and the legal framework of the End, how can the act of mercy tally with the justice of divine retribution? Is not the artist guilty of evasion?

The Catholic: He certainly steps beyond the confines of the assizes and juridical concepts of morality. The law does not deal with persons in love, the artist does. But if love be seriously considered as belonging to reality then the merely punitive aspect cannot suffice in apocalyptic creation. Love, says our artistic tradition, corrupted beyond a certain point, cannot be regained.

The Chairman: When the lover can no longer love, as for example the musician Leverkühn in Thomas Mann's *Dr Faustus*, he reaches his dissolution.

The Psychologist: His madness is final and complete because he sells his capacity for love in exchange for supernatural inspiration. A clear case of megalomania. Thomas Mann knew as well as any psychologist that the human race sits on a magic mountain where love itself acts like a fungus and brings decay. Love is a disease as things now are and the result is chaos. As the little ugly Jewish Jesuit Naphta remarks in the *Magic Mountain*: 'I permit myself to state that all justice, penal and retributive, which does not arise out of a belief in the next world, is bestial nonsense.'

The Chairman: Just so. Both love and justice need the 'as if' of eternal being, and art helps us endow to endow our relationships with the tinge of eternal values.

The Protestant: This seems to me a vicious circle from which there is no escape by art, but only by Christ's atonement. Surely you must acknowledge the dividing line.

The Catholic: And yet art mirrors the message of forgiveness whereby doom and damnation yield to bliss and union.

The Psychologist: As in the cure of the sick, the patient is remade by substituting self-acceptance for guilt.

The Catholic: It is not quite the same. Psychology moves on one level, art on another. On the stage the lover can take back the unfaithful spouse, for there the forgiving heart need not concern itself with adulteries actually committed. What is impossible in real life, because of given irrevocable alienations, is possible in that context.

The Communist: We practise amnesties more realistically than your fiction would envisage.

The Catholic: But amnesties are only a remission of punishment. Forgiveness is an act of Grace, eschatological restoration, and art alone can describe it. Mozart regards the act of forgiveness as the climax in all his operas, almost as if he believed that Christians have to return to the school of mercy and learn it afresh. Forgiveness

is for him not a mad surrender to irrational forces but rather a reflection of divine activity. It is fulfilment of goodness, the cancellation
of sin itself. When the selfish, dissolute, and jealous Count Almaviva
in *Figaro* asks his wife: 'O, angel, forgive me!' and she grants him
the pardon—of which he may be unworthy—Mozart reveals the
order of a different and higher world. Such magnanimity is divine
and a symbol, if you like, of divine mercy. In the *Magic Flute*
Mozart is quite openly symbolic, and the cosmic warfare between
light and darkness ends in the union of the lovers, albeit not without
suffering and purgation. Only when all ideas of vengeance and
violence are abandoned can the Prince enter by the portals of wisdom
and love.

The Protestant: But is this eschatology still Christian? Did
not Mozart write the *Magic Flute* as a Freemason for Freemasonry?
Christian Baptism is non-mysterious, decisive, non-magical. I will
have none of your symbolism. It is less than reality.

The Communist: This is my quarrel all the time. Why symbolism when only reality will do?

The Catholic: Because only the symbolic can unfold the
destiny of man as set forth in our tradition. God's eternity unfolds
an endlessness to which our institutions and sacraments guide the
faithful in a gradual ascent. Why should I repudiate the artistic
initiation into these realms? All the great Christian works of art
depict the striving of the soul. The Gothic style symbolizes the
ascent from earth to unimaginable perfection. Dante's *Paradiso*
beckons the ascending pilgrim from the dark wood through the stairs
of purgatory to the circles of bliss, in which individual and social
joys are one in their reflection of charity and truth. I would leave
you with this poetic vision of mankind's ascent to Heaven in an
all-embracing, God-inspired journey. This gives you the perfect
symbol of the paradox of the End, for Dante guides you by the step-
by-step ascent over the ladder of perfection and yet he retains the
absolute character of God and the transcendence of the End. Only
the poetic tradition can express this longing for eternity without
condemning our temporal nature.

The Protestant: But can a Comedy, however fine, speak of
Christ and the Cross?

The Catholic: Indeed it does! The cross is the supreme
symbol, not only for survival and Judgement. In the poetic symbolism it merges with the Rose, symbol of human, personal love,
perfected and consciously sharing in the Glory of God. Only through
the symbolism can we anticipate on earth this glory which we finally
share in Christ.

The Communist: Such symbolism befits the exiled Dante, not the freedom-fighter and responsible reformer. It transfers the political task to remote regions, inaccessible to all.

The Psychologist: Yet it helped him to solve his problems.

The Chairman: Oh, come, this is a low estimate of genius. Let us rather review the whole case of the problems of the End in the light of aesthetic symbolism. Having been somewhat diffuse so far, let us now attempt a somewhat systematic treatment.

PART III

TIMELESS PATTERNS

CHAPTER XIII

THE SYMBOLISM OF THE END

The twentieth century is known to have advanced in science and technology. What is less known is that, possibly in answer to the exaggerated claims of science as the sole mistress of culture, there has been a revival of symbolism and a new understanding of symbolic language all over the world. In the first place this has been caused by the methods of analytical psychology and the needs of clinical treatment. But symbolism is by no means only a part, and an obscure one at that, of medical studies. Its transcendence of geographical, racial, and religious barriers and its firm foothold in contemporary art, writing, cinema, and aesthetics proves that only a materialist with colossal blinkers can afford to ignore the evidence from symbolism itself. This does not mean that theologians are apt to give a ready welcome to this evidence; especially Christian theologians of the Protestant persuasion are liable to smell a Gnostic rat or, at the least, some special and disagreeable pleading in arguments which tend to be based on symbolism.

The previous chapters, however, have shown that only the most dyed-in-the-wool enemy of symbolism can hope to deal with the problems set by the End without discerning the absolutely central place which symbols occupy in the apocalyptic tradition. The critical observer may, in fact, be put off by the insidious way in which terms are used; they convey information mainly by evoking a resemblance of some sort between themselves and something beyond themselves. For example, the word 'throne' in our context at first conveys to the mind the 'throne', perhaps in some ancient Cathedral, and thence the alleged 'Throne' on which God sits in Heaven. Thus the symbol points to the thing symbolized.[1] Yet the plain man suspects that he is being cheated; his opposition is reinforced by the lack of interest or even ridicule which the linguistic philosopher heaps upon this use of words.

Such a negative attitude to symbols is, however, wholly unjustified if an attempt is made to understand the ancient world. Its language is symbolical, and apocalyptic speech is simply a matter of history. Whether the modern sceptic likes it or not he is heir

[1] Cf. E. Bevan: *Symbolism and Belief.*

to a tradition, from about 5000 B.C. to almost the present day, in which realistic pictures of many things are put down in word, painted, or sculpted, in order to bring out a meaning which is known by all to lie behind these visible things.   Sometimes the idea is primary and is made into a picture, as Goethe explained the use of symbols; sometimes the picture is primary and ideas follow.   In both instances the symbol is there, efficacious and universally understood, 'a picture book without texts'.

We are, therefore, incontrovertibly heirs to a legacy of symbols. The question remains whether we are also able to interpret its riches. Even if we refuse to adopt a totally negative attitude, which would only grudgingly consent to look upon symbols as of antiquarian interest, there still awaits us a vast choice.   We may be allegorists and claim to have a key whereby we translate the symbol into an equivalent.   We may regard symbols merely as codes to which we have no key any longer though we affirm the reality of the code.   We may approach the matter quite unhistorically and see symbols here, there, and everywhere, and thus, following C. G. Jung, detect everpresent archetypes all over the world, both in religious cults and private dreams.   Least offensively perhaps, we may see the climax of symbolism in contemporary literature and exclaim, with Rimbaud, that we copy from silence, from the night, from the unspeakable, when we speak in symbolic language.   Or if we are more scientifically inclined and yet wish to retain symbols we may acclaim the symbol as in mathematics, as the abstraction, i.e. the real, behind the appearance.

None of these approximations is wrong, for the symbol, as the word itself bears witness etymologically, is that which is thrown together.   Thus it was used in antiquity as an agreed sign, whereby men recognized each other or ratified a treaty.   For example, in the Judaeo-Christian tradition there are symbols of initiation.   The circumcised Jew and the baptized Christian carry about them signs, the former in the flesh visibly, the latter only an invisible mark of a copy of the Cross implanted upon his forehead.   It is the cultic use of the symbol which, naturally, is most prominent.   Thus bread and wine and water are everywhere used symbolically, i.e. they represent something greater than, and outside, the actual particles. In the Christian tradition an important refinement of symbolism is found in the fact that the things depend upon the word pronounced over them.   Thus the main Symbol is the Creed, the confession of faith, which governs and also elucidates the symbols which are used in liturgical association.   At the same time these symbols are themselves neutral.   They were used before Christianity was ever heard of, and they continue to be used still apart from the confessional use to which Christian liturgy has adapted them, for, as E. Goodenough rightly sums up, 'our lives are largely guided and moulded by symbols'.[2]

Owing to this complex relationship 'to translate an image into a concrete terminology by restricting it to any one of its frames of reference, is to do worse than mutilate it'.[3] Hence simple identifications—literal, allegorical, etc.—are as much to be resisted as the treatment of a symbol as a metaphor and no more. In the Christian context of the End two reservations may, however, be made: first the symbols are expressing in sense-images a spiritual reality, so that what is seen is meant to convey more than what is seen. Secondly, the act of apprehension in the cultic context supplies this necessary extra. Within this framework the interpretation of the images is free and will depend upon the origin, residence, temperament, religious training, etc., of the observer. For some the link between the sign and the evoked content is so intimate that it must be called realistic; for example, for some Russian monks the Christ enthroned in the apse of the church or the apostles shown on the iconostasis are virtually the token of their real presence. For others the picture of the Glorified Christ is more exalted than their belief in the human Christ, so that when they see an exquisite representation they may, even without much or any belief in the Divinity of Christ, be transported to an apprehension of this divinity to which dogmatically they would never assent. The symbol idealizes for them the real. Others again find, as in the Protestant tradition, that the symbol obscures the reality and that every visible expression, especially of religious and transcendental claims, must lead to a paradoxical apprehension.

The spontaneous knowledge, which comes from the apprehension of symbols, is at least as varied as the symbols themselves.[4] Adding to this richness there is, moreover, an observable ambivalence in symbols themselves, so that one and the same image comes to mean two things which are normally deemed to be opposed to each other. Among apocalyptic symbols, for example, beasts represent both majesty and brutality, desirable and undesirable qualities. The serpent, classical image everywhere, evokes the shudder of the peril associated with dragons and the thrill given by the promise of healing (on the staff of Aesculapius, god of medicine), and even of love.

In the field which concerns us ambiguity of meaning, however,

[2] *Jewish Symbols in the Greco Roman Period*, vol. 4, p. 34.
[3] M. Eliade: *Images and Symbols*.
[4] Cf. E. Cassirer: *The Philosophy of Symbolic Forms*.

may perhaps be avoided. This is due to the fact that the symbols which we shall survey are closely linked with the cult of the dead, which is, of course, really the cult of life after death. Without going so far as to claim that all ancient places of worship were originally burial grounds, which attracted worshippers because of the vicinity of the remains of the dead, there is an overwhelming mass of evidence to show that no cultic place ever existed which did not in some way cater for the passage of the dead to life. In the high places everywhere we find the symbols of Life, because there the struggle with the power of death was believed to take place. Indeed, it is the concern with the Hereafter which gave rise to the hope which the living expressed on behalf of the dead. If, therefore, we now claim that these symbols have quite a specific relationship with the Life after Death as opposed to mere fertility on earth—we are basing his claim upon archaeological finds all over the world.[5]

The Christian religion, however, uses symbolical language about the End in a very particular manner, for it is not concerned to make much ado about Life after Death in general but it must bring out its quite specific Gospel that Life is in Christ. The Resurrection of Christ as an event, and the Risen Christ as a fact, take priority over general symbols of immortality. This shift of emphasis makes a considerable difference, for it removes the End-hope from the over-concern with Death. It is true that human mortality is still the universal prelude even to Christian symbolism and it is not an accident that the proliferation of symbols is particularly striking in the catacombs, but even there one feels that Death is no longer the main actor on the stage. The new confidence, at any rate, by which men simply assert that the dead 'sleep' before the great awakening, may not be theologically quite correct, but it is an eloquent witness of the conviction that in the Living Christ all men are made alive.

Christian Symbolism of the End depends, therefore, upon the image of Christ, as it is handed down to us by word and picture. Now this tradition, as Goodenough shows, goes back in unbroken line to antiquity and may be seen as the common possession of the world into which Christianity was born. Goodenough proves his case, I think, that the emerging Christian symbolism is not un-Jewish, for the Jews themselves had, despite the prohibition laid upon the making of idols, etc., absorbed enough of the Hellenistic culture to integrate its images with the religion of the Old Testament. Indeed,

---

[5] Cf. esp. E. Goodenough's magisterial eight volumes, *Jewish Symbols in the Greco-Roman Period*, Bollinger Series, 1952–1956. 'The Jewish cult objects on graves . . . seem to indicate that the Jew hoped also to come into blissful experience of an eternal culmination of Jewish worship in heaven,' *op cit.* Vol. 8, No. 2, p. 229. 'Between the horns of "idolatry" and "mere decoration" is the *tertium quid* of symbolism', Vol. 4, p. 8.

to give one significant example, the story of Jonah was probably
from the beginning symbolic: Jonah, who is swallowed up by the
fish and then spewed out again, is a story of death and resurrection
even before it was made visible in frescoes and paintings. It would
be impossible and beside the point to enquire where the author got
the symbolism from. He adapted the common imagery in order to
harness it to the destiny of his Jonah, which is the dove of Israel.
Here the symbolism preceded the didactic purpose.

The power of the symbolism in the ancient world was such that
it could not be divorced from real life; rather, it authorized and
created the patterns of life, among which the fertility of the land
and the people was as important as the continuity of life after death.
Again we are indebted to Goodenough (text and pictures) for his
demonstration of the 'lingua franca of symbolism'. It is impossible
to speak of space-filling designs or decorative art—on tombs and
synagogues—when obviously the Candlestick (Menorah), the Torah
Shrine, the Ram's Horn (Shofar), the Incense Shovels, the Lulab
and Ethrog (Bundle of twigs of palm and citrus fruit tied thereto),
Fish, Bread, and Wine were potent forces upon which the survival
of life and institutions depended. It is equally clear that Christian
Art stepped into the same tradition of a creative symbolism, even if,
as Goodenough observes, Jews and Christians have later forgotten
their origins and 'Catholics and Jews still stand together to buy fish
of a Friday, though neither knows what the eating of fish meant
sixteen hundred years ago'.[6]

Yet within that common ground we discern also differences which
must profoundly affect our thesis of the symbolism of the End.
Although Goodenough, for example, is more sensitive than most
to the distinctions demanded by several religious traditions he gives
the impression that the basic thing in all symbols is their contribution
to, and expression of, the *Élan Vital,* especially as given in sexuality.
He is certainly right that the ancient world knew none of the prudery,
commonly associated with the nineteenth century (but also known
among people like Philo!), and did not hesitate to show phallus and
vulva. But Goodenough seems to underestimate the prophetic
history in Israel and its rightful disdain of sacred prostitution and
its denial of Baal religion. Goodenough makes it quite clear that
he is no Freudian Pan-sexualist, nor, indeed, a Jungian dealer in
archetypes, but his interpretation of practically all straight lines as
phallic symbols and all round objects as female organs—at least in
their natural environment—distorts Jewish symbolism and consequently also the interpretation of Jewish symbols in their Christian

[6] Op. cit., vol. 5, p. 53.

guise. For example, if the famous Symbol of the Fish is primarily
a phallic symbol and the fish-meal on fish-day, in North Africa,
recalls the first dance of the betrothed, found also in queer Talmudic
regulations about intercourse, we are so far from the Christian
tradition that we begin to wonder whether there is any connection.
True, the fish, like everything else, gives life and carries on life and
may look like the shape of the Phallus, but is not all this completely
absent from the Christian symbolism of the fish?

The matter is worthy of discussion, especially from our own
point of view, seeing, as Goodenough admits, that the fish is also
the symbol of the Soul as well as of the Messiah and symbolizes the
last age, because the zodiac Pisces is the last of the twelve zodiacs
of the universe. That confessions of Christ were recognizably
scratched into walls in the famous Greek letters ICHTHUS (Fish) is
well-known; the explanation for this coded sign has often been
given as a crytogram for *Iesous Christos Theou Huios Soter*, an
accidental sequence of the first letters of the words: Jesus Christ
God's Son Saviour. But an acrostic cryptogram is a pun rather
than a symbol, though it may of course associate itself with the
symbol. If Christ is represented by the Symbol of the Fish, the
matter is still further complicated by the fact that the Gospels depict
Christ as the master of Galilaean fishermen who, after his death
and resurrection, joins his friends and bids them cast out their nets.
The story in John ch. 21 culminates in the mysterious catch of the
one hundred and fifty and three fishes, a figure with a symbolic
meaning,[7] and finally in the shared meal. This Gospel context would
seem to indicate clearly that the Fish symbolism is more than a
propaganda trick of the early Christians, who use the fish as a sign on
tombs and even on walls, and different from the fertility symbolism
found elsewhere, which incorporates religious attitudes of veneration and tabu. The Christian adaptation sums up the whole historical situation in Galilee, the tradition of the Resurrection, the
commission to catch fish among men and thus to build up the Church.
In that respect the symbol is not eschatological. But in as much
as the fish symbolism also reminds us, though paradoxically, of the
Big Fish in the book of Jonah and thence is associated especially
with the Resurrection, a Sign of Jonah, and furthermore as the meal
after the Resurrection is a feasting upon Fish, we enter also upon
the eschatological scene, where the pure meal, according to common
symbolic representation, consists among other things of fish. Here

[7] For a summary of solutions to the puzzle by gematria and a suggestion which
links the 153 with the prophecy in Ezek. 47:10, cf. J. Emerton: *J.T.S.*, N.S. IX,
pp. 86–89.

however we observe that whereas Jesus and his disciples dine, according to John ch. 21, upon the fish that have been caught, the symbolism changes by making Jesus himself the Fish. This is justified by the general convention of the sacramental development; for whereas during his lifetime the disciples eat Bread with Jesus, presently Jesus himself becomes the Bread of Life. There is therefore nothing strange in the way in which the Fisherman becomes portrayed as the Fish, and the eschatological aura is strengthened by the stress on the Messianic Banquet, the future meal, which takes place in the sign of the Zodiac at the end of times.[8]

This de-sexualization of Biblical imagery, begun in the prophets and completed in the New Testament, frees the symbols from their associations with present fertility, and links them with the future. Christian symbols create and illustrate the There and Then. It is true that certain symbols are too obviously pagan to undergo this sea-change; for example, the Bull, so dear to Mithraism, gory in blood and bursting with sexuality, does not storm with his horns into the world to come. Sexuality, however, can be a symbol of reawakening life after death, just as the seed of the flower and signs of spring give an analogical portrayal of the rising life.

Animal-life features both the demonic horror and the paradisical perfection of the End. The feeling of supernatural dread regarding certain animals belongs to the early stages of Israel's existence and resembles that found in all cultures on earth. It cannot be explained by man's fear of wild animals and reptiles alone. Many animals, such as the lion, the leopard, the bear, were associated with mythological domains, and we meet them in company with Behemoth and Leviathan, which are more than hippopotamus and crocodile. With the monsters of the deep are to be grouped also such domesticated animals as the ram and the goat. The latter in particular is a reminder of desert-jinn, of hairy demons, of pagan sexuality and licentiousness. Goat-like in form these latter are really satyrs and inhabit desolate places, in company with Lilith, the night fairy who is supposed to steal and devour children. A symbol of loathsome prowling and ferocity is also the wolf, always hungry and ready to devour. Naturally vultures and certain kites and hawks are looked upon as filling the air with angry, vengeful intent, whereas locusts and cankerworms represent the destructiveness of the creeping and swarming kind, and scorpions inflict deadly pain with their sting. A whole army of the animal kingdom suggest enmity and violence, and in the apocalyptic literature they are not ornamental: they are the speaking and visible symbols of a horror

[8] Cf. also R. Eisler: *Orpheus—The Fisher*, 1921.

which extends beyond the grave. This is particularly so because the corpses of men are sometimes exposed to the attack of jackals and marauders. They create the atmosphere of a supernatural dread in the feeling about death and punishment, for they are leagued together with hostile forces in a universe which the demons have conquered.

This symbolism reaches the Christian world particularly through the seventh chapter of Daniel. Here the symbolism is allied with politics, for the lion-with-eagle's-wings, the bear, the leopard (also winged), are all tyrannies which have preceded the blasphemous Beast, which is nameless and exceeding all in horror and worldly power. Horn after horn springs up, ten in number, until a little horn holds sway. The last Beast no longer belongs to the known natural world, with its iron teeth and nails of brass. Out of this brutal monster comes the strength which challenges God's supremacy. In the Christian Apocalypse the onslaughts of the brutal enemy attain to an even heightened eschatological drama. A great red dragon, having seven heads and ten horns, has seven diadems upon his heads and lords over a third of the whole universe, ready to pounce upon the Woman and Child (ch. 12). Again a complex symbol of a compound Beast is pictured as coming out of the sea, equipped with all the features of leopard, bear, and lion, ready to attack the people of God, only to be succeeded by another horned dragon which receives worship: his number is 6–6–6 (ch. 13), a number which parodies the number 8–8–8 of Christ.[9]

The Christian bias can now be seen plainly. Against the Lamb and the peaceful Reign of Christ and his Saints there is arrayed the whole Satanic power, and the brutish images are its symbol. This is the destructive force which lies in wait to cheat and to inflict suffering. The symbolism of the wild beasts is utterly at variance with the modern interest in wild life. Now the lion, of all the beasts, is loved as the king of the beasts, and books are written and read about the few fine specimens left. The lion has become a symbol of freedom from the restraints of a suburbanized society, and what is true of the lion is equally true of the other wild beasts and even about monsters in tales. Thus the old symbolism seems to have lost its direct evocation of brutality; cruelty is associated with man rather than with beasts. Yet although this confidence towards 'real' beasts is justified when we face the cages in our zoological gardens it falls short of the deep psychological experience, as evidenced by dreams and fears. The symbol is evocative of another reality. As regards

[9] For a detailed discussion, cf. beside R. H. Charles: *Commentary on the Apocalypse*; Austin Farrer: *A Rebirth of Images*, 1948, pp. 256ff.

the world to come it is still 'natural' to pray, in liturgical fashion, 'deliver me from the lion's mouth'. The gambolling leopard, the fierce lion, the ravenous she-wolf, are still, as in Dante's *Divine Comedy,* the subterranean trinity of the condemned soul, the instinctive drive of lust, violence, and envy, which men pursue in their destructive course. The brutish faces symbolize the almost mysterious character of evil; they inspire us with the sense of numinus evil and buttress the religious conviction that cruelty is a more-than-human perversion; it receives its retribution in the realm where lust lusts upon lust, anger angers the angry, and envy envies the envious.

But the End-hope also affects the world of the brutes, and the symbols which inspire fear can also be converted into images of majesty and harmony. This ambivalence of the imagery of the lion, the calf, and the eagle stems in the Bible from the vision of Ezekiel (ch. 1), which the Christian seer reproduces in his own vision of the celestial worship in ch. 4. The four living creatures are, of course, not of this world, but their faces—among which one is human—and their fantastic appearance with eyes and wings suggests the transmutation of the horrible into the wonderful. Now the brutish is tamed, the destructive is put to godly work, the preying turns to love. This return to the golden Age of peace and harmony is part of the many prophecies of the End and in the Jewish-Christian tradition reaches its climax in the portrayal of the Messianic Age, as given by Isaiah. The force of paradox in ch. 11 is such that it deliberately reverses our inborn feelings: wolf and lamb, leopard and goat, lion and calf are led by the little child into a kingdom of perfection which in every point is unlike the world of experience.

Thus the symbol of the animals comes to reflect the healing of the split world, the split image of man, the war-torn reality of history and of tormented minds. But it is more than that, for it demonstrates the integration of opposites with which the End-hope is intimately connected. It is an open question whether this symbolism may be cited as evidence—not Biblical so much as psychological—for the rejected doctrine of universal restoration. When we identify the Beast with our shadow self we cannot help desiring to come to terms with it. This wish is best known from dreams, where the dreamer often faces his own tearing self in beastly form. Dare he confront this dangerous beast? Sometimes he may, sometimes he may not. The symbolism leaves open the final issue symbolized by the wild beasts. Some may take up the snake and play on the den of vipers, others may not, lest, like some modern snake-charmers, they may be bitten and die.

The ambiguity of this particular animal symbolism of the End never deters the visionary from his main theme: the victory of Christ. Thus the Lion of Judah has won the victory,[10] even if, in the visions of torment, lion-faced monsters punish and destroy.[11] Similarly the eagle (not to be confused with the vulture) becomes an image of one of the evangelists, St John, whose words carry the nobility and lofty grandeur of the triumphant Christ.   More surprisingly still, the horse, most apocalyptic image of images, serves the Preaching of the early Church. This animal, which came in the third millennium from the plains of Asia, appeared only late in Palestine and for the Hebrews it was always connected with unrest and war.   Only late did the Hebrews themselves master the horse and fight successfully with chariots and trade in horses. But the prophets always regarded the horse with suspicion and they insisted that not the horse, but God secures victory. In New Testament times the Jews of Palestine appear to have owned hardly any horses. Jesus entered the city on a donkey. But the horse is also the animal which draws the celestial chariot and the celestial horsemen command horses. On the red horse rides War, on the black one Famine, on the pale one Death: only on the white horse sits the crowned archer who conquers in the terrible fight, for the Rider on the white horse is the Word of God, Faithful and True, wearing a cloak stained with blood, which spells the inscription of royal Divinity.[12]

Here the conversion of the destructive symbols stands beyond doubt. A rationalistic enquiry how, for example, the white horse is to be compared with the other horses and how the faithful Rider of Peace can be found in such martial company, proves at a glance that symbolic language is not the same as logical articulation. The picture on the eternal frieze makes Christ into the leader of the destructive armies, who uses the natural terror to avenge the cause of supernatural goodness. The beasts harnessed to war are liberated from war in the greater purpose of vindication. The same process exists in the integration of the warring soul where all the chaotic forces remain what they are, but change their direction if the cure is completed. In its eschatological significance, however, the image of the wild and yet harnessed horse transcends that of the libido; the whole world of chaotic passion and overwhelming intensity of desire is portrayed in its final cosmic dedication to God.

The pagan spirit naturally resists this bending of the ferocious image to Christian symbolism. Thus D. H. Lawrence in his last work *Apocalypse* after protesting against the shoddy, moralizing tone of the Christian Book, in which, like Nietzsche, he detects the envy of the have-nots, who would compensate themselves for their

---

[10] Rev. 5:5.   [11] Rev. 9:8, 17; 13:2.   [12] Rev. chs. 6, 9, 19.

impoverished state, nevertheless proceeds to expound the images with enthusiasm. The Jews, he declares, always spoilt the beauty of a plan by forcing some ethical and tribal meaning upon designs. But he uncovers the original meaning of the truly Dionysiac symbols. 'Horses', he writes for example, 'always horses! How the horse dominated the mind of early races! You were a lord if you had a horse! Far back, far back in our dark soul the horse prances . . . he links us, the first palpable and throbbing link with the ruddy-glowing Almighty of potence: he is the beginning even of our god-head in the flesh.'

Lawrence helps us to show the precise parting of the ways between pagan and Christian symbolism. For the former the images portray the deification of our own strength, for the latter they pave the way towards redemption and the dedication of mortal man to God's eternal life, centring always upon the Son of Man who died and rose again from the dead. Thus the image of the Lion blends with that of the Lamb, not—as Lawrence writes, mocking—because 'we are always hearing a terrific roaring of lions, and we are always seeing a Lamb exhibiting his wrath. John of Patmos's lamb is, we suspect, the good old lion in sheep's clothing', but because Jesus is the Good Shepherd who has given his life like a lamb for the sheep and is therefore worthy to receive the Power which is God's.

This picture of the Shepherd and the Sheep was destined to become the classical symbol of the New Age. Its suitability is easily explained. It fulfilled the whole Near Eastern Mythology of the pastoral life, which the Old Testament reflects from its earliest times. It brought to a fine point warm feeling evoked by the spring, the shepherd festivals, the lambing season, the sacrificial giving of the lamb, the eating of the lamb. It recalled the past, it drew on the present, but it anticipated also the future. The Risen Shepherd, who gathers around himself the lambs, has passed through death and now leads the new flock to the promised pastures and the still waters of comfort. No simile could express more cogently the continuity of the new life with the old, nor the newness; for whereas all used to be hemmed in by war and violence, the new pastoral life is one of unlimited freedom and security. Again the relationship between Pastor and sheep expresses what the Church already experienced on earth as the true fellowship of the leader and his sheep, who through their following of him are united with each other. The image trans-cendentalizes and eternalizes this relationship. Yet there is in this tradition nothing mawkish. Although the picture is full of the feel-ing of final social serenity it is never spoilt by that sentimentalism of allegory which destroys the symbol. The stylized nature of the mosaics of the first millennium and the Byzantine paintings excluded this kind of decay with which we have become only too familiar.

The recovery of the symbol of the Shepherd and the flock is indispensable for the articulation of the End-hope since this image of Christ and the Church is not only the most prominent in the history of Christian symbolism but effects the conversion of pagan End-hopes to Christian belief. The Shepherd in this context is not the handsome Adonis but the Crucified who gave his life; he is not the Tammuz who rises with nature but the Risen One who rose on the third day; he is not the idyllic lover by the streams of nature, but the Almighty King, the *Pantokrator*, who as universal sovereign shepherds the whole stellar glory as his handiwork, whose staff is the rod and who holds the orb in his hands. Cosmic majesty and power liberate the image of the shepherd from the passing scene of this world to the supernatural. He stands in no need of weapons; neither the swords and shields and the accessories of heraldry, nor flags and banners, obscure the vision of his omnipotence. The Kingship of the Shepherd Christ dispenses with the all too earthly representation which the armour of men may furnish. Instead he appears before us undefended, facing the beholder, clothed in spotless white raiment. 'A sharp two-edged sword, proceeding out of his mouth', is a symbol which transforms our image of power, for it is the Word of God which defeats the armed mechanism of lies upon earth.

The face of Jesus, radiant like lightning, his raiment white as snow, links the human Jesus with the transfigured Christ, the entombed Jesus with the risen and ascended Lord. It is the picture of glory, which is made manifest in the radiance of the colour and the wonder of the priestly garment. The description of the Light of the World baffles all the powers of human speech. The garments of the glorified Christ merge with his bodily appearance. The result is a total impression of a sudden coruscation of light in which flames of fire are drawn into him, the centre, as into the Sun. The manifestation of Christ as he really is belongs still to the hereafter (the *Sol Novus*), but in the mystical perception of the radiance of the glory of the eternal Light we perceive 'thrown together' the Unity of God in his Three Persons. The apprehension of Jesus-as-He-Is fills the present vision of God with the substance which is still to be. This equation of Jesus with Saving Light (*Sol Salutis*) not only eternalizes the Innocence of the Lamb but also transmutes the pagan concept of emanations of Light to the Christian goal of life, for it is this Light which draws all the children of light unto Himself and holds out to them the same glorification.

The Christian symbolism of the final light connects with the human situation of known darkness. The exalted Christ sheds his radiance over the chaos of graves and imprisoned spirits. The sons of light are as yet in chains, just as were once the Apostle Paul and all the martyrs. The symbolism of outer darkness, with all the associated pictures of torment and the nightmarish world of monsters, belongs in a way to the symbolism of light, for in the Christian experience it is only through the 'Blood of the Lamb' that man can escape from the darkness and the prison. The raiments of the sons of God are made white by red blood, their own, which, through identification with Christ, removes them from the power of the darkness and gives them access to the celestial realm. Thus the whiteness is not obtained through 'work', or the mere washing away of filth, but rather through the reflection of Christ in sacrifice. Glory is not obtained through a secret knowledge of the emanations, nor an entry into the prisms of light by an initiation into mysteries—the pagan way, even at its highest—but through the anticipation of Christ's victory.

The *Lux Mundi* attracts all the lights of the world which reflect its glory. Light derives from light, kindling fire from fire, and in encircling rings of glory the Kingdom of God manifests its reality. The symbol of the One in the Many is eternalized in the Rainbow, no longer a broken arc, as on earth, but an endless many-tiered iridescence of complete rings. In this timeless radiation and reflection the light envelopes, penetrates, and indwells all, without diminishing or dividing its immeasurable and inexhaustible unity. Light is event and being, fused into one. The initial 'Let there be light', which flashed forth in countless ways, unfolding to sight the physical and spiritual realities, ceases at the End to be external, but becomes the inner reality. Whereas Sun, Moon, and stars were on earth manifestations of the world of fire and light which surrounds man, in the End all these phenomena of light are subjected to the pure spiritual essence and are in Christ made 'personal', i.e. the glorious face of the Son shines through and in his creation. The Light symbolism denies that there is anything base or meaningless in the world, for the whole creation is comprehended in the Light and without Light there is nothing at all. The Christ of the Sanctuary, dwelling amidst the seven Candlesticks, summarizes every aspiration which humans connect with the light. But the world below is now at last seen to be a reflection of the world above, and eyes innumerable enjoy the flood of light which proceeds from him.

The light symbolism does not destroy the conception of reality as a graded universe. On the contrary, although all things are bathed in the uniting reality, there are degrees of light-shedding circles which the apocalyptic emphasis on the figure Seven articulates:

the Lamb has Seven Horns and Seven Eyes; Seven Spirits are before the throne, there are Seven Seals, Seven Trumpets, Seven Thunders, Seven Vials. The figure Seven is not only the perfect number, the symbol of order and creation, but also that of the final perfection, the very stuff of the pattern of reality.[13] Seven is not a magical number which must somehow be made to fit into our knowledge of the universe. On the contrary, the number is the symbol of the distinct spheres of reality which together make up the whole organism of life. Thus light interpenetrates layers of coherent and yet independent substances which complete the reality of the whole. As the figure Seven was found unsatisfactory later on, it was replaced. But whereas the Gnostics postulated thousands of such hierarchies of being, Christian orthodoxy resisted such an inflationary tendency, and the classical system is that of Dante's Ten Heavens. The change of the figure shows that it has no inherent symbolical value which is irreplaceable. Seven or Ten, the orbits circle around the Primal Light as a pre-established harmony where human and angelic aspirations reach their perfection.

This theme of the Divine Hierarchy owes nothing to astrological superstitions, though it is true that it is the symbolic fulfilment of all star-gazing instincts. More important, it liberates the expectation of the End from its narrow subjective and moralizing channels. When Christ is seen as the wearer of the cosmic mantle and the stars become the playground of the angels and saints, Eschatology loses its futuristic limitation. Clearly, this is the world which already exists, and the cosmic symbol is the seal upon truth unfolded in the past, when Elisha and all the prophets 'saw' the heaven open even in their day. The imagery of the eternal Christ puts human history in its place as a mere episode of short duration, an epoch already entombed and about to be gathered into the existent reality. Ever since the making of the Divine Comedy we see human history under the aspect of this eternal order. Our world is no world at all but utter chaos and confusion, until it is admitted through the undergrowth to the spheres above. The symbols of light and order deny reality to everything that is without the hierarchy of being, unillumined by the radiance, left out of the Chain of Being. The approach to the End is the stepping into cosmic reality.

But this stepping into light is beset with perils. As in earthly experience the naked eye is blinded by the unprotected glance into the sun, and as the moth finds death in its attraction to the light, so the children of light have no direct approach to the light. If the End of men were one of absorption in the Light Stream they would

[13] Cf. A. Farrer, op. cit., ch. 2.

not have this legitimate shrinking from the light. There is, in eschatology, a Scylla of Light and a Charybdis of darkness: both spell destruction, one by blinding and the other by burying. Men must extricate themselves from between either rocks or whirlpools in order to pass on from the shadow of existence to reality. But this endeavour to get free from false attractions is beset with trial and error. Some religions commend world-renunciation and lead their devotees to failure; others make acceptance of the world easy and similarly fasten the prison of illusion. Ecstatics encourage the neophyte to make himself equal to the stars and, alas, with the deflation of the ecstasy, the light, though once attained, fizzles out and darkness reigns again.

The basic problem of eschatological mysticism is thus set by the symbol of light. In Christian thought the symbol is strictly controlled by theological teaching, especially on the Holy Spirit who alone transforms human nature and gives the interior light to each according to his capacity. Therefore repentance is the gate which leads from the realm of darkness into that of light, for God makes himself known to the penitent alone. His invisible fire bestows and sustains the visible quality of Grace which both fills and surpasses the intellect and the senses.

Granted this eschatological efficacy of Grace the light becomes accessible, and future and present merge: 'In thy light we shall see light', sings the Psalmist, and all the lovers of this famous motto would agree with St Symeon the New Theologian that 'the light already shines in the darkness, in the night and in the day, in our hearts and our minds. This light without change, without decline and never extinguished, enlightens us; it speaks, it acts, it lives and gives life, it transforms into light those whom it illumines.'

Eastern mystical theology clearly tends to circumvent the End through its emphasis on the eternal nature of illumination in the present. God is a fire which warms and kindles our hearts, and the passing of time is really irrelevant to the end of the Christian life (St Seraphim of Sarov). Love and knowledge constantly sustain the infusion of the uncreated light, and this light is the beginning of the parousia in holy souls. In that sense St Symeon can declare boldly: 'The day of the Lord will not appear to those who are already enlightened by the divine light', though the second coming of Christ will disclose the light, which at present remains hidden, among those who hate the light. There is, therefore, still an essential distinction between Now and Then, between present union and second coming, even in the mystical comprehension of the light. Then 'the heavenly fire of the divine nature which Christians receive in this world, where it works within their hearts, will work from outside' (St Macarius). This 'outside grace' (St Maximus) will chastise with the scourge of love, for it is the divine light of judgement, inseparable from eschatological fulfilment, which unfolds God as the truth.[14]

The ascent to the Light, however, is not confined to mystical language. Ritual and architecture presuppose that man passes from life to death and thence to his eternal destiny. The movement is upward, just as the steps rise in the sanctuaries to their heavenly goal. The sacred Mountain is the place where earth and heaven meet and those who would be worthy of eternal life must lift up their hearts and come up to the heights. Similarly the Temples and Churches are on raised platforms and within the sacred buildings the eye follows the vertical line. On top is the ceiling, the earthly Heaven, the replica of the eternal reality. 'There is no contradiction between the Church and eschatology, for they both belong to the same order of reality', says Fr J. Daniélou. He refers primarily to the society, but even the building must share essentially in the eschatological being of the society which worships there. The place is not self-contained in any sense. The members, priests and laity, pass through it, and so also the very masonry leads outward, upward, beyond. The closed building is only the development of the open hearth, the sacrificial altar, from whence the smoke of the sacrifices reached up as a sweet smelling savour. When Christians placed their altars inside their halls and buildings they did not deprive their worship of the transcendental function; rather, they ensured that the vertical connection was eternalized for all their liturgical activities. Here the destroying light was lit safely, no longer blinding as the Sun outside, but as the Presence of God towards whom the whole body scales the heights in prayer and contemplation.

Worship is a sacrament of the final state which Christ has already perfected in Heaven. He has passed through the veil. The veil is the necessary reminder that there is the gulf between the here and now and the there and then. The veil protects man from the Presence of God, but it also prevents him from access. Christ's passing through the veil after the rending of the veil of the Temple fulfils the ancient symbol of necessary caution and ignorance. Christ puts the End-state within reach of the worshipper for as he removes the veil he unfolds his Being and paves the way, the liturgical, traditional, safe route, towards the goal.

The Christ holds the key of admission. Clothed in his majesty he holds the key to the house of David. He has the authority to

---

[14] Cf. V. Lossky: *The Mystical Theology of the Eastern Church*, esp. chs. 10–12.

open and to shut the gate to the house of life, the Temple. But again the symbol enshrines the danger of the End, for the keys which he holds are also keys to the underworld. The key which opens and shuts lends no support to the kind of universalism which E. M. Forster so beautifully satirizes in *A Passage to India*.[15] The key excludes 'someone from the gathering', for unless it shuts the gate 'we are left with nothing'. The key is the clear sign of division— some are in, others are out—for the sake of final security.

At the same time the Christian keys are the keys of Christ, and therefore not cut to enhance arrogance. On the contrary, to get to the End by entry the password is not a mechanical slogan but penitence. That is why the key is, in a sense, deprived of its rich mythical connotation and given a somewhat practical slant. The key of Christ comes, in the Church's use, to stand for the ministry of reconciliation. Forgiveness and absolution work the keys, and nought else. A frantic search for the keys, the most common arche- typal occupation of men—as strikingly portrayed by Lewis Carroll in *Alice in Wonderland*—is not part of the ritual. The keys really reside in the approaching, striving, forgiving, and forgiven pilgrim. He is let through the impassable gates because he has come the right way. If not, no word will bring down the drawbridge, the ramparts, and open the door.

In this picture Christ himself is the Door. He compared himself to it, using here the simile from the shepherd's encampment, where the good shepherd leaves open one aperture in the walls and takes up the position of door himself. No one can get in or out without his knowledge. Thus the symbol of the Door is personalized in Christ, and every richly carved door or simple hole in cathedral or chapel demonstrates the same truth: there is but one way in through penitence, and this way is the living Christ.

Once inside the progress is both sudden and slow. On the one hand, the entry through the door is completed immediately in the acceptance of the comer, but on the other hand he stands on the threshold. There is not for him in readiness a ladder of ascent or chariots of fire. Christian symbolism is astonishingly sober in its removal of some images common to eschatology. The rainbow and the ladder, so vividly expressed in the narrative of Jacob at Bethel and recalled in the Fourth Gospel, belong only to the last stage of bliss. The ladder of ascent, on which angelic traffic is believed to unite this world with the next, is inapposite to the Christian man, for if he were to climb on it right away he would be the same man who escaped so narrowly from the open way to destruction. Here again

[15] Ch. 4.

Christian realism controls the imagination and dictates a slow, conscious, inward progress. This does not mean that the symbol of the ladder of ascent has to be discarded altogether and that the rungs of the ladder may not agree with the whole 'going-up' movement on the stairs to the heights. On the contrary, the upward movement is right, but it must be accepted with hesitation.

This hesitation in coming to the end, in achieving perfection, belongs to the Christian and also some non-Christian traditions. In fact, it is part of the institutional religious temper. It is enough, in the first instance, to open the doors, which are normally closed. We recall the cry in the Eastern liturgies 'The doors, the doors!', which puts us on our guard, as does Mozart's music in the *Magic Flute*, where the prince Tamino must undergo rebuff after rebuff before one door opens to the Temple. The removal of the veil in the heavenly sanctuary does not imply that anyone can come at any time to any locked doors and unlock them. The happy End is not to be taken for granted.[16]

In Christian terms, the willing pilgrim must prepare for and undergo Baptism. This rite is altogether eschatological in its meaning. Its precursors, in and outside the Bible, stress the catastrophe rather than the ensuing safety. In the Flood mankind was overwhelmed, and even Noah only barely escaped with the aid of the Ark. Baptism never ceases to evoke the feeling of the cataclysm at the end of time, and in this way the Fathers of the Church have rightly understood the rite. Baptism is the fulfilment, the contradiction, of the devastating Flood which reduces all life to slime and death. Just as Noah hinges the two worlds—before and after the Flood—so Christian Baptism hinges the world of condemnation and death on the one hand, and that of forgiveness and life on the other. Baptism, as Justin pointed out, is the way of escape, for here is set forth the Resurrection of Christ and the mystery of man's salvation. It is the rite, as Origen developed it, which brings Rest (Noah=Rest) to the world-weary by covering them with watery burial and raising them to fiery glory. But this translation is not a magical rite, for the divine act presupposes man's penitence (the figure eight in the Noah narrative brings out the penitential symbolism of the ogdoad in Christian thought).

The watery burial not only washes away all the unreality of human life, the layers and poses which belong to the surface, but also exposes the real man to real things. Hence, to speak in terms of Jungian psychology, water itself is the archetype of the rising un-

[16] The finest modern exposition of the symbolism pertaining to the journey in the dark is to be found in J. R. R. Tolkien's trilogy, *The Lord of the Rings*.

conscious. The rite brings to the surface at last the innermost needs of the pilgrim made for eternity. Thus Baptism is not only a religious rite, but also a psychological drama, a dying and rising, an eschatological event in the Psyche. Here the symbol and the reality overlap in the unity of experience.

But the drama is not limited to the psychological sphere. The symbolism of the Flood enunciates not only what is done in, but for, man. First, there is the Ark, which Philo regarded as a type of the human body—the bitumen representing the soul, the animals the powers and passions. But such an allegorical interpretation does not fit the Christian scheme of things. The Ark is not body nor soul, but it is the corporate, eternal ship of salvation. On it Christ ferries his members to safety. Whereas the ferryman of classical mythology takes the souls of the dead charges across the Styx to the underworld, the Ark is the ship with a celestial destination which compasses the upper oceans. From the Ark flies, and to the Ark returns, the Dove; Tertullian in *De Baptismo* changes the significance of this traditional symbol of Israel to that of the peace-bringer from Heaven. The Dove becomes the emblem for the Holy Spirit which descends upon the baptized and sustains the death-to-life movement which they enjoy as a continual benison from above. It is not that they move themselves: they are moved. The principle of attraction is now stated in Christian terms: God himself, the Spirit, attracts men by dwelling in them and moving them through the promptings of Grace. Thus the upward movement is made and sustained of God.

The olive-branch is a particularly engaging symbol of the transformation of man. The deliverance of Noah ended with this token of peace on dry land; not so the Christian voyage to the End. The old type is transcended by the new reality, for the olive branch continually puts into the life of the Church the exquisite fruition of the divine philanthropy (Chrysostom's remarkable allegory). Again the emphasis is on transformation and away from mere status. The baptized are on the move towards an End in which love is as yet to be fulfilled in peace, and the olive-branch is the token of the promise, the spur towards the goal. All these symbols show—especially on the early frescoes of the second century—that the soul does not rise 'as by nature', but by Grace and Promise.

The progress of the pilgrim is a journey within as well as without: the sacramental symbols are not external milestones only, to indicate the distance covered on the heavenward journey, but serve as figures of the inward perfection attained. Ultimately the journey and the state of the traveller are as one. This principle of

13

the correspondence, between the objective reality and the subjective fruition of this reality, guarantees that we do not indulge in a free mythology or a world of fairytales where the hero traverses woods and fields, meets with gnomes and giants, fights with beasts, and enters enchanted gardens. The symbolism of the End, it is true, cannot dispense with these altogether and therefore may give rise to a suspicion that the Christian religion and *Alice in Wonderland* and the *Epic of Gilgamesh* are all the same in their pursuit of the unattainable, beyond the door, behind the high wall, and out of reach beyond the water. The symbols are, in fact, common to all humans, but in the Christian setting, which is a progress towards the Centre they are the outward signs of an inward reality.

From the Flood of Baptism, therefore, the pilgrim continues on his road to the consummation. He is now ready to enter Paradise, the original home of Adam, the state between earth and heaven, the garden where man is at home, to dig, to sow, cultivate, and reap the fruits of his endeavour. Paradise has been allegorized by almost all who have meditated on this elusive term, which implies work and life and earthly conditions on the one hand, and ease and enjoyment of a celestial kind on the other. Paradise recalls the golden age which no one has ever known except in his dreams. Paradise conjures up the perfect garden, the lyrical sight of flowers in blossom and streams trickling through mosses, of bird and insect life stirring in the hedges. Here it is agreeably warm and yet cool enough to keep away passion. Paradise is, in fact, the innocence that was, and is lost, the life that might have been, the concord which could have kept at bay every hand which lifts up weapons of destruction. Paradise, however, is not only the enclosure of all nostalgic regrets and yearnings—though it must be this romantic thing too—but also the final destiny without which all strife is chaotically meaningless. To enter here is a necessity, the fulfilment of hope.

The Greek-speaking Christians could not resist the allegorizing of Paradise. Philo had declared Paradise to be the name for virtue, the symbol which betokened wisdom; the trees are the virtues, the animals the passion, the woman the sensation, now happily blended into felicitous unity. Ambrose equated Paradise with the soul and referred to the four rivers as the four cardinal virtues. The allegories help to stress the inward connection between the symbol and the human condition. Unless the soul has attained itself to a co-ordination of its ingredients and can harness the passions and the sensations, as well as the virtues, to its spiritual self, it cannot present that harmony which will find in the world outside the place where all contradictions are reconciled. The blending of innocence and passion, of passive yielding and active desire, of female and male characteristics, agrees with the apocalyptic picture of the harmonious existence between savage and defenceless animals. Paradise is not a tidy park where every distinction is obliterated and life is regulated to such as an extent that the roses are 'painted' (a wonderful touch in *Alice in Wonderland* which brings out the artificiality of such a 'garden'); rather, formality and spontaneity—the two opposing principles in creation—blend, as in the soul, to produce something which is better than the old state of innocence. Paradise regained is not the old place, though it is also that: it is the fulfilment of the aspirations of Man, fallen, conscious, aware of good and evil, passionate and now disciplined by the higher good.

The Paradise of the End, therefore, embraces the idea of the harvest too. All the seasons are summarized in the symbol, very much as in Haydn's work *The Seasons*. But whereas Haydn ends on the melancholy note of decline and winter, so that the good things of the harvest will see the people through to the next spring, the Christian symbol of Paradise takes the best of each: the asperity of winter, the pulsating sap of spring, the full radiance of summer, the crop of autumn: all are gathered in. The harvest and the End are one. The symbol enshrines the truth that nothing is lost and that all inward treasures are imperishable and continue to contribute to the cultivation of the world with life. There is no end to this harvest.

The myth of Paradise is further rendered Christian by the Christians' acclaiming Jesus as the Gardener. Here again the metaphors are often used loosely, for Jesus is also the Vine, and Israel or the Church are compared to the Vineyard. The emphasis throughout is on fruitfulness and harvest. Growth alone is not enough: the End determines the value to be accorded to the growth. Christ acts as the life-giving sap and through him the garden is growing God-ward. No plant grows for its own sake but every individual growth finds its place in the wholeness of the garden. Christ imprints upon the formless garden the form of perfection. Therefore he is not only the life-giving principle but also the gardener who surveys, prunes, and directs the growth. The harvest is gathered by him, but it is not a harvest which is taken away, for when he takes he also gives, thus restoring the original rhythm of seedtime and harvest to the spiritual creation. In the Paradise regained everyone who gives of himself also receives himself. Thus the earthly event of growth and self-fulfilment are wholly transformed into the divine type of husbandry and service.

This concept of eternal life, i.e. of an ever-renewing seed and ever-continuing work, culminates in the Tree of Paradise, which is perhaps, as the focal point of the Paradise Myth, the most fertile source of symbolic interpretations. The tree stands firmly implanted in the tradition as the Tree of Life with which is contrasted the Tree which bears the fruit of self-knowledge, and therefore of death. Originally the two trees were probably one, but in Genesis ch. 3 one Tree brings life, another Tree causes the Fall. Upon the latter's stem there coiled the serpent and from thence issued the cause-and-effect: the serpent beguiled Life (Eve) and Life handed the fruit, sweet but disastrous, to Earth-Man (Adam). Under the trees the pagans discovered each other's nakedness; there played the harlots, worked the wizard, enchanted the sorcerers. The Tree and the cultus were indivisible. The tree symbolized sex. Yet the same symbol, just because it combined life and shame, also incorporated the genuine sap which rises to every branch, gives colour to boughs and fruit to the hungry: symbol of beneficence and of rising aspiration. The tree is royal and divine, full of mystery and consolation. Out of its roots comes Messiah, out of the stem of David comes the shoot of salvation.

Thus the Messianic use of the tree image depaganizes the fertility symbol and retains the upward sweep, by which the image combines the rooted earthliness and the flight to heaven. Here is more than a vertical line in the abstract: the living trunk with its rich foliage represents the organic striving towards the light. The symbol also combines the tragic destructiveness—for trees die, are chopped down, or burnt to cinders—with the theme of majestic growth. In the Bible it stands for the uprooting of evil, root and branch, and for the planting of good, trunk and crown. There is hardly a case history of dreams which does not relate to the fate of the tree, good or bad. From the point of view of psychology the tree is the classical example of an ambivalent symbol.

In the light of this welter of associations the Christian imagery needs to be more precise than usual, for without harnessing the tree to Christian revelation it might quite easily support the Gnostic theory that as the tree grows higher so the pilgrim through purified knowledge will reach heaven. The Christian tradition counters this easy assumption by linking the tree of Paradise with the tree of the Cross, 'one and only noble tree'. Here is a typical case of a symbol which is put into the crucible of theological criticism and comes out looking very different. In the light of the second tree, which also combines themes of shame with those of glory, there can be no question of natural growth and salvation by knowledge. Indeed, the knowledge which led to the first disaster is also responsible for the crucifixion: Christ who carries the Cross is the Saviour who is not known by those who are blinded in their own knowledge. By hanging on the tree Christ transforms the symbol of the Tree, for he himself is the true Root of Jesse and in him the tree of David alone continues to live. Thus he joins the earthly to the heavenly in his own person and those who enter Paradise find there the Tree of the second Adam, whose fruit no longer corrupts. The Tree in Paradise now stands for that knowledge of him who is the truth. The universal symbol of life had to be robbed of its mythical quality by the historical impact of the Cross, but the sacredness of that Tree—venerated even for its wood in relics—also establishes the truth of the symbol of man's attaining to the conscious knowledge of God—a knowledge which is not against, but for God.

The upward procession of man, then, is sustained by the downward condescension of God. From the garden of Paradise the pursuit of the centre leads to the walls of the City. The New Jerusalem is portrayed as eternally in heaven; it is not built on earth but it comes down to meet man. It is the celestial type of all cities, the pattern of community made perfect, the throbbing heart of every feeling and thinking society. The City is man's consummation of all cities because it is also God's City. Order and harmony feature the design from time immemorial. The symbol can only be fully grasped in its contrast to all the human perversions of corporate life. Earthly cities are essentially the parody of *civitas*, but the *urbs coelestis* is the dénouement of the Babylonian counterfeit. Jerusalem the New can afford to be free, for her freedom springs from her devotion to the truth. The whole Biblical history with its foundation, conquest, defence, betrayal, surrender, rebuilding, pomp, and lawlessness of Jerusalem stands in the background with concrete demands of justice and brotherhood.

The City symbolizes the universal victory of all the civic virtues, such as prudence and fortitude, without which mankind is degraded to a lawless mobb. But its very shape, its ramparts around the limits of the city, the towers and gates, also demonstrate that this *Polis* is a closed city and by no means the haven for all and sundry. The subtlety of the imagery cannot admit anything flavouring of vulgarity or demagogy; indeed the false gods of 'Bread and Circuses' are as alien to the conception of the City as the Babylonian pomp and the adulation of human government. The City is not a final term of flattery to our existent politics or a sanction of compromised politicians. This eschatological imagery, above all, lives by contrast rather than by analogy. Only in as much as our present institutions resemble the celestial pattern can we speak on earth of an anticipation of the City of God.

Yet, notwithstanding this necessary reserve, the City is the Fatherland of all true men. As we have seen, this idea of *Patria* is deeply embedded in human consciousness and to 'get home' is the desire of all. 'Light's abode, celestial Salem' attracts throughout the centuries all those who are fired with any vision of destiny whatsoever. It is more than any local fatherland, it transcends the natural instinct of wishing to return to the womb, although that instinct is certainly most likely to apprehend the City set on high. Again we can see how Christian symbolism transforms, and with it transforms our understanding of, the common symbolic forms. Patria is no longer the return to the point of origin, the beginning of the circle, the closing of another epoch, the goal which is also the starting-line. Instead, the very heart of the City is new, not yet visited, hardly heard of, beyond any conception or imagination. The splendour which attracts us here is the unprecedented. We may call it the fulfilment of all the shadows of reality which, on earth, we have perceived in the drama of liturgical worship. For this City is dominated not by a town-hall and administrative buildings, not to speak of works and offices, but all the streets lead in silent magnificence to the Throne and to the Temple. But Palace and Temple are no longer two different buildings, for at last the contest between secular and spiritual power has ended. The Throne is in the Temple.

Here the symbolism of the sanctuary almost sinks under its own weight, and we are not surprised that a dual tradition tries to convey to us the unspeakable. On the one hand the centre of the City is pictured to us in glowing terms of royal presence. The very streets are paved with precious stones, and gold, pearls, and jewels adorn the buildings. On the other hand we are invited to look more closely and, lo, there is no more Temple and God himself is amongst his people. The cultus is done away, for the Lord of the cultus is also the Priest of the heavenly sanctuary, the Son who eternally presents his offering to the Father with the glorious Spirit. The duality of the conception only serves to enhance the celestial glory of the whole cultic symbol: church, temple, pillars, throne, liturgy and altar are all caught up into the eternal pattern of the angelic, cherubic, seraphic homage.

This duality adumbrates the whole theme, for even the Rock on which the City is built fuses contrasts. On the one hand the Rock is the simile for the unchanging and avenging God, who crushes all under him and who bruises those who stumble upon him, and on the other, the Rock is the place of refuge from the storm. Again, the Rock is hard and unyielding, yet the Rock also provides water when struck in faith. The rock is unhewn and under the open sky serves as the altar for pagan sacrifices, yet it becomes, in our context, the orderly foundation for the City, the Cube itself, which mirrors all the perfections which man attaches to symmetry. Thus the picture of the divine society takes up the prophetic theme of the Rock which God has laid, be it as a foundation or to crown the building as coping stone which holds the walls together; the Stone, which the builders rejected, displays the right proportion, the eternal congruity of all parts from which beauty derives. Jesus is compared to this Rock, foundation and pinnacle of building, and the architectural figure promptly draws upon all the members of the eternal society as the stones with which the building is completed. This City, and above all the Temple in the City, is alive and the living stones, duly arranged in their fitting order, make up the walls. Thus this symbolism, not unlike that of the rays of light and their interplay, takes hold of the interpenetrating solidarity of all to bestow an eternal place to each.

It might be supposed that everything belonging to the world of stones, precious or ordinary, might fail to live up to the process of transformation without which eschatology cannot be portrayed. This is not so, for the stone, as indicated in the expression of 'the philosopher's stone', stands always for the human yearning for transformation. The alchemist seeks to make gold out of the vulgar material. Thus when Jerusalem is bedecked as a bride with smaragd, rubies, and other glowing crystals we have reached the journey's end in the search for transformation. The jewels express the heavenly fecundity expected of the bride, for it pertains on earth to pearls and shells to set forth the future fertility, the transformation to life through conception, pregnancy, and parturition. By adorning the heavenly Bride with precious stones this imagery of fertility is also translated from its associations on land and at sea to the final reality.

The final scene in the Temple abounds in cosmic symbols. All earthly appurtenances of worship are reinstated to unfold their meaning which, on earth, often failed to be made manifest. In this setting the living stones attend on the Lamb at the Banquet. On earth eating and drinking had, even within the setting of the Christian Eucharist, obscured the Communion with God, and the Liturgy had been severed from its correspondence to the heavenly reality. In Corinth, for example, even within the first century, members had gathered and stuffed themselves in accordance with their wealth and rank in society. Jung, the parson's son, describes in his Autobiography the boredom of a first Communion. Everywhere the Eucharistic rite has partaken of the sinfulness of the human condition, so much so that liturgical studies can never be pursued without the closest attention being paid to political developments and abuses. The history of the Reformation, for example, proves that the one rite (the Mass), which was designed to be independent from the flux of power politics, had, in fact, become the centre of military designs and conquest. The formula *Cuius Regio Eius Religio*, which at length brought peace to Europe, was an earthly compromise, which left the Latin Mass for the Catholic regions and the Lord's Supper in its various reformed shapes to the Protestant princes. Thus in every Christian land the Eucharist, instead of symbolizing unity and transcendent love, could not but demonstrate disunity and competing interests. The Table of Food and Drink is by its nature, as all symbols, ambivalent, for it brings together all the warring instincts of man. Communion may be for peaceful purposes, it may also be the prelude to destruction. The symbol of eating in its logical extension leads to the devouring tiger. The empty and unhappy non-loving self cannot fill others but would rather gnaw, bite, masticate, and digest so as to fill up the aching vacuum. The symbol of the banquet, however formalized in the Eucharist, and stylized in art, cannot disguise the depth of savagery which earthly reality throws up as against the eschatological hope of the Meal of the Good Shepherd, the Lamb's High Feast.

Our interpretation of the Banquet is not helped by the abundant evidence from the tombs of many races. Wherever the dead, or at least, the corpses of formerly prominent men, were not burnt or exposed to vultures, but carefully buried, their monuments contained vessels of all sorts which, among other things, provided food and drink for the departed. These provisions were, of course, only tokens of the sustenance which the dead would need in the world to come. Yet the custom itself draws attention to the materialistic conception of the hereafter. Among the rewards to which men looked was a doubling of all their joys on earth. If they had enjoyed good food and drink on earth, then, they judged, the celestial state must provide for an endless round of banqueting. The token foods and the jugs of wine in the tombs were themselves a symbol of the hope of such carousals.

The prophetic tradition had, however, stripped the symbol of the Messianic Banquet from such earthly expectations by insisting in the most uncompromising manner that 'man does not live by bread alone'. This anti-pagan slant did not intend to add opulent dainties to the mere expectation of bread. On the contrary, dainties came into the category of superfluous and harmful vanities. Bread became a symbol of the Word, the cause and sustenance of all real life. Similarly wine, condemned often for its abuse in drunkenness, was freed from its associations with intoxication and came to stand for the spiritual joys of life. The depaganization was completed in allegorization. On the one hand sinners were threatened with the Bread of Tears and with the Grapes of Wrath, whereas the righteous were invited to come forward to that banquet which only the clean and dedicated may share. When the call went out 'Come, buy, and eat: wine and milk without money . . . eat the good, delight yourselves in fatness!', it was directed to those who had by their decision already manifested a thirst for the spiritual and an appetite for 'real' bread. In this new tradition of the Kingdom of God a break is made with the natural which cannot satisfy. The earthly appetites and their foods always fail, always come to an end, always require replenishing: the celestial food is called 'angels' bread' because it lasts. Its nature is no longer material.

It may well be objected that such an allegorization kills the symbol altogether. If such basic patterns as eating and drinking and such direct images as bread and wine no longer mean at all what the words convey we reach the bankruptcy of the imagery. There is some justification in this criticism provided by history. The rise of Islam in formerly Christian countries certainly proves that the spiritualization of living symbols is beset with perils and that a diluted eschatology, above all, leads to an unconscious protest among the humble followers of religious belief. They do not consent to be fobbed off with empty promises: they want Heaven here, and Heaven hereafter. This demand assumes that the Marriage and the Banquet really take place and that the gratifications of appetites, already experienced on earth, must—only on a larger scale—be granted at the End. A superior smile at such materialistic literalism is out of place and only proves once again the gulf between sophisticated sublimation and literal End-hopes.

Historical considerations, however, rescue us from the horns of this particular dilemma. The pre-Christian sectarians, at Qumran and elsewhere, as well as the ordinary friendship guilds in Palestine, did eat bread and drink wine together in a way which owes nothing to the pagan mysteries nor to allegory. For them bread and wine were the real sustenence of the Kingdom of God and not metaphors for something else. As they met together in solemn assemblies they showed forth the perfect order and loving relationship which they held to be the ultimate reality. The Passover Feast, we gather, was more than a domestic banquet and not less than a Messianic Feast. The blessings over the unleavened bread and over the several cups of wine not only looked back to the past redemption, nor confined themselves to the present fellowship, but also looked forward to the future when the Sacred Meal would be consummated in the Reign of the Messiah. Against this background Jesus shared his life-giving sacrifice with his loved ones, but the Meal was also a real expression of what was still to come: the eternal consummation of the Kingdom. In the New Covenant bread was eaten and wine drunk, not as a memorial to a dead departed friend, but as an anticipation of the End. Until this consummation Jesus would not drink again of the vine. The 'Until' dominates the scene, and it is the 'Until' of the End which answers to the 'Now' of history.

The picture of the marriage-supper resolves the tension between the 'Until' and the 'Now'. Until the union of God with his people there remains the hunger and thirst, for the symbol of the Bread and Wine asseverates the lack of food, the famine and starvation of the waiting and enduring people of God. As a Sign of the End the supper reflects not so much the institutional life of the Church or the admitted pagan propensities of eating and drinking to excess, but rather the trials of the righteous. The consolation 'they shall hunger no more, neither thirst any more' obviously appeals only to those who have hungered and thirsted after a righteousness which eluded them, and not to those who had regular meals and more. The Messianic Banquet conjures up the sufferings of all the starved and maimed of mankind, who despite their sufferings did not abandon hope but looked forward to that hour when 'the Lamb which is in the midst of the throne shall feed them'.

If then the Banquet returns to the ancient theme of the vindication of the righteous it goes also beyond it, for it closes the epoch of ordeals and marks the turning-point towards the new Age when man is permanently sustained by God. Yet this sustenance, couched in the symbols of Bread and the Wine and centring upon the Lamb, is not to be separated from the mighty acts of God in Christ who declared himself to be the Bread and the Vine. Jesus the Bread is Jesus the Word: now the physical and the spiritual symbols blend in a new unity, the reality from which all temporal sustenance, as we know it under earthly conditions, is derived. Jesus the Vine is Jesus the Wisdom: the red juice of the grape prompts an awareness of Jesus the Lamb, the sacrificial victim whose blood poured forth from his open wounds. Thus Christian symbolism brings together all the different aspects of the atoning work of Christ as they are eternalized in the members of the divine society who gather round their Bread and their Wine and feast on Him. The conception of the first fruits heightens the mystical awareness of the Presence of Christ in each and all. The sharing in the Body and Blood of Christ, which on earth is a cherished but ambiguous institution, is freed from its anticipation and brought to the full realization. Sacrament becomes Reality.

At the feast the Host still remains Judge and King, thus checking the note of conviviality with the solemnity which pertained to the original night when the Last Supper was instituted. Then the man who was to betray the host was also at table. Since then many have followed the invitation who were not eligible. The final picture of the Feast, therefore, combines with that of the Judgement when the guests are scrutinized and some are rejected, while others are admitted. The Marriage Feast is, therefore, symbol also of the exclusiveness of the universal love and of the secret of God's will, choosing this one and rejecting that one.

This predetermined and inscrutable Counsel of God is symbolized by the age-old image of the heavenly Book. The art of writing in our ancient cultures was never divorced from the sacred sphere; in their scrolls men endeavoured to record and perpetuate the text of heavenly tablets. Wherever God was believed to have spoken by prophets, their heirs and successors formed a school and founded a tradition. The old is handed down, the new is added, and the result is the sacred scroll. Thus in Israel there grew up a veneration for the scroll, the sweet substance of the divine words, and when scrolls yielded to the making of books, these came to symbolize God's timeless speech. The book, however, does more than reproduce laws and prophecies: it predicts the future out of the divine wisdom, it unfolds the state at the End of the world. When men recite their liturgical texts out of the book they look back to the mighty acts in order to prepare themselves for this glorious future.

As all other symbols the book also suffers from abuse and dilution. Sorcerers and astrologists kept their records, long before the book became completely secularized and divorced from, and even opposed to, the things of the spirit. The book can betoken human ignorance, lack of understanding, hopelessness. Hence the apocalyptic tradition also acknowledges the existence of the book which is 'sealed', which no man can 'open', because no one can be found who is worthy to read it. The heavenly Book is only for the heavenly reader, for the inspired who comprehend the mysteries of God's election. Therefore Christ is appointed to open the Book and to pronounce the final Judgement out of it.

The Book, once opened and its contents proclaimed, divides men according to their names. In the heavenly book every name is recorded and the deeds of everyone are set against the names. Thus there is a Book of Life which records the names of those eternally predestined to Life, while the missing names imply exclusion and expulsion from the banquet. This use of the Book as a threat is, of course, well known from the world of dreams, where special fear is engendered by the experience of 'not finding' the needed text or spell. On the other hand, great relief is afforded by the guarantee of the written name, recorded and found in the printed page. The desire of men to see their names written in print certainly supports the image with authority even at a time when men have lost faith in Judgement.

The ambivalence of Judgement—rejection and approbation—is further brought out by the use made of 'vials' in the context of the final disclosure. From the vial there flowed the oil which made kings; from the vase were poured libations and costly perfumes, often in connection with the final rites of the dead. The smell of decomposition, which always seems to contradict the eternal destiny of man, could in a way be kept in check by the overpowering odours of Arabia. Thus the bowl of spices is an instrument used in matters of life and death, for it is the cup full of life-bestowing matter applied to the realm of decay. When the visionary sees the Lamb with the Book of Life unsealed he portrays the twenty-four elders prostrate before the Judge of the world 'having harps and golden vials full of odours, which are the prayers of saints'. The sweet fragrance of perfumes yields to the stark realism of Christian suffering, for the vials are, as all the other images, depaganized and tell of the Christians' struggle. Thus they become a symbol of division, for, in the hands of the avenging power, the truth, poured out of these vials, as from the scales of Judgement, falls upon the world of devilish tyranny and deceit. The vials, through their contents poured out from above, recapitulate the whole history of divine indignation and finalize the scornful contempt with which human history is shown in its nakedness. Thus the vials of the angels of wrath—symbolizing sickness, blood, fire, darkness, drought, pollution—correspond with the vials of the Saints who, standing beyond sickness, blood, fire, darkness, drought and pollution, have achieved the 'It is done', the triumph of the Lamb and, in presenting themselves to God, pour out the praise of the martyrs.

The Banquet, the unsealing of the Book, and the offering of the homage of the prayers of the Saints like incense, are accompanied by the fearful sounding of the angels' seven trumpets. Their piercing notes now convert the image of the Judgement to the sphere of music. It is a music of a special kind, for it has no strings nor soothing woodwinds in it. The trumpet combines the low-pitched, staccato, or prolonged note which used to summon the tribes to war as well as to feasts. The trumpet, whether actually a horn or the straight

trumpet of metal, as reproduced, for example, on the frieze of the
arch of Titus in Rome, is meant to give the certain, irrevocable signal
of alarm.   Now its military and cultic character is harnessed to the
sound of dread which chills the blood, for as it utters its threats it
sums up all the voices, thunderings, and earthquakes, which in
apocalyptic literature are the signs of that inner fear and trembling
with which man must meet his doom.   This is the music of the *Dies
Irae*—the *Tuba mirum spargens sonum per sepulchra regionum*—
which summons man before the throne.   The trumpet-call symbolizes
the timelessness of all events, for it rings through the ages whose
termination it announces.   It is the divine answer to the triviality of
life, the deafness of indifference, the refusal of the heroic and all-
transcendent.   Thus it has entered the Christian heritage as the one
symbol which requires no explanation though it has become separated from war and cultus.   It lives on in sacred and secular music.
The trumpeter in the orchestra gives vent to the long tradition of the
universal awakening to the finale.   In this respect the part played
by the trumpet in Beethoven's *Eroica* settles the validity of the
symbol for ever.

The musical part played by the trumpet also shows how the
note of the fearful judgement sounds at the same time the note of
relief, the hour of liberation.   Just as in the wars the final trumpet
announces victory to one side, and as in the cultus the trumpet
breaks in the New Year, and as in the Christian religion the trumpet
calls the elect to their victory and renewal—'for the trumpet shall
sound!'—so the trumpet announces in the soul the return from doom
to light.   Beethoven epitomizes this double validity when in his
Fidelio it is the trumpet which proclaims for the condemned
Florestan the advent of the Governor who will bring about retribution and speedy release.

The eschatological symbols stress with increasing vehemence
how great is the loss of the doomed and the gain of the saved.   But
all sense impressions of touch, taste, eye, nose, and ears fade into
nothing until they are focused upon the personal relationship, for
ultimately the loss is not of things but of love which permeates everything and comes from God.   The image of the Beautiful Lady, Virgin
and Mother, brings the paradox to the finest point.   It is used
sparingly in the Christian Apocalypse, but with increasing confidence
and devotion in post-Biblical times when the image of 'Our Lady'
becomes representative of all tender emotions, chaste desires, wise
thoughts, and the Church's perfection.   But this somewhat institutional respectability may obscure the apocalyptic fervour and place
of the symbol, and the world owes much to Michelangelo that in

the *Last Judgement* he boldly sets Her in the centre of the Judgement Scene, beseeching for mercy in the awful moment of the utterance of the Word which condemns. The image of the Lady, though rightly a personification of Wisdom and of the Church, ceases to be real when it is factory-made and sentimental. It evokes no transcendental marvel when it is part of the embroidery of harmless religious furniture. The Apocalyptic visionary, however, stands in the true tradition when he suddenly sees 'a great wonder in Heaven: a woman clothed with the sun, and the moon under her feet, and upon her head a crown of twelve stars'. These mysterious words raise the whole issue of the female symbol in religious history.

It is embedded in paganism. The worship of sexuality and fecundity, portrayed on so many temple walls and depicted in the figurines of the Ancient Near East, answered to the earthly passions. The cultus of the Divine Mother—Artemis in Ephesus, Cybele in Phrygia, Astarte and Anat in Syria, Isis in Egypt—offered fertility against bloody oblations and prostitution. The many-breasted goddess found her victims. The so-called chaste virgin huntress knew how to destroy. The Mother Image, far from extending assurances of cosy help, draws the children to their undoing. It is the open womb, source and origin of life, which after life-giving becomes an avenging pit, the dark shaft into which the insane hurl themselves in their need for protection. The Mother, in the unflattering opinions of all psychologists, has to be overcome if the child is to live maturely and independently, and before the advent of psychology Goethe used 'the Mothers' as a symbol of dread in *Faust* II.

The Judeo-Christian heritage knew no goddesses, on earth or in heaven. The God of the Lord Jesus Christ has no consort. The feminine symbol had been excluded with the prophets' victory and only the memory of the painted ladies, of the Jezebels, lingered on. The Apocalyptic visionary looks to the End when the mockery of lascivious religion shall be exposed in all its shameful nakedness. This exposure he paints in the fall of the personified Babylon. The great whore sits upon many waters as the universal representative of the consorts of power, the source of all spiritual fornication. The woman sits upon a scarlet coloured beast, full of names of blasphemy, having seven heads and ten horns. The allegory recapitulates the long tradition of the abuse of femininity. The woman is monstrous, for the archetypal monster supports her. The secular power in its totality—monolithic in power, but composite in its abuse—is not now the centre of our disgust, but the Woman allied with the Beast. She is the parody of beauty, colourful, impressive, in a blaze of purple; she sparkles with the sheen of gold and pearls; she is very rich. But she is the harlot and everything she holds is filthy. She is, like all goddesses, the antithesis to Virginity and Motherhood. She is neither chaste nor motherly affectionate. She bestows her favours promiscuously and for hire. She has no children and if she had she would smother them, beat them, torment them, sell them. She is the feminine principle of the devouring selfishness and utter vanity. She portrays the End of humanity in its artificial, commercial, and hard cruelty.

The symbolism ignores the finer shades and only knows black or white. In opposition to the grotesque Jezebel stands the sun-adorned Lady, the true Woman, the second Eve. This vision of the star-encrusted Mother of the Child has been indicted as a pagan pastiche, an intrusion which no Jew or Christian could have written.[17] But the figure is not an invention, a contrived image of a sun goddess, but rather the cancellation of the whole cruel imagery and its substitution by the genuine picture of the holy Virgin, the unique one, the Madonna of the Incarnation, who in holding her child shares in the Passion and in the sufferings of all mankind.

In the Christian setting, therefore, the image of the God-bearing Lady is not merely the reverse of the all-devouring Goddess, but the symbol is given its historical setting of Nazareth and Bethlehem. This Lady is none other than Mary, who conceived the Son by the Holy Ghost and laid him in the cradle of the manger. The Lady who is bedecked with the Sun, Moon, and stars is none other than she who stood under the Cross. The Lady who fled into the wilderness and in whose house the young Church met heads the throng of the innumerable saints. The humble little maiden, who said 'Be it to me according to thy will!', is the same as the mystic Rose, the Queen of Heaven, who eternalizes meekness and generosity, zeal and liberality, chastity and fruitfulness.

Few are those who can comprehend the final mystery of the God-bearing image. On the one hand the grip of history is heavily upon some, and in seeing only Mary-in-history they see a historical fact and repudiate her titles to honour. In doing so they deprive themselves of their own god-bearing image, the vital symbol, the inner experience, which leads out of objective history and mere facts to the eternal sphere of reality and love. On the other hand there are those who in ignoring the Christian setting of the Mother of Jesus in the Gospels forget that she is the Hebrew Lady of a Hebrew boy and would substitute the true image with a counterfeit of pagan origin. Thus the Madonna of many statues and of many pilgrimages still retains a great deal of human dross, and in the hands of

---

[17] Cf. R. H. Charles on Rev. ch. 12.

unscrupulous vendors and organizers the Virgin-Mother reverts to the days of Artemis and Astarte. Between these two errors—in which we detect the two enemies of symbolism: literalism and loose allegory —or rather beyond these two errors, lies the truth of the eternal Feminine which, in the person of Mary, has been redeemed and has been exalted. She who made herself a servant is Miriam, the Lady of the Sea, Mistress of all true human aspirations and devotion.

In that greatest of all eschatologies, in Dante's *Divine Comedy*, the Ascent is near its end when the pilgrim has passed through the nine Heavens of increasing glory and finds that his own God-bearing image, the loved and loving Beatrice, merges with the highest glory and light of the Virgin within the infinite circle of the petals of the snow-white Rose. Thrones with Saints dominate the picture, but there are still some vacant thrones, for the Celestial Rose is not yet filled to the utmost capacity. Here the symbolical passes, as it must, into mystical contemplation, for the End of all things is God. The master of contemplation, St Bernard, is the new guide of the pilgrim who falls into a stupor of amazement. The Virgin Mother is enthroned Queen, not to demand homage for herself, but to welcome the loving ardour of the heart in her angelic radiance. Here is the state of ecstasy, which mankind has darkened in self-love, made good again by the divine Transcendence itself, for the Virgin Mother is herself one of the redeemed humanity who in her adoration directs the rays of light to the infinite source of all goodness. She who never desired any glory for herself radiates the glory of him who is Glory.

In this mystical realm the symbolism of the End loses all its paradoxes, its shades of grim revenge and doom. Here the symbol becomes event, for it is freed from the limitations which we impose upon its truth. Here the symbol leads to adoration rather than comprehension, for the face, whose 'radiance alone can grant to thee the power to look on Christ', lifts up the pilgrim's gaze in the direct vision. In varying degrees of excellence all the children of God reflect the Grace which flows from the centre: Eternal Light which is the Love that moves the sun and the other stars.

PART IV
FORMULATIONS

CHAPTER XIV

THE DOCTRINE RESTATED

Symbolism relies upon mental pictures which, if successful, make visible the invisible. Symbolism relates a variety of complementary patterns and brings together contradictory images. Symbolism can bring within our grasp the incomprehensible by way of suggestion. It articulates in words what it evokes in feeling. It draws upon past and forgotten types and it opens the door to the unknown. Symbolism, therefore, is in every phase of its operation the direct opposite to doctrine in general, for doctrine avoids pictures, patterns, images, and types; if it speaks about the past, it does so historically, and if about the future, it fizzles out by the process of logical abstraction. This opposition of subject-matter is also often reflected in the masters of their respective crafts: the symbolists detest doctrine, especially Christian dogma (of the Protestant kind), the dogmatists do not especially try to understand what they suspect to be the obscurantist pitfall of imagery.

It may be assumed that none of our five interlocutors would respond favourably to the symbolism of eschatology. The Chairman should be most nearly engaged, but if we know his sort he would refuse to accept the impact of apocalyptic imagery. His rationalism would stand in the way of his imagination. The Psychologist would welcome the material as familiar old stuff, but he would sniff at the jump from neurotic symptoms and therapeutic possibilities to the theological inferences that things really are what they seem. The Protestant would like the Biblical descriptions but would most certainly jib at the thought that universal archetypes exist outside the Bible and inside the unregenerate mind. The Communist would just laugh in derision and let the mumbo-jumbo go with the rest of Capitalist clap-trap. Only the Catholic, if he be of a certain enlightened type, would comfortably behold the images in the mirror of humanity. As he insisted in the Dialogue, he would regard them as he regarded the arguments from behaviour, phenomena, thought, ethics, and aesthetics, viz. as analogies of being. But even he would think twice before he admitted the pictures to a process of ratiocination.

It is indeed questionable whether this process can still be upheld. May we, it must be asked, feed into the computer a series of pictures

in order to expect by way of return an orderly argument in the form
of sentences? Our doubts cover not only eschatology but all aspects
of Christian theology. The Gospels of Matthew and Luke, for
example, tell us about the birth of Christ in a sequence of well-known
pictures: can the dogmatists derive from them an abstract doctrine
of the Incarnation?

From the beginning the Christian affirmation—that doctrine can
be formulated and taught—rested upon an optimistic belief that the
human tongue is equal to some of the task. The Bible itself bore
witness to the eternalization of the event by the word, First Moses,
Isaiah, Ezekiel and others saw, then they apprehended, spoke, re-
peated, and finally wrote. The transformation of the picture into
the sentence grew up spontaneously and soon the word outstripped
the event in durability and significance. Similarly Christian doctrine
grew out of the preaching and by one generation's comment upon
what it had received. One may marvel now at the fecundity of the
dialectic of the centuries when men spoke lest their silence be
interpreted as indifference or cowardice.

In the last analysis the need of the moment gives authority to
doctrinal bravura. The symbolical patterns are not only there to be
enjoyed or chewed over, but they lie dormant in order to create
and interpret. The eschatological symbolism requires restatement
precisely because the one-sided 'here and now' dogmatism of the
twentieth century is likely to destroy us all, body and soul. An
all-too-dormant eschatology is a danger to our political and spiritual
health. But a doctrinal restatement needs buttresses stronger than
pragmatic considerations alone. It must test the veracity of the
apocalyptic imagery—and invite its criticism, even though it
attempts to convey its magnificence—by rendering in cool, detached
language the substance of its symbolism. The quest for truth
justifies the comparative tedium of a summary of nearly a hundred
theses: a tedium which is relieved, I hope, by the foregoing insights
into transcendental experience.

*   *   *   *   *

1.   The expectation of the End is part of the Christian Gospel
of Hope and not an optional article of belief. It must be preached
as the climax to the whole body of revealed truth. The End-hope
is not the preserve of cranks and sects, nor is its abrogation a sign
of sophisticated superiority. Christian eschatology is necessary to
the existence of Man as a rational, political, emotional, creative,
morally responsible, and religious creature. The needs of the whole
human race and the divine promise converge in the final fulfilment.

2.   Eschatology is not a formulation of fossilized beliefs but an attempt to systematize religious texts, traditions, and experiences which belong to Christian history, as well as to accommodate all elements of human activity and apprehension which contain an element of finality.

3.   The End is outside the realm of direct experience and cannot be demonstrated. It is 'not of this world', but rational analysis and an effort of the imagination can penetrate behind the curtain and speak with some authority on the future-behind-the-present. The End is not a realm of fantasy but a reality which may be explored validly, always on the supposition that we possess a critical sense which enables us to discern truth from fabrication.

4.   The trustworthiness of such a doctrinal formulation depends upon its inner coherence and its agreement with the general framework of doctrine. Particular statements made in one section of theology must not be incompatible with the whole. This interdependence provides therefore a check in the perilous field of apocalyptic thought.

5.   Such a regard for doctrinal coherence must not iron out what to us appear to be paradoxes and ambiguities. Theological language uses words which are taken from common experience transcendentally. This analogical use enables us to articulate theological propositions which go beyond merely negative assertions, such as 'God is not . . .'. But the anological use of terms—such as 'Father', 'Son', 'Love', etc.—demands a full dialectical awareness. The term 'End' is no exception: it must be seen as opposed to the Non-end and as related to many distinct ends which occur in human experience.

6.   This analogical use of the term End ensures that all doctrinal conclusions remain open to criticism and invite further discussion. Every statement—the 'I say' of St Thomas—is confronted by counterstatement—the 'They say on the contrary' in the *Summa Theologica*. This dialectic of Pro and Contra is particularly appropriate in eschatology.

7.   The term 'End' must be exposed to the general bombardment of possible relevant attacks. The present techniques of research will influence doctrine by setting a scientific tone. Moral axioms of the present age will create a mental climate. Yet it does not follow that all contemporary assumptions must necessarily be regarded as right in theological work.

8.   Apocalyptic thought has always tended to oppose contemporary and popular trends. This traditional opposition does not

exclude error, but if we expose the End-hope to modern demands we must also be prepared to reverse the process and expose modern postulates to the unchanging aspects of eschatology.

9.   While Christian doctrine may be forced to stand against contemporary thought it cannot be prepared to oppose facts which were not known to former generations. Statements about reality, which are as good as accepted as facts, must also be admitted as evidence. The new conceptions of the Universe, in as much as they come within this category, will change accepted traditions about the End and create a new climate of thought.

10.   The outstanding point of departure is the Copernican revolution—though not intended at the time to be revolutionary[1]— and the birth of modern astronomy. The impact of these is not lessened by the observation that we do not know when and how the material universe was created, nor how it is sustained, nor whether it will end. The enduring controversies and the crop of empirical data are not likely to change the heliocentric description of the universe nor the conviction that our solar system, in which the earth is a humble member among many planets, is only one among a very large number in our galaxy, and that our galaxy is only a member of a very large number of galaxies.

It is obvious that the doctrinal approach to the End cannot now be identical with that of St Thomas or anyone writing before A.D. 1600, for practically all the relevant conceptions about space and the position of the earth then held are now known to have been wrong. Only one conception really remains which, in a drastically changed manner, may still be called valid today, viz. the assumption that everywhere and at all times the physical universe is One in its framework of natural laws, so that what must be postulated to be real here will also be real there. Hence a modern eschatology need not jettison its confidence that we are on earth already physically members of a much larger world.

11.   The effect of the new world-view, however, is clearly designed to disprove details of eschatology in a very radical manner, if only because the whole naivety of the conceptions of 'Heaven above' and 'Hell below' is now seen to belong to the nursery of myths. This three-tiers universe is now dead. In the past writers, such as Dante, were in any case not content with a simple three-tiers arrangement, but evidently regarded the 'below-centre-above' division of space as a convenience and not as a scientific fact. There is therefore something a trifle exaggerated and humourless among the so-called 'de-mythologists', such as Bultmann, who would bracket

---

[1] As Koestler and others have shown.

Christian eschatology with Mythology, simply because it contains such terms as Heaven and Hell.

12.   Furthermore in defence of tradition it must also be remembered that a not inconsiderable body of writers in antiquity, beginning with Plato, seem to have held the view that the earth rotated around the sun.   The loss of the heliocentric hypothesis caused a grave setback in Christian theology, for this knowledge would have obviated some of the absurdities of the celestial and subterranean topography.   But error does not imply that all connected metaphysical axioms, held by traditional theology, are *ipso facto* to be discarded.   Thus the principles of correspondence—i.e. that the earth reflects realities found outside the earth—and that of teleology—i.e. that the earth exists for a purpose—need not be invalid because they are in medieval theology embedded in much erroneous non-science.

13.   The findings of astronomy can only be considered irrelevant to doctrine, and to eschatology in particular, if theologians disown an interest in the world as it really is and are content to theorize about an inner world which has no connection with the Universe. Such a view can be defended on the grounds that religion is a spiritual activity and that spatial categories are irrelevant to its concern.   But a purely spiritual concept, unaffected by categories such as stars and galaxies, is no longer traditional in any sense, since by virtue of the doctrine of the Creation the whole world is dependent upon God and included in the process of salvation.

14.   The scientific world-view must cause a conception of space in eschatology which altogether widens and transfigures the somewhat parochial traditional images of Heaven and Hell.   There are no 'below' and 'above' realms, nor Seven, Ten Heavens, nor an infinite number of graded spheres.   Instead the space at 'the End' is unimaginably large, immeasurable, and as far as we can give a name to it, infinite (though it may actually be 'finite' mathematically speaking).   Thus modern conceptions of space support the Biblical and traditional language which dwells on the incomprehensible nature of the Universe.

15.   A corollary of the new dimensions, which must widen eschatology beyond recognition, is the limitation of the concept of the End.   Whereas the pre-scientific theologian could hold quite happily that the trumpets would sound and the whole Universe quaver and melt in the final catastrophe no such view can now be entertained.   Instead it must be asserted that it is extremely improble that a Universe of these dimensions will be affected one way or another by human affairs.   If the earth, for example, were to suffer total destruction, either by natural means (collision or

explosion) or by human means (weapons so powerfully destructive that nothing can survive) it is less than probable that such a local catastrophe would cause physical effects beyond this planet. Again, if mankind succeeded in establishing posts on other planets of this solar system it might take its genius for destruction thither but again not beyond. Thus it follows that the old fantasy which dreamt of a world-cataclysm can no longer be entertained. But this limitation of the End to this earth and its inhabitants happens to have the advantage that the cosmic relevance of religion can now be apprehended in better ways. Instead of the wholly negative view of the Universe as a hostile force in a fallen world there comes to the fore the positive expectation that the Universe is part of the providential rule of God who links the destiny of man to its superb order.

16. This apparent restriction of the destructive element, by the elimination of the world cataclysm, merely restates the Biblical tradition that the Universe 'declares the glory of God' and that it is meant to be a permanent manifestation of spiritual energy. It does not abrogate that part of eschatological doctrine which dwells upon the re-making of all things and the restoration of man in harmony with the world, for the present interpretation of the Universe postulates that the process of creation is constantly in operation. Since the Universe is not a piece of clockwork which God has left to its own devices, but rather the Creation which he sustains with his Word and his Spirit, it is both more reasonable and in line with true eschatology to confine the notion of cataclysm to the world over which man has control.

17. This affirmation of the Universe must itself be limited by the fact that vast conflagrations have occurred and will occur in all parts of the Universe. Together with this elemental destructiveness of a dramatic kind we must also include the so-called running-down of energy or the principle of entropy. The Universe is therefore itself also the scene of a process of terminating 'Ends', just as it exhibits signs of creative energy. The absolute future of the Universe is unknown to both science and theology.

18. Traditional eschatology measured the 'Before' and the 'Hereafter' in clock-time. The story of the coming End was governed by cycles of time or world-epochs which, so it was thought, measure the history of all existence from beginning to end. Thus seven thousand years spanned the gulf from Alpha to Omega. This evaluation of time has become as meaningless—except as a parable—as the measuring of pre-Copernican space.

19. The effect of dimensional time on theology is comparable with that of space. On the one hand the perspective is widened to

an incomprehensible degree: the whole concept of world-epochs has to go, and with it the notion of a measurable concept of time in an eternal setting. Thus religious ideas like the Kingdom of God and Eternal Hope can no longer be contained within the narrow definitions of 'Before', 'Now', 'Hereafter'. The subtle distinctions of succeeding events in an eschatological time-table can no longer be regarded as meaningful. The theologian has now the enormous advantage that he need no longer concern himself with such problems as, for example, the relationship between the soul after death to its state after judgement. The refusal to provide a consistent thread on which to hang apocalyptic events does not imply an indifference to chronology as such.

20. The dimensional concept of Time makes it impossible for man to envisage an absolute End. We apply to the future our categories of duration, but this future, though calculated in thousands of millions of years, cannot reach an End in, or of, Time. Time is not an ontological reality, but ceases with the time-keeper. The end of Man, or even of all energy, is not the absolute End.

21. The absolute End can only be postulated as a transcendent event which God imposes upon the Universe. God can end time and space, because God is not involved in duration and extension. Finality is a term which is only meaningful when applied to God who is exempt from all transformations of energy.

22. By ascribing to God the power to end the known order we reiterate the tradition which views the End itself as a transcendental, i.e. supernatural and non-physical, 'event' by which God ushers in a new order of absolute cosmic perfection.

23. The End is therefore unique, comparable only to God's acts of Creation and Redemption. In the 'final event' God is the Subject who addresses Man the Object.

24. Man has knowledge of the End analogically. The knowledge of death, in particular, partakes for man of finality. Death is therefore the focal point of man's apprehension of Beginning and End.

25. The place of Man in the eschatological purpose does not derive from his position as an animal in the Universe, but from God's creation of Man in His own Image. The order and meaning of earthly existence reaches its climax in Man's destiny, for Man represents the apex, the 'break through', of Being in creation.

26. The fallen state of the human race partly explains the forward movement implied by eschatology. The Son of God Jesus Christ has already attained to the Order which lies beyond the future. It is towards the Adam re-made that Man moves by the Power of

the Holy Spirit. Man is not the maker and measure of, but Christ draws Man towards, his fulfilment.

27. The central place assigned to Man in Christ does not contradict the importance given to angels in the final state. As it is difficult to contemplate even now a world empty of intelligent beings, i.e. in other parts of the Universe, Man cannot be the sole inhabitant of the world to come who can respond consciously to Reality. The belief that Man is not alone in the Universe runs consistently through the Christian tradition. The Beginning and the End of creation includes a spiritual order, namely of Seraphim, Cerubim, Thrones, Dominations, Virtues, Powers, Principalities, Archangels, and Angels. An identification of these hierarchies with life on other planets is not to be entertained.

28. The supernatural basis of eschatology blends with a strongly historical expectation of future developments. History has a more direct bearing upon the End-hope than scientific hypotheses and philosophical analysis. Sandwiched between the wide, open, uncharted spaces of an eternal topography and the narrow, closed, and specific earthliness of history, it is the spiritual activity which links the latter to the former, turning historicism into expectation.

29. In this Christian tradition there is kept alive the hope of the End of history which coincides with a Return of the Lord Jesus Christ from Heaven. This *Iterum Venturus Est* cannot be stated in terms of literal materialism or of metaphorical spiritualization. It was originally understood as the conquest of history. The Return of the Lord is the symbol of victory over historical evil.

30. The Return of the Lord is the manifestation of divine Judgement with power. This exercise of triumphant goodness is universal, for the defeated hostile powers on earth represent the whole force of the supernatural principle of evil.

31. Christian eschatology, by holding out the hope of the conquest of hostile forces in history in a final onslaught, foreshortens the clash between good and evil. It belongs to the tradition to identify the Enemy in the passing framework of history and to discern Antichrist on earth.

32. Antichrist wears a mask of Christ and his kingdom is the counterfeit of truth. Antichrist changes the supernatural future into a radical ideology of this-wordly power, bestowing omnipotence upon a totalitarian society in which materialistic ungodliness and licentiousness flourish. It is the state of the self-seeking rich, the oppressive and boastful. In our day the spoliation of the countryside, the pollution of the waters, the slaughter on the roads, the defilement of cities, the pervasion of everything with noise, the build-up

of military stockpiles, condition human life to the dulling accompaniment of television and radio. This inhuman compulsion of the human spirit portrays the rule of Antichrist.

33. Warfare, mass extermination, torture, starvation exhibit the demonic quality of the Antichrist in history. In these outrages the fallen powers externalize their inward rebellion against God and use men as tools for their purposes.

34. The End-hope is the only weapon left to men wherewith to defeat the victory of Antichrist, for eschatology furnishes the victims with a trans-historical reality in which history—with its dark symbols—is overcome. Evil is relegated to the temporal level, as opposed to eternal reality; the worthlessness of Satanic power is seen against the sovereignty of God, the earthly rule of the Beast is opposed by the celestial glory of the God-Man, and the victims receive the consolation of vidication. This conquest is one of Faith.

35. The evidence for this supra-historical Faith is found in history, for history itself provides its own judgement, showing by its results that the triumphs of ungodliness are passing. In retrospect the idols of the masses are seen in their contemptible nothingness, for the monstrous nature of the crimes also reveals, in subsequent trials, the incredible hollowness and stupidity of the actors.

36. In contrast to the exposure of the devils stands the evidence for the victory of the martyrs. The long line of names testifies to the possibility of the conquest over demonic compulsion. Men and women, and even children, prove that in considering the End they can through death make good their escape from the shame of historical existence.

37. The final conquest of history resides in the principle that history is not endless, as a succession of events, but ending and therefore meaningful. The evolutionary advance from the cave to the technical society leads, owing to a failure of moral control, to a final break-down in history. But this winding-up of the historical process also marks the dawn of the new age.

38. On the level of historical existence mankind is condemned; the approbation of human existence comes from without the historical sequence. In saying 'No' to the things that are, Eschatology pronounces a 'Yes' to the future, to the things as they ought to be. The End-hope justifies the moral assumptions from which condemnation and approbation derive.

39. The eschatological judgement is not the product of a moral superiority on the part of religiously inclined experts, nor the ill-humour of soured failures in the world, but the evocation and demonstration of divine justice.

40.   God's Justice manifests God's triune Being in a dynamic manner.   It authorizes law, inspires righteousness, and rebukes sin. Mankind is in a state of condemnation until the End of historical existence, in as much as human nature is drawn to sin.   The Ten Commandments and the seven so-called Mortal Sins describe the field of wrong-doing appropriate to historical existence.

41.   The end of this existence is non-existence, and Death is therefore the natural end of mankind.   Since 'all have sinned and fallen short of the glory of God' all men are liable to extinction.

42.   This universal annihilation is cancelled by God in the intervention of Christ who by his sacrifice on the Cross has reconciled Man to God for eternal existence.   The condemnation of mankind is annulled in the approbation of Christ whom God raised from the dead.   Thus an event in history has rescued man from non-existence.

43.   Although Christ is central to Man's salvation it does not follow that all who claim allegiance to Christ are automatically saved and that all who are outside the Church are necessarily condemned.

44.   The End-hope embraces the whole of mankind with a future of condemnation and salvation.   Heaven and Hell are not Christian prerogatives but constitute a universal truth.

45.   Salvation and Condemnation are not events external to Man.   The forensic setting of indictment, trial, prosecution, defence, judge, verdict and sentence is the outward scene in which tradition expresses the universalism and objectivity of the inward experience of the End-hope and End-fear.

46.   In the process of Judgement every individual appears not only as himself but also as a member of a family, tribe, race, nation, party, place of employment, culture, technical environment, and religious society.   Thus every individual brings to the Judgement a reflection of the corporate body.

47.   While the Impersonal outlives the individual on earth and has a greater claim to lasting importance than any individual on earth, only the Personal can be held accountable in Judgement.   It is the Judgement which bestows upon personality an inherent and permanent worth.

48.   The abiding worth of individual personality derives from its potential apprehension of God.   Whereas institutions and techniques are subject to permanent change, only the human spirit can come to fruition in eternity.

49.   It is impossible to locate the so-called nucleus of human personality which represents a person for eternity.   There resides, however, in persons the transcendent capacity for truth, goodness,

and beauty which lifts the soul out of its immediate and perishing environment.

50.   This estimate of personality, however, does not exclude those members of the human race who appear to hold no link with this transcendent world.   All men must appear before the Throne of God to give an account of themselves, irrespective of their wishes and talents.

51.   Unlike St Thomas we have no longer to answer the question at what age and in what circumstances the dead are raised by pointing to a specific date in the physical and mental flux which features man's passage from birth to death.   In the ever-changing constitution of the body the real self expresses itself in desire.   This desire emanates from the soul and furnishes the body with a continuum throughout its life span.   This continuum the Bible calls the Face of Man, and some writers credit the eyes with man's seat of perception from which there radiates the personal and living desire, while others fasten on the heart as the centre of the will and the emotions.   The whole personality is formed by the sharply engraved imprint of free decisions which the character of man registers, as in the making of a portrait; in this cumulative acquisition of character the brain acts as the centre of passive responses to, and active stimulations of life. There is then a total residuum of permanent human personality which is known by its manifold and complex desires and which hastens on to its End as a given goal.

52.   The condemnation of wickedness and of the wicked at the Last Assizes presupposes the immense complexity of personality, to be exposed to final scrutiny.   Such an assessment of character is known to us on earth in part from analytical psychology, which deals with material sunk deep down into the unconscious and brought back to the surface by the narration of dreams, painting, or other acts of free association.   Unremembered acts and desires of the past, together with their frustrations, are carried forward into the future. Whereas religious self-examination never gets beyond remembered sins the scrutiny of personality as it really is discovers the deep motivation of guilt.

53.   The final Judgement on personality is therefore the crisis of Man at the point of his real existence.   The self is not judged only for acts committed or omitted, but for the controlling desires which prompted these acts.   Hence the act of Judgement is not so much a trial in a court-of-law but a confrontation of the self with reality.   In man's self-exposure he is measured not only by his works but by his innate reality.

54.   The Judgement is the fulfilment of all human desires since

the most deep-seated of all is that of receiving approbation. Judgement is not entirely forced upon us from outside but consistent with our attitude to life, which consists of what St Paul called 'Boasting' or 'Justification'. This Boasting is nothing else but the wish of baby and child to be in all things approved and praised, and of the adult to be found in the right.

55. This desire for approbation establishes not only our characteristic attitude to God, the world, and ourselves, but also the aggressive will to power which always turns to destructiveness, whether in fantasies or acts of violence. This murderous and suicidal aspect of self-justification may be equated with original sin, the inevitable residue of guilt in the common state of personality. Man comes therefore to the Judgement as a paradoxical creature, who in trying to please brings to exposure a self which deserves condemnation. In seeking approbation he finds condemnation.

56. In this final spectacle of the divided personality wickedness and sin co-inhere and cause the deformity of the real self. The condemnation of this deformity agrees with the final approbation of virtue, for only by exposing the delusions of unreality can the integrated self exist. Judgement is an act of healing.

57. The therapeutic nature of Judgement enhances the seriousness of this searing process of the 'dividing asunder of soul and spirit . . . naked, manifest, and open'.[2] The fear of the Judgement is the fear of pain. But the conception of punishment in Judgement is not confined to pain, administered from outside, authorized by God, and inflicted by demons. The nature of the punishment is as complex as are the delusions under condemnation.

58. Earthly forms of punishment and pain are relevant only in a very restricted manner. Retributive measures and exemplary threats are clearly meaningless when the innermost causes of conduct are exposed. The dread of the Judgement lies in the fact that man can make no satisfaction for the past.

59. The act of condemnation, inevitable as it is, points towards restoration. As on earth the patient needs to be made aware of himself as he is, and must learn to accept responsibility and give up delusions, and in so doing turns on his own past and accepts atonement and reconciliation which are not his own, so the final condemnation has in it the possibility of reconciliation and restoration.

60. This inner act of acceptance is not the sorting out of oneself in a Paradisical clinic nor a merely subjective decision for self-improvement, but it is objective justice forced upon man. The coercive element is painful, though for the good of Man.

[2] Heb. 4, 12–13.

61. The quality of the 'torment' is known to us through earthly analogies: tension, pressure, friction, burning, etc., on the physical plane, loss of liberty and other privations outside the physical plane. Pains may be distinguished by the intention which are their cause. The eschatological pains are part of a necessary good and coalesce, by anticipation, with the final joys.

62. The pangs of the New Age are not only inflicted on, but also sought by, Man who is condemned to be restored, for the Restoration of Man takes part in the rhythm of Judgement as prefigured in the Bible: Exile and Return, Death and Resurrection, Crucifixion and Glory. The human will is perfected by finalized mortification.

63. The Perfecting of Man does not stand in isolation but is flanked with loving relationships. Hence prayers confirm the interdependence of all men and good works the validity of personal ties. Eschatology not only condones but requires the extension of prayers and good works into the eternal scene, for they are tokens of successful self-transcendence.

64. The growth in perfection presupposes an interim-state. Such a state—whether called Purgatory or by some other name—used to be inferred from premises now outdated, such as the time between the death of the individual and General Judgement, or between the Millennium and the Final Reign of God. The real reason for the postulate of an Interim State is to be found in the potential perfectibility of Man.

65. The interim-state must not be confused with the so-called 'Second Chance', i.e. a wholly untraditional speculation that sinners may alter the course of their lives through new decisions. On the contrary, the necessity for the interim-state arises out of the ethical impasse that good decisions failed to reach fruition on earth. The life which is meant to develop Christ-like perfection cannot be contained in a static, frozen End.

66. The interim-state and the possibility of perfection depend upon the existence of Heaven and Hell as the final transcendent poles of reality. These symbols eternalize all religious distinctions and aspirations.

67. The concept of Hell raises the greatest difficulty because the Christian Religion is not dualistic. Hell as an eternal realm of evil is unthinkable.

68. The reality of evil, however, is such that it cannot be disposed of as the *Privatio Boni*, rendering Hell a harmless figure of speech. Evil, as exhibited in man's shadow self and symptoms of mental disease, as chronicled in the history of the degradation of

man, and as practised as rebellion against God, is felt as the absence of God.

69. There is no reason to deny that evil will undergo punishment proportionate to its wickedness. The punishment consists of the exposure of the depraved will to the light of God. In its preference for darkness the evil will dwindle into the orbit of nothingness. This process of damnation, begun on earth, reaches its ultimate after death in deluded self-love, impotent destructiveness, loss of personality, and the total absence of Grace.

70. The only claim of such evil and its punishment upon an eternal 'place' is that it is remembered as past and overcome. The victory over supernatural evil does not commit us to a belief in the eternal existence of nothingness.

71. The vindication of the righteous and the triumph of the Church do not support the belief in eternal damnation. The state of perfection shrinks from finding any joy in the perpetuation of the sufferings of the wicked. On the contrary, the spectacle of the damned in eternal torment clashes with the vindication of righteousness and the joys of Heaven.

72. Our revulsion against eternal damnation, as given in unending torment, does not imply the revival of the ancient Origenist heresy of universal salvation. The *Apokatastasis* of the devils and the submission of Satan to God cannot be entertained, for the total absence of Grace, freely rejected and persistently outraged, is not a temporal accident but a metaphysical fact which disallows a return to reality.

73. The fear of condemnation is not conducive to good actions and is not an instrument of education of any value. The prospect of torment and punishment may even attract the unbalanced and feed their sadistic and masochistic tendencies. History gives many examples of ruthless tyrants who laughed the idea of subsequent punishment to scorn. This does not mean that they were right, but it shows the inherent weakness of moral threats. Hell as an eschatological threat does not serve as a moralizing concept.

74. On the contrary the incentive of eternal rewards as a first step towards the affirmation of the future can be maintained without qualms. A positive and wholesome goal gives direction to the good will, especially when operating under strain. The Principle of Hope is a rational and emotional part of life and its transcendent apprehension of the future does not contradict the needs of human personality.

75. The justification of the Principle of Hope rests, however, on the objective reality, which is called Heaven in theological dis-

course. Heaven must not be viewed as the counterpart to Hell. Our fondness of symmetrical arrangements, if apt to suggest a God-Satan, Heaven-Hell, Good-Evil parallelism, must be resisted. Just as Satan is the personification of nothingness, so Hell is the spatial and temporal figure of nothingness. Heaven, however, is not the figure of reality, but it is the divine order from which, and in which, all reality co-inheres.

76. Heaven is the word for all real perfection, existent apart from human apprehension and articulation; it expresses all that lies beyond human experience as the fulfilment of that experience. Heaven is thus not only the End which succeeds all human space and time, but it is the objective and eternal dimension which bestows meaning and eternity on all partial intimations and endeavours of humanity.

77. Heaven, being the term which represents perfection and fulfilment of all transcendent desires, is nevertheless not solely the traditional *Patria* for humanity, but it is also the cosmic consummation of reality. Heaven is not a man-centred universe projected into eternity but the total reality in which mankind has by God's Grace found a 'place' in common with such myriad forms of reality as are to us as yet unknown. Thus a hierarchy of Being, not human but related to Man in perfection, makes up the eternal Reality.

78. Heaven being this eternal Reality and fulfilment of all right human aspirations is by no means to be confused with God. Although sometimes the Christian tradition uses the words imprecisely and makes Heaven = God there can be no such identification. God is subject, heaven object, in the transcendental relationship: God made it, sustains it, sees it, and fills it. He is the Lord of Heaven. The triune God is above the Heavens, as Creator and Lord. Heaven is therefore the End of man since it is the appointed reality where man can apprehend in a variety of ways the Glory of God.

79. This celestial End has been gained by Christ in that he 'cleansed' the Heavens from the defilements of angelic evil. Reality, in God's eternal design, is incompatible with all forms of evil and Christ has already completed the final conquest of transcendental enmity. The celestial reward is none other than a conscious and joyful share in the triumph of Christ and in his cosmic reign.

80. Christ's subjugation of Death has brought into existence for man not a survival of his faculties but the resurrection of himself into a new world. The vindication of the righteous and their approbation for eternity lies beyond present human experience. The Resurrection of the Flesh as a dogma merely insists on the abiding

15

identity of Personality in the progress from Glory to Glory. It has nothing to say on the decomposition of the earthly body or the disposal of corpses, for it expects the soul to be clothed with a celestial body. This body is alive with the former activities brought to perfection. The risen man can see and hear in a way not possible on earth. It can move and penetrate its new world. On the other hand it no longer requires anything outside itself and is prompted by no instinctive need, except to continue in its love and service of God.

81. The End of Man envisages a continuity with earthly aspirations and a discontinuity with earthly occupations and needs. The concerns of property and self-defence cease to exist, but the new life is still human in the pursuit and cultivation of loving relationships. The highest good consists of a state of active rest in which God is worshipped in company with the whole family of the redeemed and glorified, who reflect the Love which they have received. The Deification of Man is not Man's usurpation of God's unique sovereignty but his attainment to the *Summum Bonum* to which God has called him in Christ.

82. The transcendental nature of Heaven does not preclude it from being more than a philosophical concept of perfection. Heaven is the End of all simple goodness, the childlike hopes of man, the enjoyment of the universe of nature as given to us in flowers, the intimation of rest given in sleep. In as much as our natural desires on earth transcend our immediate selfish designs they also find fulfilment in eternity.

83. More particularly does Heaven give the seal of eternity to our religious activities and apprehensions. There is already on earth a way of self-transcendence which reaches its highest expression in ecstatic enthusiasm. This way, often abused and engendering pagan worship, if inspired by the Spirit of God and made subservient to the truth, finds in eternity a positive reality to which it has an affinity.

84. The ascetic way of perfection by denying itself gratification on earth in food, entertainment, sensual pleasures, and by putting a bridle on its natural desires, also attains to perfection and fulfilment in eternity, in as much as the restraint, discipline and deliberate creation of a vacuum made in time can, like an empty vessel, be filled with that newness of life for which the old life had been an appropriate preparation. Thus the principle of sacrifice is seen to lead not to loss and denial of life, but to gain and affirmation.

85. The continuity of experience is foreshadowed in the partaking of the Sacraments on earth. In Baptism the re-birth to

spiritual Christ-likeness prefigures the status of the eternal humanity, and in the Eucharist the transcendent Christ lifts the community to the celestial altar and sanctuary, from which every Eucharist receives form and content. The Eucharist is, therefore, an institution on earth which will not cease in eternity, in as much as the celebration of God's Mysteries in the Death and the Resurrection of Jesus Christ is the focal point of the eternal redemption. While the imperfections of ritual and other shortcomings of liturgy belong to our earthly disorder and must, together with it, vanish, the heavenly liturgy, freed from spatial and temporal limitations, unites men and angels with God in felicitous harmony.

86. The Presence of God in the final state of mankind is the reason and form and content of existence. The radiation of God's Light never diminishes His Essential Being and is reflected in the many grades of perfect felicity. The union of Man with God shares in a totality of blessedness which is continually sustained by the work of the Holy Spirit.

87. This reflection of God in the in-Godded brings to fulfilment the life of individual love and of all individual strivings on earth. Love on earth never fails to raise problems of separation, for all loving relationships are subject to imperfections and to natural partings. Thus parental and marital affection, even when guarded by absolute faithfulness, have in them the germ of failure just because of the transcendent nature of personal love. The fact of human mortality always seals on earth the transitory character of loving and being loved. Love on earth defies definition and resists permanent consummation. The act of loving is bound up with acts of non-loving, hesitations, and even exclusions. Love is never known apart from those very conditions which militate against its fullness. Thus love on earth is never free from a tragic content, isolation, and lack. The eschatological affirmation of God's consummation of blessedness in himself is also an affirmation of the eternalization of human love. It gives dogmatic sanction to the universal anticipation of lovers and loved that eternity provides them in God with an eternal consummation of loving relationships. But this consummation is not a mere repetition of intimate relationships but an all-embracing divine Yes to all human loving, free from exclusive ties and prejudices. The in-allness of Christ, i.e. the mystical indwelling of Christ in his Church, while retaining the precious diadem of personality, integrates the countless jewels into the corporate adornment of himself.

88. This consummation of all love also perpetuates all services rendered and all values cherished on earth. The promise that nothing

will be lost is fulfilled in the preservation of all human endeavours approved by God. Music, poetry, and art belong to the eternal reflection of the divine perfection and do not perish.

89. The concept of consummation does not limit the endless increase which is implied by Love and Light made perfect, for it belongs to their perfection that they never cease to grow since they reflect God's Being. The eternal union—which is not absorption—does not maintain a static relationship but creates an ever-wider sphere of glory.

90. In this setting of cosmic perfection the Kingdom of God sets forth the Power of God as the hierarchic principle in which the lower serves the higher to the constant joy of both. The earthly abuses of power, which have made power one of the most obscene distortions of reality, are now seen in their absurdity and worthlessness. The principle of true power is, however, already visible in the cosmic order of the Universe. The End is also the beginning of the glorification of this created order, so that all parts of the Universe reflect in their parts the Light-Love of the Whole. In the display of true order the ideal is the real.

91. The remaking of the world according to God's Law does not brush aside the Sacrifice which has achieved the vindication of truth and love. In the centre of all sacrificial loving and giving stands the Crucified as King and it is he who heads the throng of martyrs and men defeated in the cause of righteousness on earth. The meaning of human history is at the End made clear by the simple act of reversal: the abasement of the proud and the exaltation of the humble. The Christ-death is only now seen to be also the Christ-life, and it is this blend of the tenderest sorrowing and consolation which tradition associates with eternal life. The place accorded to the Blessed Virgin Mary and to the Saints in the future assures us of the constancy of Christian feeling in the vastness of eternity.

92. This recapitulation of all things under Christ implies that the End is not the savage ending of all things but their return to the Source. The fragmentation of energies and the errors of appearance end in the gathering-up of power and truth in Christ, the Fullness of God's Word and Wisdom. Of this fullness men had already received rays of light, as in contemplation and mystical prayer. But then the Glory of God concealed his Being. After the End the Vision of God is direct and life-giving.

93. In this new world Reality is now seen through the mind of Christ and what was hitherto only known as absence of energy, or as a vacuum in the experience of solitude and dark silence, is now apprehended as eternal peace. The complete accord of the creation

with God renders all relationships and activities serene, for all contradictions are cancelled in the vision of the One.

94.   The final harmony is such that no positive affirmation in
human speech is left to describe it, in as much as the simultaneity of
all things seen in God can only be expressed in negative terms.   In
the last state there is no division between event and meaning, between
reality and apprehension, between activity and passivity.   At the
end stands the great simplification of the supreme Oneness of God
comprehended by the Spirit-filled and in-Godded.

95.   When the desire of all rests in the attained Good, when the
End is with the Beginning made One in Christ, and when the Christ
and the Spirit within the Glory of the Father establish the final
ecstasy eternally, then at last everything outside God enters into His
Majestic Love with adoring gratitude.

BIBLIOGRAPHY

P. Althaus, *Die Letzten Dinge. Lehrbuch der Eschatologie*, 1957.

J. Auer, *Das Eschatologische, Festschrift Kardinal Faulhaber*, 1949.

J. Barr, *Biblical Words for Time*, 1962.

K. Barth, *Church Dogmatics*, esp. vols. III/2, III/4, IV/2.

G. R. Beasley-Murray, *Jesus and the Future*, 1954.

J. A. Beet, *The Last Things*, 1897.

N. Berdyaev, *Slavery and Freedom*, 1943, Pt. IV.

E. Bevan, *Symbolism and Belief*, 1938.

E. Bloch, *Das Prinzip Hoffnung*, 1960.

C. D. Broad, *Lectures on Psychical Research*, 1962.

R. Bultmann, *The Theology of the New Testament*, 1955.
History and Eschatology, 1957.

E. Cassirer, *The Philosophy of Symbolic Forms*, 1953.

R. H. Charles, *The Pseudepigrapha of the Old Testament*, 1913.
Critical and Exegetical Commentary on the Revelation of St John. 1920.

N. Cohn, *The Pursuit of the Millennium*, 1957.

O. Cullmann, *Christ and Time*, 1951.

J. Daniélou, *From Shadows to Reality*, 1960.

C. H. Dodd, *About the Gospels*, 1958.
New Testament Studies, 1953.
The Parables of the Kingdom, 1936.
The Background of the New Testament and its Eschatology (ed. W. D. Davies and D. Daube).

M. Éliade, *Images and Symbols*, 1961.

A. Farrer, *A Rebirth of Images*, 1949.

J. E. Fison, *The Christian Hope*, 1954.

H. Frankfort, *Before Philosophy*, 1949.

E. Fuchs, *Zur Frage nach dem historischen Jesus*, 1960.

E. Goodenough, *Jewish Symbols in the Greco-Roman Period*, 1952–6.

K. Heim, *The World: its Creation and Consummation*, 1962.

L. Hodgson, *For Faith and Freedom*, 1957, vol. II, ch. 11.

C. J. Jung, *Symbols of Transformation*, 1956.

K. E. Kirk, *The Vision of God*, 1931.

R. A. Knox, *Enthusiasm*, 1951.

W. G. Kümmel, *Promise and Fulfilment*, 1957.

P. L. Landsberg, *The Experience of Death*, 1953.

V. Lossky, *The Mystical Theology of the Eastern Church*, 1957.

A. Malraux, *Metamorphosis of the Gods*, 1960.

J. Marsh, *The Fulness of Time*, 1952.

P. S. Minear, *Christian Hope and the Second Coming*, 1954.

T. W. Manson, *Studies in the Gospels and Epistles*, 1960.

S. Mowinckel, *The Psalms in Israel's Worship*, 1962.
He That Cometh, 1956.

W. Nigg, *Das Ewige Reich*, 1944.
W. Ölsner, *Die Entwicklung der Eschatologie von Schleiermacher bis zur Gegenwart*, 1929.
J. Pelikan, *The Shape of Death*, 1962.
J. A. T. Robinson, *In the End, God . . .* , 1950.
    Jesus and His Coming, 1957.
W. H. Salter, *Zoar, or, The Evidence of psychic research concerning survival*, 1961.
P. Schütz, *Parusia, Hoffnung und Prophetie*, 1960.
U. Simon, *Heaven in the Christian Tradition*, 1958.
    The Ascent to Heaven, 1961.
E. Staehelin, *Die Verkündigung des Reiches Gottes in der Kirche Jesu Christi*, 1951.
G. J. Whitrow, *The Natural Philosophy of Time*, 1961.
A. Winklhofer, *The Coming of His Kingdom*, 1963.
A. N. Wilder, *Eschatology and Ethics in the Teaching of Jesus*, 1950.

Articles on Eschatology and related topics in :
    Dictionary of the Bible.
    Die Religion in Geschichte und Gegenwart (2. and 3. Auflage).
    Encyclopaedia of Religion and Ethics.
    Jewish Encyclopaedia.
    Reallexikon für Antike und Christentum.
    The Catholic Encyclopaedia.
    The Oxford Dictionary of the Christian Church.
    Patristic Greek Lexicon, ed. G. W. Lampe, 1961.
    Scottish Journal of Theology, Occasional Papers 2, 1957.
    La Venue du Messie, Bruges, 1962.
    World Council of Churches, Evanston Report, 1954.

INDEX OF PERSONS AND DOCUMENTS

INDEX OF PERSONS AND DOCUMENTS

INDEX OF SUBJECTS

INDEX OF SUBJECTS